Consuming Fashion

Dress, Body, Culture

Series Editor **Joanne B. Eicher,** *Regents' Professor, University of Minnesota*

Books in this provocative series seek to articulate the connections between culture and dress which is defined here in its broadest possible sense as any modification or supplement to the body. Interdisciplinary in approach, the series highlights the dialogue between identity and dress, cosmetics, coiffure, and body alterations as manifested in practices as varied as plastic surgery, tattooing, and ritual scarification. The series aims, in particular, to analyse the meaning of dress in relation to popular culture and gender issues and will include works grounded in anthropology, sociology, history, art history, literature, and folklore.

ISSN: 1360-466X

DRESS, BODY, CULTURE

Consuming Fashion
Adorning the Transnational Body

Edited by

Anne Brydon and Sandra Niessen

Oxford • New York

First published in 1998 by
Berg
Editorial offices:
150 Cowley Road, Oxford, OX4 1JJ, UK
70 Washington Square South, New York, NY 10012, USA

© Anne Brydon and Sandra Niessen 1998

Berg is an imprint of Oxford International Publishers Ltd.

Library of Congress Cataloging-in-Publication Data
A catalog record for this book is available from the Library of Congress.

British Library Cataloguing-in-Publication Data
A catalogue record for this book is available from the British Library.

ISBN   1 85973 964 4 (Cloth)
        1 85973 969 5 (Paper)

Typeset by JS Typesetting, Wellingborough, Northants.

Contents

Acknowledgements

All of these papers originated as conference presentations at the Canadian Anthropology Society meetings held in Montreal in 1995. The session was co-organized with the help of Nicholas Packwood, and the editors would like to thank him for his participation. The Faculty of Social Science, University of Western Ontario has generously helped with much of the pre-production costs, and the University of Alberta has assisted with the cost of the preparation of the index.

Introduction: Adorning the Body

Sandra Niessen and Anne Brydon

In her article 'The F Word' (1991), Valerie Steele queries why academics dress so badly. Her aim is deadly: she strikes at the heart of an academic conceit which presumes that the lofty mind's pursuit of truth is above any base attention to the arts of the body. Fashion and clothing have for a long while remained scholarly unmentionables. The unwillingness of social analysts to recognize the power of how people – of how they themselves – clothe, decorate, inscribe, perform and otherwise gesture with their bodies is, for the editors, a central fascination to analyse for its root assumptions and avoidances. Ironically and unintentionally, in skirting these disquieting topics, the power of bodily performances is made manifest. Perhaps it is the power of the uncontrolled, undisciplined, expressive body which clothing, fashion systems and adornment all in diverse ways reveal, play with, defer, disguise, restrain or otherwise modify to express many forms of desire – including sexual, sensual, hierarchical, aesthetic – that makes some faint hearts wish to push the issues raised by material culture's en-rapture of the body into the dark corners of their awareness.

Academic denial of the body has marginalized the topic of clothing and fashion within mainstream social science, driven there by strongly-rooted assumptions inherent to the Enlightenment's rationalizing project. That project has separated realms of experience into subjective and objective, treating the former as the superstructure, the frill on the dress, the useless ornament, the indulgence to the feminine which is tolerantly bestowed by the masculine while its mighty attention is directed at other, more weighty matters. In the academy, often the mirror of common sense assumptions, those disciplines lacking the legitimacy guaranteed by the ideology of pure science and granted to the natural sciences, biomedicine, engineering and other 'hard' practices, strive for authority by means of the appearance of 'hardness'. This entails avoiding anything which might be too difficult to categorize or contain, or which might be construed as feminine and hence subjective, soft and secondary. Fields such as Home Economics where the study of fashion has its academic roots and its longest history, and Physical Education where the body is and must be central, are involved in endless struggles for credibility even when the university's pursuit of knowledge is touted as universal. So well do academics learn society's lessons during their formative years that they write these lessons into curricula and the political structures of their institutions.

Only recently, as some of the conventional barriers of academe crumble, have fashion and clothing matters been more incisively pursued and more credibly received. The academy once again mirrors changing social norms: demands for social recognition and respect issuing from the socially marginalized – women, gays and lesbians, ethnic and aboriginal groups, religious sects, visible minorities, former colonials – have infiltrated even conservative institutions of learning bringing with them new ways of knowing, behaving, speaking and bodily performance; the power of visual media is being unleashed and explored through film and advertising, inspiring unprecedented scrutiny of their cultural and political messages; dress codes have become increasingly diverse as individual expression is championed over hierarchical expression; and not least, the explosion of commodities in an increasingly material world has been met with an explosion of scholarly interest in commodification – and the body and its adornment are a lucrative site for both. The power of bodily adornment has forced itself upon aware-ness through clothing acts of rebellion and resistance, as Hebdige (1979) has so cogently demonstrated. Those who manipulate it successfully, whether the 'in' crowd at school, the political leader's spin doctor, or Phillip Knight of Nike, can accumulate greater symbolic and economic capital than ever before.

As academics also begin to mine this rich vein, they do so, not surprisingly, within new fields which blur conventional disciplinary boundaries. Earlier writings within a positivist tradition by social psychologists, clothing and art historians, folklorists and sociologists (e.g. Brenninkmeyer 1963; Flügel 1930; Hurlock 1929; Webb 1907) have been expanded upon as theoretical advances reveal interconnections between material culture and social forms. In their first moralizing manifestations, social analyses uniformly condemned fashion. Feminists critiqued the sexual politics and gender oppression inhering in clothing which hobble and confine women. Marxists critiqued the fetishism of fashion and the ideology of conspicuous consumption. Psychologists treated fashion adherence as pathology. But the hermeneutic turn slowly emergent during the 1950s and 1960s recognized the greater complexity of human thought and creativity, bringing forth analyses of meaning, and interpretive and performative strategies. Without abandoning social critique, diverse writers (e.g. Craik 1994; Finkelstein 1991; Gaines and Herzog 1990; Hollander 1978; Kaiser 1990; Kunzle 1982; McDowell 1992) were nonetheless able to give theoretical weight to how people understand their own thoughts and actions in relation to body decoration. In the last ten years scholarly presses such as Berg, Routledge and Duke have recognized these developments with specialized series about the body, fashion and dress and, in the case of Berg, introduced a specialized journal, *Fashion Theory: The Journal of Dress, Body and Culture*.

Awareness of these developments, peppered with experiences of marginalized sessions and isolation in our respective fashion-related intellectual pursuits, inspired a discussion of solidarity and strategy amongst Anne Brydon, Sandra Niessen and Nicholas Packwood at the Canadian Anthropology Society (CASCA) meetings in Vancouver, 1994. We began to conceptualize a large, diverse CASCA conference session which would draw together scholars concerned with issues of the body, fashion, clothing and material culture, and which, by virtue of its size, could not remain ignored by conference attendees. From this beginning, *Consuming Fashion* grew into a successful event at the 1995 CASCA meetings in Montreal. This book is a compilation of most papers given during that session.

The essays in this volume are diverse. They scrutinize particular items of adornment: shoes, bowties, the nude model's mantle; they scrutinize the act of wearing these items, the compulsion, conformity, and creativity involved in adorning the body. They are about the present and the past, the industrialized world and the economically marginalized. They concern ideology, seduction, north–south relations, and cold hard cash. This diversity is indexical because dressing enacts one of the most complicated acts of daily existence. Dressing negotiates between the intensely personal and the prescribed and constructed layers of the social. Dressing both hides and lays bare body and soul. It is fraught with all the contradictions and tensions entrenched in universal, local and increasingly, also global social processes. The diversity of this volume, in short, has reason and method.

Early fashion theorists such as Simmel (1957) and Sapir (1937) brilliantly articulated the social and psychological processes of change in bodily adornment during their own times and cultures, and bestowed upon the local processes familiar to them the label of fashion. Despite what was then conventionally perceived (and is still commonly perceived today) as the danger and decadence of fashion's frivolity, fashion was nonetheless considered to be the exclusive purview of 'civilized' nations. Clothing systems of the colonial Other were considered to be non-fashion, or fashion in negative image: sign of the child-like mentality of the prototypical 'primitive'.

The category 'fashion' was reserved for an industrial, mass-production and consumption system. Thus defined, fashion mirrored the familiar and insidious dichotomies of large- vs. small-scale, literate vs. non-literate, developed vs. undeveloped, and people with history vs. those without.

Extrication of the fashion concept from this out-moded wisdom has happened slowly despite innumerable analyses demonstrating the racist, classist, and sexist underpinnings of us vs. them thinking. Cannon's essay in this volume contributes to a cross-cultural, non-Eurocentric understanding of fashion processes starting to appear in the literature (cf. Hendrickson 1996; Niessen 1993; Schevill et al. 1991). Using archaeological and ethno-historical data, he examines principles and mechanisms of change in taste amongst First Nations peoples of North America during the early colonial contact period. While other contributions to this volume do not critique conventional understandings of fashion as explicitly as Cannon, they all draw on ethnographic knowledge to examine social, political and cultural processes shaping changing styles of clothing and other bodily adornments. Here the diversity of the volume works well with the details of experiential knowledge: a nude model carefully selects the time and place to slip off her robe, thereby controlling how her identity will be perceived by a drawing class (Roe); a stroke of genius resides in the moment a nun chooses to announce her interest in a pair of red shoes (Sullivan); a gay man has the option of changing his life by pulling on a pair of white trousers (Higgins). These are fashion stories distinctly parallel to the tales told by Cannon about the 'highly volatile' taste in beads and cloth of Aboriginal Peoples.

As the wearers of clothes, we have the latitude to perform, but also the ineluctable burden of performance; we have no option but to be on the social stage over which most people typically have little control. This is the central issue addressed by Gordon Roe in 'The Body of Art and the Mantle of Authority'. The feminized-because-objectified nude model sitting for artists must work strategically and skilfully to create a social climate of safety when the mantle is slipped off. The challenge of retaining personal authority when stripped of clothing and acting the body pure is but a sharper manifestation of how identity is negotiated in daily existence. It brings to mind the student who earnestly told the class that his dreadlocks were an aesthetic and a style and would we please read them as such, and not as a sign that he is Rastafarian – so that he could feel understood and more comfortable amongst us. He was trying to establish a convention.

No discussion of fashion and clothing can escape the centrality of gender, sexuality and desire to their meaning and use, and many contributors to this volume assist in shaking apart any easy assumptions about male–female difference to expose the struggles involved in constructing sexual/gendered identity. In 'Sensible Shoes', Anne Brydon reminds us of the sexual power of the stiletto and the long-toed winkle-picker, the blatant machismo of the Doc Marten, the suggestiveness of a foot slipping into soft leather, the decadence of closets full of shoes. In doing so she sensitizes the reader to life's choices even – or especially – the most fundamental choices of sexuality and gender which may also be slipped on and off. Along the way, she demands that we recognize who wears the shoe and how, in order to ensure that analysis of material culture does not reify or fetishize. In this way we acknowledge that cognition is social, and that meaning resides in practices which frame the object, and not in the object itself.

The wearer of clothing must know the meaning of apparel items and be skilled in performing the nuances which shape their interpretation. Rob Shields points out in 'A Tale of Three Louis: Ambiguity, Masculinity and the Bowtie' that the wearer of the bowtie had best master its art, if virile elegance is his goal, in order not to come across as the servant or buffoon. The bowtie typically adorns all three of these personae. The bowtie's historically-constructed ambiguities create challenging cultural codes, and remind us that individual choice can never escape social constraint. The actor must 'get it right' to situate himself comfortably in his time and place.

The challenge for the wearer may be to hide within convention as a strategy to mask the unconventional self, or it may be to resist conventions in order to create space for personal identity. In 'À la Mode: Fashioning Gay Community in Montreal', Ross Higgins tells how both options have been, and continue to be, employed by gay men in Montreal. In fact, they situate themselves relative to two settings, straight and gay, simultaneously. Subtly and/or blatantly they adorn themselves with their affiliations and disassociations, thereby identifying themselves socially and psychologically. Higgins' essay makes a salutary counterpoint to cultural studies' focus on more flamboyant subcultures of gay community – drag queens, cross-dressers and transvestites – and in so doing demonstrates ethnography's strength at revealing the less visible practices of everyday life.

Higgins' article makes an interesting parallel to Rebecca Sullivan's 'Breaking Habits: Gender, Class and the Sacred in the Dress of Women Religious'. Women religious, too, collaborate with others of like orientation to construct their own community's norm so that they can place themselves relative to socially-dominant norms. They adorn themselves in an eccentric femininity which proclaims chastity and devotion and 'the look' of the wife of god.

None of these strategies is as easy as slipping on a pair of loafers. The dress has to be right for the stiletto; so too the hairdo and the demeanour. The dress of the nun involves her habits, the frequency of laundering, the demarcations of where private ends and public begins, the legitimacy and boundaries of personal taste, the melding of spiritual conviction and daily practice. These are the all-involving questions which engulf the habit's wearer cognitively, emotionally and culturally, revealing the profundity of the act of changing clothes and exposing the depth of the root where the two English definitions of 'habit' merge.

Fashion habits are instilled early and deep, according to Jeanne Randolph. 'That Barbie-Doll Look: A Psychoanalysis' draws on object relations theory to unpack the psychic complexities underlying compulsions to change styles of adornment. Randolph's provocative argument that considerable aggressive energy can be socially sanctioned if displaced onto an obsession with fashion and appearance is insightfully revealed through visual analysis of Barbie™ trading cards and colouring books. She shows how representational codes can dress up the separation and alienation inherent to consumer desire. She is careful to point out, however, that playing with Barbie™ need not lead blindly to a shop-til-you-drop fixation, and that a healthy child has a wealth of creative resources with which to subvert the cult of Barbie™. Nonetheless, this perspective on consumer desire introduces a much-needed psychological complexity into social analysis which resonates well with the essays by Li and Skoggard.

Xiaoping Li's fascinating exposition in 'Fashioning the Body in Post-Mao China' reveals how vulnerable women are, even later in life, to the capitalist construction of femininity which has only recently appeared in China. Her paper helps us to see the similarities and differences between Chinese and Western manifestations of modernity. There exists in the world today monumental corporate encouragement to perform financially-profitable gender stereotypes. And so the performance of gender becomes all-involving, even on a global level. Nike's success, as described by Ian Skoggard in 'Transnational Commodity Flows and the Global Phenomenon of the Brand', is in having peasants throughout Asia and Southeast Asia scramble to meet the consumer needs of North Americans, and in having consumers seduced by the Nike miracle of Michael Jordan. The deepest psychological urges are manifested in the broadest global trade networks.

Despite acknowledging Western fashion as an industrial product, conventional fashion theory tends to separate its glitz from the sweat of its production. After all, it was the wives of the nineteenth-century industrialists who were caught in fashion's thrall, while their husbands merely wore utilitarian suits symbolizing their seriousness and industry (e.g. Hollander 1994; Rouse 1989). Also a legacy of Enlightenment thinking, the art of displaying fashion has been kept separate from the craft of its manufacture (Hardy 1995). This has allowed fashion theorists to locate fashion in Euro-

American society without acknowledging the global ties which inhere in the production system. Perhaps the narrower, conventional definition of fashion persists because industrialized fashion itself thrives by separating and masking the conditions of its production. Spectators have always swooned over the fashions of media stars without a thought for the drudgery involved in stitching the outfits together (Nielsen 1990); glitz and sweat have always gone together, but the former gleams in the spotlight while the latter is hidden backstage.

Ian Skoggard brilliantly pulls the two into close proximity to emphasize the mutualism in their separateness. Nike, he points out, has achieved the acme of success by manipulating the distinctiveness of the worlds of production and consumption. Labourers in the Taiwanese countryside work hard 'to supply a bottomless North American market' and accumulate wealth. Consumers in North America, on the other hand, 'just do it', thoughtlessly following the compelling advertising slogans of miracles and success through sports shoes. Skoggard offers an understanding of the fashion machine as comprising halves, in a relationship of complementary imbalance, with the balance of power in the hands of corporate mediation. His analysis provides an interesting parallel to Paul Smith's (1988) reading of the Banana Republic clothing chain, and resonates with Brydon's discussion of the Bata Shoe Museum. Xiaoping Li's description of fashion in China, and Randolph's insights into the formative power of 'playing Barbie' convince the reader that power does not reside with the consumer. In this light, the historic and economic weight of the established norms render heroic, as well as inevitable, acts of apparel resistance in the construction of the self by women religious, gays, nude models and Chinese peasants, in the selection of a non-Barbie doll and in slipping on a different pair of shoes.

There are no bastions of exclusion from the producer–consumer link. On the isolated eastern Indonesian island of Flores, handweavers compete within terms set by large-scale production, and 'modernization' appears to be a process in which both the production and consumption of local indigenous textiles are increasingly informed by global trends (Niessen 1996). People begin to wear Western clothing, their indigenous clothing is commercialized for decorative and functional purposes such as wall-hangings, upholstery and tailored dress. Molnar, in 'Transformations in the Use of Traditional Textiles of Ngada (Western Flores, Eastern Indonesia): Commercialization, Fashion and Ethnicity' depicts a struggle to compete for identity, status and economic survival in social and economic climates receiving their impetus for change from outside. How and why the textiles are still made, the materials from which they are constructed, and where they are sold are strategies used to jockey for economic and social identity in a rapidly changing context. On non-mechanized looms and far from the centres of fashion – and the centres of fashion production – these people still must struggle to accommodate the rhythms of an external fashion system by adapting with their own fashions.

Condemnation of fashion is a condemnation of history. Celebration of fashion exclusively as creativity, resistance and freedom is similarly deficient, obscuring the realities of social inequality and dominance. If conventional academic boundaries between disciplines leave out the body, they also fail to articulate the link between the peasant in Honduras and the suburban shopper in Vancouver, and between the materiality of the earth and our own bodies. The essays gathered in this book represent ways in which their various authors have struggled to ground their analyses in the immediacies of human cognition and experience while theorizing beyond to point to the legitimacies of alternate modernities.

Implicit to all these essays is a recognition that conventional understandings of self, subject and society are inadequate to explain the interconnections of cultural and economic systems inherent to fashion and clothing. Taken as a whole, this volume argues that political economy is inextricably linked to the ways in which subjectivities are negotiated and produced within a complex interplay of cultural processes and everyday improvisational acts themselves situated within structuring forces of economic, political and social power. Such a recognition entails mobilizing theoretical frameworks capable of articulating human will and desire as they are influenced by and respond to the ethnically-diverse, transnationally-networked, politically-fraught world of consumption and production.

Current transformations in global capital and the coming together of multiple modernities confront us with new analytic concerns. How we negotiate these within our mythologies and our modes of interpretation will have unpredictable effects, but we can modify their prejudices by acknowledging that adornment in itself is neither moral nor ethical. Rather, it is the ways in which bodily adornment figures in the relationship between the embodied self and social history which lead us to perceive adornment's implications.

Bibliography

Brenninkmeyer, Ingrid (1963), *The Sociology of Fashion*. Köln: Westdeutscher Verlag.

Craik, Jennifer (1994), *The Face of Fashion: Cultural Studies in Fashion*. London and New York: Routledge.

Finkelstein, Joanne (1991), *The Fashioned Self*. Cambridge: Polity Press.

Flügel, J.C. (1930), *The Psychology of Clothes*. London: Hogarth Press.

Gaines, Jane and Charlotte Herzog (eds) (1990), *Fabrications: Costume and the Female Body*. London and New York: Routledge.

Hardy, Michele (1995), 'A Phenomenological Approach to Women, Craft and Knowledge: the Embodied Embroiderer in India.' Unpublished MA thesis, Department of Human Ecology, University of Alberta.

Hebdige, Dick (1979), *Subculture: The Meaning of Style*. London: Methuen.

Hendrickson, Hildi, (ed.) (1996), *Clothing and Difference: Embodied Identities in Colonial and Post-colonial Africa*. Durham: Duke University Press.

Hollander, Anne (1978), *Seeing through Clothes*. New York: Viking.

—— (1994), *Sex and Suits: The Evolution of Modern Dress*. New York: Alfred Knopf.

Hurlock, E. (1929), *The Psychology of Dress*. New York: Ronald Press.

Kaiser, Susan (1990), *The Social Psychology of Clothes: Symbolic Appearances in Context*. Sec. ed. New York: Macmillan.

Kunzle, David (1982), *Fashion and Fetishism: A Social History of Corsets, Tight-lacing and Other Forms of Body-sculpture in the West*. Totowa, N.J.: Rowman and Littlefield.

McDowell, Colin (1992), *Dressed to Kill: Sex, Power, and Clothes*. London: Hutchinson.

Nielsen, Elizabeth (1990), 'Handmaidens of the Glamour Culture: Costumers in the Hollywood Studio System.' In Jane Gaines and Charlotte Herzog (eds), *Fabrications: Costume and the Female Body*. London, New York: Routledge.

Niessen, Sandra (1993), *Batak Cloth and Clothing: A Dynamic Indonesian Tradition*. Kuala Lumpur: Oxford University Press.

—— (1996), *Wood-based Crafts and Agroforestry in Northern Thailand: A Human Ecological Perspective*. Unpublished research Report #1, Maejo University, University of Alberta Agroforestry Project. CIDA Linkage Project.

Roach, Mary Ellen and Joanne Bubolz Eicher, (eds) (1965), *Dress, Adornment, and the Social Order*. New York: John Wiley and Sons.

Rouse, Elizabeth (1989), *Understanding Fashion*. Oxford: BSP Professional Books.

Sapir, Edward (1937), 'Fashion.' In *Encyclopedia of the Social Sciences*. New York: The MacMillan Co. pp. 139–44.

Schevill, Margot Blum, Jane Catherine Berlo, Edward B. Dwyer (eds) (1991), *Textile Traditions of Mesoamerica and the Andes: An Anthology*. New York: Garland Publishing.

Simmel, Georg (1957), 'Fashion.' *American Journal of Sociology*, LXII(6): 541–58.

Smith, Paul (1988), 'Visiting the Banana Republic.' In Andrew Ross (ed.) *Universal Abandon: The Politics of Postmodernism*, Minneapolis: University of Minnesota Press.

Steele, Valerie (1991), 'The F Word.' *Lingua Franca*, April:17–20.

Webb, Wilfred Mark (1907), *The Heritage of Dress: Being Notes on the History and Evolution of Clothes*. London: E. Grant Richards.

Sensible Shoes

Anne Brydon

The productionist bias and taint of moralism found in conventional anthropological studies of material things draw attention away from people's relations with their own artefacts and possessions. Yet if we are to account for the phenomenon of consumer demand in modernity we need to understand the ways in which ordinary human desires are in part constituted through the medium of things and objects. In this essay, I cast the shoe (boot, sandal, slipper: all variants of footwear) in the role of explanator in order to elaborate upon the expression and narration of human desires by means of a category of clothing. Whether as fetish, sign, metaphor, *objet d'art* or collectible, shoes mediate between body and place, between self and other, in the continual, necessary human desire to situate identity within its realm of experience. Shoes may stand for an unattainable whole, a lack or a longing. And the shoe collection, while objectifying this continual lack, may also make imaginable completion and wholeness. This desire to which I refer, then, is not limited to sexual longing or the craving for status: rather, it is a fundamental component of human sociability, a need as real and material as for food and shelter (and, yes, clothing) to render lived experience meaningful, ordered and complete. It is also a desire only occasionally fulfilled, one motivating a myriad of practices and performances in the fabric of human history.

Do we limit what can be learned about dress if we think of it only as bodily adornment? Can anything else be said about clothing, in this case shoes, if we consider it more broadly as one category of objects through which human relations are mediated? In what ways, both on and off the body, can shoes be used to express identities and transact gender and class relations? These are some of the questions which are appropriate to a cultural analysis seeking to connect fashion and clothing to other aspects of social life. In the following discussion I take up these questions by examining various contexts in which shoes articulate identity, whether as metamorphosing sign, sexual fetish or institutionalized collection.

At the same time, I want to engage the reader in speculation about the ways in which humans interpret their objects, and the necessity for cultural analysis to recognize these various interpretive modes through its own selection of theoretical perspectives. I conceive this essay, finally, as something of a story, a story about desire and longing: about a modernist longing for authenticity – of both self and shoes – in a world of copies and knock-offs, about the desire of the shoe collector to narrate footwear as objects of consumption while re-narrating social memories about the social relations of their production, and about the re-fashioning of shoes as metaphors, *objets d'art*, souvenirs and sexual substitutes in the dream-work of existence.

School Shoes

What I described earlier as the productionist bias of anthropological approaches to things is clearly and concisely detailed in the work of Arjun Appadurai. In Appadurai's view, outlined in the introduction to *The Social Life of Things*, objects, goods, products and artefacts are distinct and categorically separable from commodities, and further, 'commodities represent very complex social forms and distributions of knowledge' (1986:41). Intent on rescuing the term 'commodity' from its typical usage – referring only to the products of Western capitalism – he argues that understanding in what ways commodities have social lives requires examining not just *how* commodities are exchanged, but also what the objects themselves are and how '. . . meanings are inscribed in their forms, their uses, their trajectories' (ibid.:5).

Despite recognizing that commodities are intricately social, Appadurai's interest nonetheless lies foremost in economic systems, wherein objects are construed strictly as tokens of exchange. Such an analytical distinction, however, limits discussion and fails to deal with the ways in which objects come to be meaningful. While I do not deny the relevance of the economic, the emphasis on exchange value skirts the other ways in which individuals and groups experience the worth and meaning of objects and possessions. While such objects are most likely commodities in some contexts at certain times, it is only in situations where purchasing or disposing of them is at issue. But what of those other times, when the object is displayed, worn, carried or otherwise used? How then is value and worth construed? Does the continual emphasis on monetary value and its relationship to status and power actually help us to understand material culture in its ordinary manifestations in everyday life?

The motion of exchange is not the only place in which to observe the contexts and forms of humanly-endowed meaning embuing an object, as Igor Kopytoff argues (1986). Kopytoff proposes a different approach to studying objects, one which more emphatically engages with the recognition that objects are also created culturally and cognitively, and that they move in and out of the state of 'being' commodities. Objects exist in a tension between their commonality and their singularity, he states, between commodity form and personal possession. His approach emphasizes the *biographical*, and conceives of objects as having life histories. These life histories can be quixotic and idiosyncratic: objects can be diverted from their life paths in acts of creation or destruction, of plunder or theft, by appropriation or transformation from sacred into tourist art or archaeological artefact, or turned from workaday thing into *objet d'art* or collectible. In this way, objects accrue meanings like surface encrustations; their meanings and uses mutate and play one off another in a manner analogous to the multivocality of ritual symbols (Turner 1967).

Such an insight is particularly useful to keep in mind when examining objects in contemporary society. In modernity, an object's contestability is greater; the social constrictions of small-scale societies which helped to limit the social meaning of a class of objects have lessened to allow individualized tastes and choices to predominate. The likelihood is greater that within any given society, and at any given moment, one object can carry several meanings for different individuals and groups. Context becomes integral to understanding.

Kopytoff's idea of tracing the biographical life of things is more useful for my purposes if wedded with contemporary understandings of narrative as developed in the field of literary criticism. 'Narrative' in conventional discourse analysis refers to a type of text, usually separable from description, exposition, argument or persuasion. In this essay, I am borrowing from Susan Stewart's booklength essay *On Longing*, wherein she defines narrative as 'a structure of desire, a structure that both invents and distances its object and thereby inscribes again and again the gap between signifier and signified that is the place of generation for the symbolic' (1993:ix). Objects themselves are dumb; it is we who animate them with significance by means of the statements we make about them. Narratives invent significant objects, and those objects in turn solidify experience and translate desire into material form, thus making possible history and memory.

Narrating shoes can be another way of narrating the self by means of shoes. Yet as Stewart notes, the relationship between shoe and narration – between signified and signifier – is ambivalent and endlessly mutable. Similarly, the relationship between self and outside world in the context of modern individualism and self-fashioning is equally ambivalent and mutable.

Since the time of Beau Brummell, the idea of the self-fashioned individual, someone using items of clothing in symbolic and representational ways as evidence of their accomplishments and attributes, has had far-reaching consequences (Finkelstein 1991). In effect, a social space opened for the life history of the shoe to intervene, diverted into politically-nuanced codes of adornment and the exigencies of self-creation.

To return this point to the topic at hand, that of human desires and identities and the objects which articulate them, I argue that the pursuit of authenticity in modernity is displayed while displaced onto, amongst other things, shoes. One has to look no further than the footwear choices of academics to see the ways in which identity, narrative and shoe style are used to articulate the politics of gender and status. Scholarly footwear figures in academic standards and codes of legitimacy. Particularly for women academics, who have had to negotiate clothing codes established by their male colleagues, choosing shoes which communicate intellectual credibility is not an easy task, given that some displays of fashionability may be judged as inappropriate. On a level playing field, any footwear would be suitable. But in the rocky arena of academe, women have to watch their step. Ironically, shoe politics can only be possible when there is choice, but choice for women is constrained by the trope separating mind from body and relegating the latter to the margins of intellectual respectability.

The footwear codes of the academy are not arbitrary; instead, they connect inextricably to the unmarked white male voice of authoritative knowledge. The fashion historian Valerie Steele, in an analysis of scholarly dress codes (1991), raises a pertinent question in this regard: why is it the case that, when clothing choice is not officially sanctioned for them, professors nonetheless dress so uniformly and, I might add, so badly? Her response rings true: that in all likelihood such a striving for blandness is an extension of the Cartesian mind–body split. To draw attention to the body by means of stylish or somehow 'extravagant' clothing would be to suggest a diminished intellectual capacity. The great mind of the genius, so this logic goes, is indifferent, indeed oblivious to the body and its ornament. Scholarly authenticity, then, is coded in footwear notable for its unnoteworthiness. Never mind that these same renunciators of clothing style will nonetheless spend freely on the sensual pleasures brought by food and wine, travel, stereos and computers and more.

To underline her point, Steele observes that outside the university high heels for women are viewed by both men and women as representing authority, and that female executives often wear the highest heels. Yet in universities those same shoes are viewed as lacking in intellectual weight. The preferred footwear for the female academic is the flat, the low pump or

the brogue: sensible shoes, slightly orthopedic but otherwise not acknowledging the body and its sensibilities. It mimics male dress, a masquerade to
avoid the appearance of femininity, and an inversion of the too-frequently
observed masking of intelligence behind an excessive performance of
femininity.

So what about sensible shoes? When I first gave this paper as a public
talk at an academic conference, I wore black stilettos – and a brightly-
coloured ensemble to match – to assist my treading upon that invisible but
palpable line of defence between academic sense and aesthetic sensibility.
The sensible shoe (as opposed to the comfortable shoe, which is a separate
category) intertwines with the separation of mind and body characteristic
of Western theorizing. Sensible footwear draws its significance from its
opposition to the ambiguous, bodily evocations of the stiletto. It does so by
mimicking the unmarked quality of the male shoe, and by denying or ignoring
the body which the stiletto so resolutely emphasizes.

This dissociation of style from intelligence is easily contradicted. One need
only think of the nineteenth-century dandy who combined a cultivated style
of dress with brilliant repartee and the fine art of verbal *badinage*. Oscar
Wilde, for one, demonstrated wit and elegance of both body and mind, a
talent which enhanced rather than detracted from his brilliant social
commentaries. Nonetheless, I have heard it frequently repeated by male
colleagues that they do not participate in fashion. They claim to choose
footwear and other clothing items as if they could, by the power of their
own will, remove them from any pre-existing systems of meaning. Their
wardrobes, one is to assume, are purely functional and express only their
owners' lack of interest in how they clothe their bodies. I am reminded of
similar claims made by Le Corbusier and members of the Bauhaus School,
defenders of the self-confidently-named International Style of modernist
architecture. Glass and steel skyscrapers, they insisted, were 'purely'
functional, transcending the shallowness of surface style to achieve an
authentic expression of utilitarian good. Ideology in action is always
fascinating to observe, and the intellectual gyrations necessary to defend
this curious logic attest to the powerful hold that the unmarked nature of
male dress has on members of the academy. One need only break that code,
by wearing the 'wrong' shoes, to demonstrate its strength.

If we consider this narrative of white masculine denial as a strategy of
power, then the logocentrism (to use Derrida's term for the repression of
difference and uncertainty in Enlightenment rationality) of standard academic
dress becomes apparent. To deny, for example, the existence of a social
language of footwear while at the same time enforcing it – in other words,
to assert the ability to step outside any language of adornment and to speak

one's identity without using it – is equivalent to claiming the possibility of total understanding, of an absolute truth. But to admit that one's choice of shoes is not an absolute value but an imperious act, is to acknowledge the possibility of situated difference and one's own delimited identity. To have a body is to admit to not being omniscient.

Such a masculinist point of view has been well expressed by otherwise excellent fashion analysts, James Laver (1969) and J.C. Flügel (1930). They have argued that the 'great masculine renunciation' which occurred early in the nineteenth century with the creation of the male suit, had placed men outside of fashion. Fashion was, according to these authorities, a woman's domain, and consequently less important, less intelligent, more rooted in bodily states and emotions, and expressive of childlike emotions and/or neurotic, infantile tendencies. A few decades later, many feminists accepted this characterization and located women's liberation and empowerment in the rejection of fashion as both constricting (tight clothing, high heels) and inherently racist and classist (since fashion is associated with privilege and wealth) (Wilson 1992).

Significant Shoes

Unlike premodern societies where sumptuary laws and social collectivity ensured that dress, ornamentation and body modification signified for members of the same society or social group an unambiguous message of membership and status, modernity's individualism and consumerism have made codes more ambiguous and more subject to misinterpretation, mutable meanings and contestation. It is not possible to assume any longer that dress as a cultural phenomenon necessarily defines categorically a person's identity geographically and historically, as is typically argued in the field of fashion history. Increasingly, transnational flows of goods and media images render group and cultural boundaries permeable. Whereas this may give the appearance of superficial sameness, it is necessary to recognize that these goods and images can take on radically divergent meanings upon reception in different social and geographical locales. Cultural analysis, then, must be more intent than ever at revealing the gaps between signified and signifier, to explore the myriad ways in which meaning is constituted by the clothing sign.

Considering shoe-buying habits reveals something of the ambivalence of self and collective identities in modernity. This is an ambivalence between the desire, on the one hand, to find a genuine expression of one's self and, on the other hand, the realization that any identity in modernity is arbitrarily constituted and thus never truly authentic. This contradiction is at the root of modernity's anxiety, the social distinction between authenticity and reproduction, and is the principle of alterity specific to the modern self. While fashion provides the codes for displaying one's authentic self through display of ranked value and taste, distinction, expertise and judgement (or deliberate denial of same), the logic of fashion also entails the desire to imitate, to reproduce the fashion sign in order to 'speak' a comprehensible code. It further plays on the tension between surface and depth, the idea that the self is hidden behind an adorning mask which, while needing to be stripped away to reveal the innermost soul of the person, also yields clues to what lies beneath. Disclosure and disguise.

To return to the topic of the stiletto, it can be argued that, for its part, it can never remain unmarked and unremarked. Instead, it tells a story about its wearer, but one which is open to several readings. The stiletto is an evocative symbol of both submission and domination, and as Mary Douglas (1966) has argued, any phenomenon which blurs categories and transgresses boundaries is dangerous to any established order. And although high heels (for both men and women) have been around in Europe since the sixteenth century, the stiletto with its needle-point heels of reinforced steel is fundamentally a shoe design of modernity, a postwar phenomenon self-consciously breaking with the past and tradition.

Social proscriptions have dogged the heels of the stiletto's advance since its first appearance during the 1950s. In that decade, the stiletto was the footwear of sexual freedom. For many women of the period it represented divine decadence and defiance. It symbolized the world outside the home, the freedom of rock and roll, and release from post-war austerity. Moralists argued that stilettos led to depraved behaviour when young women adopted them to rebel against their parents' plan for their good fit, whether into sensible shoes or sensible marriages.

The comedian and actor Sandra Bernhard's bravado commentary on her high heels, accompanied by her bad-girl photograph taken by Annie Liebowitz, gives one take on the power of stilettos, and challenges the assumption that they are strictly the shoes of victimized women:

> When I walk out the door in a good pair of heels, and I'm not talking about that kitschy crap that you can buy on a trip to Frederick's of Hollywood but a really solid set of heels from Manolo or Prada Chanel Clergerie, I never feel vulnerable, there's no time for any weakness, I feel focussed strong secure, my stride is potent and no one hassles me when I'm standing on the corner hailing a cab, you'd better believe I'm the first fare he'll throw on his brakes for . . . Because I demand respect and my heels back me up . . . (1996:192)

7

But as always, context is everything. Bernhard is a woman of power and with enough connections to be granted space in the *New Yorker* to narrate her self by means of her shoes. She is empowered by crippling footwear, and has the social and personal autonomy to perform her self in shoes beyond the price range of the average shoe-buyer.[1] This is not to deny the truth of her narrative; instead it points to the difference between lack and completion that the shoe's relation to the embodied self wearing it articulates. For Bernhard, the stiletto completes how she sees herself and how she wishes to be seen, and expresses what Brenninkmeyer defines as *elegance*: 'the ability to shape clothes around a central thought' (1963:168). There is, presumably, a continuity running from surface to depth, from the mask of clothing to the inner reaches of being.

Another relation between stiletto and self is equally imaginable, a relation of lack, contradiction and powerlessness. When women are forced against their wills by men in their lives to don stilettos and/or other erotic clothing, in order to ensure their continuing fidelity, economic support or to stave off violence, then clearly the stiletto is figuring in codes having nothing to do with authenticity, autonomy or self-fulfillment. Feminists have countered attempts to see erotic clothing as straightforward and healthy expressions of sexuality, and have argued convincingly that, reinforced by pornographic imagery, women are manipulated into conforming to the masculine gaze, to introject male desires into how they perceive and clothe themselves. In this narrative, the stiletto is the epitome of women's oppression, wherein the Birkenstock sandal is to the stiletto as the authentic is to the spurious. One cannot be a feminist and empowered and balance atop four inches of needle-sharp steel at the same time. Flat, wide shoes and heavy boots symbolize the rejection of the tortured sexuality that the stiletto represents. This parallels the footwear choice of turn-of-the-century suffragettes, when women embodied their emancipation with the adoption of a unisex boot style. For bourgeois women, this meant leaving behind the delicate slippers and high-heeled shoes which had effectively limited their social and physical movements.[2]

Therein lies the contradiction generating feminist debates about female sexuality, debates that trickle into everyday life to underlie polarized celebrations or condemnations of the stiletto. The fallacy here lies in the fact that the meaning of things (always deemed singular) is assumed to be a property of the object itself rather than cognition or feeling. The possibility that two contradictory things might both be true depending on circumstances

1. In 1995, a pair of Manolo Blahnik shoes sold for anywhere between US$450 and $2600.
2. This observation is made in the Bata Shoe Museum's show, *In Step*, curated by Jonathan Walford.

challenges the drive to catalogue experience into discrete categories. The stiletto, then, erupts forth from any narrative seeking to contain it. It is dangerously transgressive and hence desirable and potent in its uncontainability.

This transgressiveness carries through into the interplay between sensations of pleasure and pain aroused by wearing stilettos, and which make them the footwear of choice for S&M aficionados. In *The Sex Life of the Foot and Shoe* (1977) Rossi states that stilettos make a woman look and feel sexy, by altering her body posture and facilitating a stimulating friction. He shares this interpretation of the stiletto with other commentators on shoe design. Describing the effect on a woman's body of Manolo Blahnik's stilettos, one author claims they 'change the anatomy by drawing the legs out. You get one, long, pointy line falling from the hipbone all the way down to the toe cleavage. The girl ends up looking like a sketch.' (Collins 1995). Rossi's and Collins' descriptions don't alter cramping calves, crushed toes and the periodic shocks of pain running up the spine of their wearer. Extended wearing of stilettos can lead to atrophied calf muscles and make the wearing of other, lower heels difficult. But the crippled woman with mincing steps is enticing to some men in the way it suggests vulnerability. For others, the longing to submit to the spiked heels of a dominatrix walking across their prostrate body makes the stiletto wearer the powerful inflictor of pain onto another person.

High heels and stilettos have not always been worn by women. High heels were first worn in Europe towards the close of the sixteenth century, and then first by men. Their purpose was to lift their wearers, to make material their class standing and thereby inscribe the spatial metaphor of class onto their bodies. In the eighteenth century, high heels for women became more popular, perhaps coinciding with the bourgeois family's need to place daughters into upwardly-mobile marriages on the basis of appearances rather than lineage. This trend went along with changes in attire and the arrival of dressmakers into middle-class life, and the uses of clothing and footwear as signs of emergent individualism.

In contemporary times, drag queens and transvestites prefer the highest stilettos, foregoing comfort to achieve a look of drag sexuality. In the movie *Priscilla Queen of the Desert*, three drag queens travelling across the Australian desert have a giant silver stiletto sandal atop their bus, a shoe that gives a masculine gendering to a quintessentially feminine foot attire. At the same time, that giant stiletto was a proclamation directed not just at the small, narrow frontier towns of the outback, but to the land itself. It was a gesture celebrating the exuberant freedom of drag taste.

Within the logic of twentieth-century fashionable footwear, there is no greater opposition than that between the stiletto and the Doc Marten comfort boot. That distinction itself plays into the codes of dress used to perform gender and class identities. The life history of the Doc Marten makes more apparent Marx's sardonic comparison of the commodity form to the religious fetish, suggesting that both displace the value of human labour and social relations onto objects: the products of the capitalist formation.

The Doc's original air-cushioned boot design was developed by Dr Klaus Maerten in Germany in 1946, immediately following the Second World War. He designed it as a comfort shoe for older women, and its purpose was prosthetic, to correct feet that had suffered from the poorly made footwear available during the war. An Englishman, Bill Grigg, eventually persuaded the German manufacturer to give him the licence to manufacture the boot in England for British workmen, which he started to do in 1960 (McDowell 1989). He set up shop in the town of Wollaston near Northampton, a region having a significant history of shoe and boot manufacture going back to the seventeenth century, but that was experiencing economic decline as the footwear industry was transferred to Third World countries.

Not long after they began to be made, Doc Martens were picked up by British skinheads; their 'bovver boots' were to bother the bourgeoisie with their outrageous affrontery of good taste and the status quo:

> Aggressively proletarian, puritanical and chauvinist, the skinheads dressed down in sharp contrast to their mod antecedents in a uniform which . . . [is] a 'kind of caricature of the model worker': cropped hair, braces, short, wide levi jeans or functional sta-prest trousers, plain or striped button-down Ben Sherman shirts and highly polished Doctor Marten boots (Hebdige 1979:55).

The skinhead look played upon the downward mobility of the displaced working class of England, displaced by the same transformations in industrial production that affected shoe and boot manufacturing in Northampton. The Doc Marten, as part of a complete look, manifested an unsettling, rebellious response to unemployment. Through what Hebdige calls the ostensibly incompatible sources of the white working class and Caribbean immigrants, skinheads invoked an image of working-class community. Skinhead identity demarcated the boundary between a collective self and the middle-class other. Its referral to a lost authenticity, however compromised by nostalgia, makes that identity exemplary of existence in modernity, what with the ubiquity of estrangement.

Sometime during the 1970s, the Doc Marten began to disperse through the population and out of Great Britain. Middle-class youth, in a familiar gesture of appropriation, came to covet the Doc Marten as a token for transgressing their class position while still living within its comforts. This act blurred the boundary between the classes to mimic the look of working-class alienation. With the Doc it became possible to commodify rebellion, making it a consumer object rather than a social movement, a safe means of transgression sanctioned by middle-class shops benefiting from their popularity.

But the history of borrowing the Doc does not end there. Feminists and lesbians wore Docs to subvert malestream expectations of female propriety and to relish the feel of power that big boots can give. Gay men began to wear them in the performance of macho masculinity: wearing the signs of heterosexuality while performing its ambiguities. Further, in the late eighties and nineties, streetwise young women wore their Docs with baby doll dresses and frills, an equally ambivalent statement of prepubescent sexuality combined with a fashionable grrrl rage.

The manufacturers of Doc Martens responded to the boot's popularity by commodifying its image and increasing the number of products sold. In 1993, the Doctor Marten Department Store opened in the upmarket shopping district of Covent Garden, London. Its four storeys of retail space not only sell boots and shoes but also watches, pencils and pencil cases, binders, T-shirts, jeans, backpacks, jackets, shoelaces, boot treatment products, a guide to the streets of London and a hair salon where one can presumably get more than a buzz cut. In that same year they launched a line of clothing 'inspired by British workwear'. The store itself refers to the industrial roughness of the boot: price tags are cut from aluminum, leather hides are used as change room curtains and bench coverings.

Docs themselves now come in 150 different styles and in a range of colours, textures, patterns, including gold and silver lamé, paisley, gingham, flowers, pastels, velveteen, glitter black, silver or lilac, lace, tartan, nubuck red, mustard, eggplant, cobalt blue or lime green. One highrise style has printed across its surface in courier typeface: 'Unlaced'. There are desert boots and beatle boots and corporate shoes that, while still possessing the patented sole, are more suitable to wear with a business suit. Children's footwear comes in miniature versions of the 1460 in classic black but also flowered versions: mary janes with thick soles, or in gold or silver lamé with rainbow coloured laces, or in red, black, or white patent leather. On each child's shoe the brown rough paper tag reads 'their future's not only in their hands'.

Across every product label, the word 'Original' is emblazoned. The relationship between the original Doc Marten and 'The Original' copyright – a relationship between mimesis and alterity – is ironically mixed up in the Doc Marten narrative. In another dizzying twist, myriad other manufacturers now imitate the look of the Doc. Like the cowboy boot before it, the Doc has become removed from its working man's roots. The multiplying images and their ephemeral meanings render impossible any singular claim to authenticity, including the claim of subcultural resistance on which the Centre for Contemporary Cultural Studies has placed great theoretical weight. For an authentic culture of resistance to exist, the boundary between us and them needs to be more firmly entrenched, and not continually played upon and shifted in the performance of divergent identities.

Desirable Shoes

The relationships between self and object expressed in the Doc Marten narrative suggest excess, displacement, over-valuation, error, difference and deviation: in short, the traits associated with (commodity) fetishism. The idea of fetishism resonates powerfully with the shoe, but it often blurs a necessary distinction between it and eroticism, a distinction premised upon the way in which the shoe is associated with the body. Cross-culturally, the foot is one of the most frequently eroticized body parts (other than the genitals) along with hair, hands and eyes. For Bataille, the fetishization of the foot and shoe are exemplary of the attraction to the base, to the excess of debasement.

Shoes can be sexual without being fetishistic. Although there are clearly types of footwear carrying strong erotic messages, the difference between erotic shoe and fetish shoe lies not in the shoe itself but in the individual's relation to that shoe. Erotically, the shoe serves as a metaphor for the desired other; fetishistically it stands on its own, a substitute for or displacement of the other. The individual's relationship, however, is strongly shaped by social discourses and the ways in which the shoe draws on bodily form. For example, the male equivalent to the stiletto dating from the early 1960s is the 'winkle-picker,' with its elongated, intentionally phallic, pointed toe. Its predecessor was the fifteenth-century 'poulaine' which also had an exaggerated toe of even greater length, sometimes curled at the end and stuffed with horsehair to retain its shape. In that era the sexual symbolism of the shoe was more overt and strong, and its erotic message was to suggest the virile qualities of its wearer.

Shoe mementos – objects imitating the shape of the shoe – can also be erotic: according to Mary Trasko, sixteenth-century Italian potters made hand warmers 'in the shape of women's shoes, which noblemen cupped in their hands both for warmth and to enjoy pleasant recollections' (1989:11). Flügel (1930:27) notes that shoes are phallic symbols as well as symbols of female genitalia. Unlike the male necktie, hat, collar, coat and trousers, and the female girdle and garter, the shoe, he suggests, is 'ambisexual': the intimate insertion of flesh into an opening of leather, silk, kid or satin versus the seductive enclosure of foot's flesh with caressing fabrics. Folk knowledge associates foot size with size of genitalia. The length of the male winkle-picker and poulaine counterposes the snug-fitting, pinching female shoe. Small feet on a woman suggest a slender virginal opening, and in order to achieve the appearance of such, women have been known to wear shoes that are too small. A few women have been reported to have had little toes removed in order to fit, Cinderella-like, into tiny shoes. The fact that, in the original French version of the Cinderella story, the slipper was made of fur, not glass, suggests that Prince Charming had more on his mind than returning lost footwear.[3] Trasko reports that 45 per cent of American women have, at some time, worn undersized shoes.

Chinese footbinding represents the epitome of the emulation of the small foot. To the Western imagination, it was a form of exotic body mutilation comparable to other 'oddities' such as Mesoamerican tooth-filing, African scarification, and Japanese tattooing (Mascia-Lees and Sharpe 1992). In Levy's (1972) examination of the practice, it is difficult at times to ascertain what were the actual circumstances and receptions of footbinding, and what is Levy's 'anthro-porn' rhetoric, a titillating blend of exotified difference and moral horror. Nonetheless, the reality appears to have been more complex and nuanced than any blunt declamation of its misogyny reveals. Fortunately banned in 1911, footbinding was practised most typically on aristocratic women for reasons of status and for enhancing their sexual attractiveness, since the tiny crippled foot was highly eroticized in Chinese culture. The foot was used by men as a secondary sexual organ; he used the cleft created in the woman's foot to masturbate. Surrounding this practice were various seductive arts to increase the foot's desirability: it was kept hidden from all save the husband, wrapped in silk and encased in delicate, embroidered lotus slippers. Unwrapping it was considered to be seductive and erotic, as was the man taking the foot into his mouth.

These are examples of the erotics of foot and shoe, but what of fetishism? The term 'fetish' has several, interrelated meanings. As Dawn Ades (1995) has pointed out, unlike the word 'taboo' also associated with nineteenth-century investigations into the 'primitive,' it is a word that comes from no culture or society. Rather, it arose in the borderlands, a pidgin term for a Portuguese misunderstanding of sacred West African objects. By the nineteenth century, it was a term taken into popular usage in Europe. In an era

---

3. In the Bata Shoe Museum's publicity literature, reference is made to an historical translation error which confused the French word *vair* (white fur) with the word *verre* (glass).

well-informed by rational discourses of the Enlightenment, it came to signal the irrational. Marx used 'fetish' to satirize excessive desire for the consumer object. He conceived of commodity fetishism as comparable to the 'savage' mistaking the idol for the god and, in semiotic terms, mistaking the sign for that which it represents. The idea of the fetish, rather than describing any existing object, is a means for encoding the distinction between appropriate and inappropriate, us and them, civilized and primitive, deviant, outside.

The idea of fetishism was also taken into psychological discourses during the nineteenth century to indicate sexual deviance from a presumed norm. In sexual fetishism, the object represents and substitutes for the woman's body. This gendering is intentional, since it was assumed at the time that only men could be fetishists. The Freudian conceptualization of fetishism theorized its origin in the son's recognition of the mother's missing penis. With castration anxiety at its root, female fetishism was not conceivable, at least to Freud, who argued that women could not be sexual fetishists, but were more inclined to be shopping, that is, commodity fetishists.[4]

Fetishism begins with a singular moment, a powerful coming together of chance events to produce a singular, transfiguring moment which associates first sexual desire with a specific object. Although the original moment is forgotten, it is endlessly reproduced through the fetishization of the object (Ades 1995). The fetish object must be present (even if only in the imagination) in order for sexual gratification to take place. The object can be the only other with which the fetishist engages sexually. That object is over-determined; it is likely to be associated with certain body parts such as hair, foot or eyes, and/or made of particular materials such as leather, fur or rubber.

Artists have used shoes to play upon their erotic, fetishistic and debased meanings.[5] For the surrealists, Freudian analysis provided a means for exploring the relationship between the individual, culture and the unconscious. As the surrealist André Breton noted, the fetish object is more than utilitarian; it provokes an intense experience that gives the object itself such power: the imagination experienced as real (Ades 1995). One goal of surrealist art was to bypass the conscious mind by means of the tactility of the object and to provoke a visceral reaction and recognition of what lies beneath the surface in the unconscious.

A work which so effectively produces such a jolt in the viewer is Meret Oppenheim's 1936 sculpture *My Governess, My Nurse, My Nanny*. A pair

---

4. Steele (1996) summarizes feminist debates on this issue and acknowledges that whereas some women are fetishists, it is nonetheless a predominantly male practice.

5. Steele (1996) does an excellent job of articulating the relationship between fashion and fetishism, and in particular how this plays out in footwear.

of women's high-heeled white pumps lie together and inverted on a silver serving platter. The shoes are trussed like poultry, complete with white paper drumstick caps on each of the heels. The radical juxtaposition of shoe soles with the suggestion of roasted meat prompts an association with female flesh, bondage and debasement. The provocative title further suggests the domination and submission of the child to the female authority figure who once had intimate contact with its body, and for whom the child might have felt the first stirrings of desire. The bondage hints at the child's longing to invert the power relation with the governess, a repressed fantasy of illicit and powerful sexuality crossing the boundaries of class.

In Canadian artist William Eakin's whimsical play on male and female stereotypes (Fig. 1.1), a pair of men's brogues – footwear associated with the business suit – are made to look clownishly large when juxtaposed to slender, female 'legs' made of rose stems. Eakin's artwork plays everyday objects off each other, not in the manner of the surrealists exposing the unconscious, but rather as a means to reveal and satirize outmoded cultural habits such as rigidly demarcated gender differences (Brydon 1995).

Figure 1.1. Canadian artist William Eakin uses men's shoes to satirize middle-class male stereotypes.

Anne Brydon

Collectible Shoe

I have until now been considering shoes as singular or paired objects. But what of shoes which are part of a collection, either privately held or displayed in a shoe museum? How are these collections narratives of desire and longing? Following Susan Stewart, I see the relation of narrative to the collection, and more so, to the museum, as implicated in nostalgia, and that the shoe collection, the exaggeration of ownership, is a technique for fulfilling a yearning which is the ache of nostalgia, a yearning which by definition can never be satisfied. In Elsner and Cardinal's (1994:1) terms, collections are 'bastions against the deluge of time'. The urge to collect and categorize is not simply the effect of capitalist accumulation, but is much older: 'in the myth of Noah as ur-collector resonate all the themes of collecting itself: desire and nostalgia, saving and loss, the urge to erect a permanent and complete system against the destructiveness of time' (ibid.).

Collections and museums, although related, are not the same thing. The act of collecting manifests the maturing of the individual's self-identity. Children start to collect at age five or six. Developmentally, it gives them a world they can control. They decide what is good and what is not, what to keep and what to pass over. Collecting not only expresses who they are, it participates in the process of locating their sense of self in the flux of experience.

Collecting any object, shoes or otherwise, is also a means of returning it into circulation by bestowing value upon it. Unlike the 'vulgar' accumulation associated with, for example, Imelda Marcos' infamous shoes – now, incidentally, the central attraction of the Marcos Palace Museum, making material and visible the Marcos regime's corruption and excess – the collection is a means of recognizing the unappreciated, neglected and forgotten object. Collecting and displaying items of footwear thus transforms them from something to which no one paid attention to something admirable and interesting, and usually quite separate from the individuals who wore them. Susan Sontag (1992) considers collecting a virile activity, with its will to possess and bestow value on things.

Museums as public institutions displaying one or more collections, play a social role as sites of moral education. Their display of objects renders them significant as repositories of history and knowledge, value and taste. Museums display objects as representative of the other, an appeal which is strongly rooted in the West, although not exclusive to it.[6] The museum

---

6. For a non-Western example, see Gell's (1986) discussion of the Muria of Madhya Pradesh, India.

collection as an ethnographic exercise of scientific inquiry was part of a Victorian evolutionary drive to accumulate facts about other peoples as they were ostensibly poised on the brink of disappearance in the face of the so-called forces of progress. Finally, museums strive to tame covetousness through the regulatory narrative of social history, tying its collections to ideas about art, science, taste and heritage.

There are several shoe museums throughout the world. Some, like the Bally Museum of Switzerland, are associated with a single shoe manufacturer while others, like the Northampton Shoe Collection, are located within historic sites of shoemaking. In the museum, shoes are taken from one context and made to fit into new narrative schemes. The case of the Bata Shoe Museum of Toronto, opened in 1995, exemplifies many of the themes of identity, authenticity and modernity I have taken up in this essay. Its collection of over 10,000 shoes links to its founder Sonja Bata's moral and aesthetic ambitions and the transnational reach of her family's manufacturing company. In its public displays, the museum evokes nostalgic pasts and attempts to establish narrative closure on that past by focusing on the shoes as representative objects of social progress and cultural aesthetics. In the process, the social history of shoemaking is distanced and drained of the local conflicts which shaped that history, and in which Bata Industries has played a significant role (Brydon 1998).

Bata Limited is a successful example of commercial globalization and market domination. Until recently, it employed 65,000 people, with 65 manufacturing units and 6,300 stores in 60 countries, and sells more than one million pairs of low-priced shoes per day. The Bata family had been shoemakers for eight generations when Tomas Bata began Bata Industries in Czechoslovakia at the end of the nineteenth century. He transformed the family's local trade into an expanding industry, following on the philosophies and practices of American industrialists, notably Henry Ford. The relationship between the business and its workers was and is benignly paternalistic, and driven by a modernist belief in progress. Before his accidental death in 1932, Bata had laid the groundwork for the expansion of his footwear industry into the colonies of Europe. His son Thomas J. Bata continued and expanded upon the company's global mission to 'shoe the world'. By manufacturing cheap shoes of plastic or locally available materials, Bata aimed to saturate the markets of Third World countries, and in the process wipe out small, local and traditional manufacturers and replace them with ostensibly progressive industrial manufacturing plants.

Sonja Bata married Thomas J. Bata when she was nineteen years of age. She abandoned her ambitions to become, in her words, 'the world's greatest architect' when she accompanied her new husband to Canada, where Bata had relocated after escaping the Nazi occupation of Czechoslovakia and set up its own company town of Batawa 150 km east of Toronto. Her shoe collection began as a working collection, a means for learning the techniques of shoe manufacturing so that she could participate in the running of the company. She later began to collect shoes from those parts of the Third World where Bata factories were displacing local footwear manufacture. This became part of her salvage mission: to preserve and document the indigenous way of life that Bata Industries, as part of the globalization of industrial manufacture, was helping to destroy. She is also an art collector, and the particular form of art she collects happens to be shoes. Thus, connoisseurship mixes with technical knowledge and moral duty as the basis of the collection.

There is no denying that Sonja Bata is a hardworking, serious, even driven businesswoman. In this she is exemplary of the modernist individual Max Weber described as the product of the Protestant work ethic. She is determined that her museum will be a testament to the viability of privately-funded museums, a politically contentious issue at a time of dwindling government funding for social and cultural programmes. Bata situates her museum squarely in the centre of the free enterprise narrative, the one which calls upon the leadership of the heroic entrepreneur to represent morally uplifting examples while engaged in its egoistic craving for the immortality bestowed by the museum's 'ark'.

The Bata shoe collection exemplifies the excess of ownership which is the collection, while as a museum narrating shoes as a separate category of object, it denies both the eroticism of footwear and the circumstances of its production. Once entered into the collection, any item of footwear is removed from the realm of bodily adornment and enters into a new life phase: none of these shoes will ever be worn again. However, they do enter a fantasy realm for their viewers. By means of narratives on the display's signage giving singular interpretation to each item, the viewer is invited to imagine all the nostalgic beauty of costume. In so doing, by focusing attention on the object itself, the museum's display avoids uncomfortable questions about Bata Industries' role in dominating shoe manufacturing worldwide.

The permanent installation *All About Shoes*, a show which reviews footwear through the ages and cross-culturally, is more problematic than the other temporary exhibits in its ambivalent status between personal collection and museum exhibit. As the first display designed for the museum, it betrays the totalizing and objectifying drive of a collector who is determined to amass the largest, most comprehensive collection in the world. Backed by her family's wealth, Sonja Bata has been able to outbid many other collectors and museums, and has effectively raised world prices for collectible shoes.

The irony here lies in the fact that no Bata-made shoes are displayed in the Bata Shoe Museum, presumably since their mass-produced blandness and disposibility run counter to the exclusivity associated with the handcrafted, exotified shoe. The narrative of authenticity versus artificiality once again holds sway in this collection, serving the added purpose of not only accumulating cultural capital for Sonja Bata and, by default, her family's company, but also of glossing over any representation of factory production and its aura of imitation.

All About Shoes makes virtually no reference to industrial production. A tableau *Tools of the Trade*, located in a corner of the exhibit towards its end, simulates a cobbler's shop by displaying tools and other equipment along with costumed mannequins taken from various societies and eras. The tableau's narration freezes shoemaking in time and erases history and difference: 'Until just over a hundred years ago, images of artisans engaged in the manufacture of footwear showed how little the craft changed in seven thousand years . . .' Two videos, made by the Colonial Williamsburg Foundation, describe 'Traditional Shoemaking' and 'Modern Shoemaking'. In the former, still photographs show the stages of making shoes. In the latter, contemporary computer technologies of cutting and assembling are praised for their efficiency of decision-making, and prevention of inefficiency and danger. Only one human operator appears in the video, and the viewer is left with the mistaken impression that progress from tradition to modernity has been seamless, frictionless and for the betterment of everyone, displaced worker and millionaire factory owner alike.

Notably missing from the Bata displays are the exaggerations and symbols of the erotic body. While the exaggerations of fame and status are present – for example, a pair of platform shoes worn by Elton John – those of sexuality are not. Although fetish shoes exist in the collection, they are not on display. A pair of medieval poulaines are on display, but they are interpreted by the accompanying text as being inspired by the spires of Gothic cathedrals. A pair of Chinese lotus slippers are similarly de-eroticized in their description referring only to their role in symbolizing status. In the catalogue, a photograph of winkle pickers are described simply as a 'hit with hip young men and women'; a lithograph of a fetish boot by British artist Alan Jones is narrated without mention of its obvious sexualization; lotus slippers are passingly referred to as 'sexually attractive'; sixteenth-century Venetian chopines are described as aristocratic but without mention that they were also favoured by courtesans, a fact which the curators of the Victoria and Albert Museum's costume display have no such qualms about noting.

Conclusion

The invisibility in the Bata Shoe Museum's displays of the signs of both eroticism and the relations of production locates that institution within bourgeois narratives of morality and progress. The museum effectively legitimates Bata Industries through its celebratory narratives of civic participation, a gesture itself dependent on the self-regulation and containment of modernist individualism. The moral body is disciplined, rational and labouring. But that body cannot experience its own pleasures without its desires being mediated by the commodified, reified object. The collectible shoe, desirable by virtue of its singularity, when brought together in the museum with other shoes similarly desirable for their singularity, provides an odd analogy for the contradiction confronting the modernist individual who desires a singular presentation of self in an era characterized by repetition and mass consumption. Singularity and authenticity of self, built as they are on a contradiction which is inherently ideological, must be negotiated in an unstable field of possible meanings and displaced longings.

Just as the physiology of the neck overdetermines the symbolic potency of the necktie (cf. Shields, this volume), so too do the foot's physical properties intersect with narratives of identity to form a highly volatile symbol. The shoe (and its bodily polar opposite the hat) is a form of clothing which lends itself to sculptural elaboration around what is fundamentally a hole, an absence or lack, the space which the foot (or head) will occupy. The pleasurable comfort promised by the Doc Marten joins with discourses of social rebellion whether real or simulated, while the distorting pain of the stiletto blurs the boundary between female empowerment and disempowerment by means of its erotic potential. Academic footwear, oddly enough, depends on the existence of fetish footwear's abundant sexuality in order for its denial and displacement of the body to be persuasive.

Artists who utilize the image of the shoe in their art, or make art of shoes, draw upon these complexities and ambiguities. They can depend on their audience having already internalized the codes necessary to respond both intellectually and viscerally to the shoe. In terms of Turner's (1967) model of symbolic multivocality, the shoe embodies the twin semantic poles of socially normative meanings and orectic physiological evocations. The shoe, arguably more so than any other clothing item since it is the most ubiquitous, expresses and mediates the prime forces acting upon the individual in modernity. It is in this way, whether on or off the body, whether singular or part of a collection, that the shoe narrates all the anxieties of the modernist self as it engages in its relentless search for unattainable completion and certainty.

Bibliography

Ades, Dawn (1995), 'Surrealism: Fetishism's Job.' In Anthony Shelton (ed.), *Fetishism.* London: The South Bank Centre.

Appadurai, Arjun (1986), 'Introduction: Commodities and the Politics of Value.' In A. Appadurai (ed.), *The Social Life of Things: Commodities in Cultural Perspective.* Cambridge: Cambridge University Press.

Bernhard, Sandra (1996), 'Why High Heels?' *New Yorker*, 72(2):192–3.

Brenninkmeyer, Ingrid (1963), *The Sociology of Fashion.* Köln: Westdeutscher Verlag.

Brydon, Anne (1995), 'Dumb Things.' In *Home Sweet Home.* Lethbridge, Alberta: Southern Alberta Art Gallery.

—— (1998) 'Out of Step: Toronto's Bata Shoe Museum,' *American Quarterly.* Forthcoming.

Cekota, Anthony (1968), *Entrepreneur Extraordinary: The Biography of Tomas Bata.* Rome: University Press of the International University of Social Studies.

Collins, Amy Fine (1995), 'Fashion's Footman,' *Vanity Fair* (May):148–60.

Derrida, Jacques (1981), *Positions.* Alan Bass, trans. Chicago: University of Chicago Press.

Douglas, Mary (1966 (1994)), *Purity and Danger.* London: Routledge.

Elsner, John and Roger Cardinal (eds) (1994), *The Cultures of Collecting.* Cambridge: Harvard University Press.

Finkelstein, Joanne (1991), *The Fashioned Self.* Cambridge: Polity Press.

Flügel, J.C. (1930), *The Psychology of Clothes.* London: Hogarth Press.

Gell, A. (1986), 'Newcomers to the World of Goods: Consumption among the Muria Gonds.' In A. Appadurai (ed.), *The Social Life of Things: Commodities in Cultural Perspective.*

Hebdige, Dick (1979), *Subculture: The Meaning of Style.* London: Methuen.

Kopytoff, Igor (1986), 'The Cultural Biography of Things: Commoditization as Process.' In A. Appadurai (ed.), *The Social Life of Things: Commodities in Cultural Perspective.* Cambridge: Cambridge University Press.

Laver, James (1969), *Modesty in Dress.* Boston: Houghton Mifflin.

Levy, Howard (1972), *Chinese Footbinding.* New York: Bell.

Mascia-Lees, Frances E. and Patricia Sharpe (1992), 'Introduction.' In F.E. Mascia-Lees and P. Sharpe (eds), *Tattoo, Torture, Mutilation, and Adornment: The Denaturalization of the Body in Culture and Text*, Albany: SUNY Press.

McDowell, Colin (1989), *Shoes: Fashion and Fantasy.* New York: Rizzoli.

Oakes, Jill and Rick Riewe (1995), *Our Boots: An Inuit Women's Art.* Toronto: Douglas and MacIntyre.

Rossi, William A. (1977), *The Sex Life of the Foot and Shoe.* London: Routledge and Kegan Paul.

Sontag, Susan (1992), *The Volcano Lover.* New York: Farrar Straus Giroux.

Steele, Valerie (1991), 'The F Word,' *Lingua Franca*, April:17–20.

—— (1996), *Fetish: Fashion, Sex and Power.* Oxford: Oxford University Press.

Stewart, Susan (1993), *On Longing: Narratives of the Miniature, the Gigantic, the*

Souvenir, the Collection. Durham: Duke University Press.

Trasko, Mary (1989), *Heavenly Soles: Extraordinary Twentieth-Century Shoes.* New York: Abbeville Press.

Turner, Victor (1967), *The Forest of Symbols.* Ithaca: Cornell University Press.

Wilson, Elizabeth (1992), 'Fashion and the Postmodern Body.' In Juliet Ash and Elizabeth Wilson (eds), *Chic Thrills: A Fashion Reader.* Berkeley: University of California Press.

2

The Cultural and Historical Contexts of Fashion

Aubrey Cannon

Fashion, in some sense, has characterized human culture since the first adornments of the Upper Palaeolithic. Although the processes of fashion comparison, emulation and differentiation are more noticeably apparent in the rapid changes that characterize systems of industrial production, the same processes are observable or at least inferable in most cultures. In most non-industrial contexts, however, the operation of fashion may be limited to a relatively narrow range of circumstances, and these have been documented in only a few rare cases. One exceptional example is the North American fur trade. European fur traders documented in precise detail their efforts to satisfy what they saw as the ever-changing Native fashions for beads, cloth and other items of adornment. The universality of fashion is therefore evident in its general definition as an agent of style change, in the recognition of circumstances that regularly promote its operation and through its documentation in particular ethnohistoric contexts.

The Universality of Fashion

The applicability of fashion to small-scale non-industrial cultures depends in part on its definition. In separating fashion, as a process of continuous change, from short-term, ephemeral fads, Blumer (1968), for example, largely removed fashion from the domain of 'traditional' societies. Unfortunately, this definition excludes the systematic changes in style that occur in all cultures. These are neither the result of continuous fashion change, nor are they the inconsequential result of randomly-occurring fads. In smaller-scale societies, systematic style change may only occur sporadically as it is activated by circumstances, and continue only so long as the conducive conditions exist. A more inclusive definition of fashion therefore must encompass the

basic process of style change, without the requirement that it be the continuous process evident in recent Western industrial societies.

Broadening the application of fashion concepts also requires a shift in
understanding of its basis. Explanations of fashion, as defined for recent
Western contexts, typically focus on its psychological motivation and social
purpose (Blumer 1968; Sproles 1985). Its psychological basis, which is the
desire to create a positive self-image, is recognized as widely if not universally
applicable cross-culturally, but the social role of fashion is often restricted
by definition to those societies that exhibit a clearly-defined class structure
(McKendrick, Brewer and Plumb 1982; Simmel 1904:138). This definition
is unnecessarily restrictive, and ignores pervasive but much more subtle
distinctions in status based on personality, wealth and skill. These are equally
capable of giving rise to fashion-based differentiation and emulation,
especially in circumstances where the basis for prestige recognition is
uncertain or undergoing change.

Fashion develops in all contexts as the result of the assertion of self-identity
and social comparison (Simmel 1904; Wiessner 1989). Individuals use visual
media to indicate to themselves and others whether they think they belong
with another individual or group, or whether they consider themselves
another's equal or superior. These expressions may involve an infinite range
of comparisons depending on degrees of similarity or distinction, but the
essential process of comparison remains the same in all contexts. The first
beads from the Upper Palaeolithic, dating to ca. 30,000 years ago (White
1989), therefore are testimony to a common human desire to gain recognition
as a separate identity by setting oneself apart visually.

The fashion process can also explain the diversity and changes of styles
that characterize all subsequent culture history (Wiessner 1989), up to and
including our own time. Unfortunately, because fashion is normally seen as
a more recent and specifically Western development, its role in the creation
of style among smaller-scale societies is generally unrecognized. In these
contexts, group and individual styles of dress and adornment are more often
attributed to conservative traditions and the representation of social roles
(Blumer 1968:342; McKendrick et al. 1982:34–7), and fashion is considered
of little consequence within these social and cultural constraints (Appadurai
1986:31–2; Simmel 1904:138). The myth of traditional conservatism (e.g.
Simmel 1904:136) is so firmly entrenched that long-term changes of style in
small-scale societies are almost never attributed to simple fashion. Instead
they are considered the result of external forces such as acculturation
(Quimby and Spoehr 1951), or are attributed to unknowing selection of
random variation (O'Brien and Holland 1990), though both explanations
tend to minimize the role of human intention and choice.

Ethnographers may not recognize the fashion process because they witness cultures over relatively short periods of time. Archaeologists do not have the same excuse, but the evidence of prehistory is a much better record of the outcomes of style change than of the processes by which it occurs. Historians and sociologists, in contrast, can examine detailed documentary evidence to seek the origins of fashion in the more recent histories of European cultures. As a result, fashion has come to be seen as synonymous with the spirit of individualism and consumption characteristic of Western European industrial capitalism. Historians generally trace fashion to the nascent capitalism and later industrial economy of post-Medieval Europe (McKendrick et al. 1982; Sombart 1967), though some trace the specific origins to a particular time and place, such as the court of Elizabethan England (McCracken 1988). These efforts, however, may mistake particular social and political uses of clothing style for a more fundamental process of social comparison, which is evident throughout human history. They also tend to confuse the fashion industry with the fashion process. Although industrial production encouraged and enabled fashion consumption, the industry grew initially on the basis of consumer demand and a process of social comparison that already existed (Mukerji 1983).

Contexts for Fashion

The underlying unity of the fashion process in all cultural contexts from the prehistoric, to the ethnographic, to the recent historic and contemporary is the manipulation of appearance to enhance or maintain a positive self-image (Wiessner 1983, 1989). This may depend on conformity in many social contexts, but fashion and culture change depend on an ability to derive some positive value from distinctions in appearance. This may not be possible in the majority of circumstances in small-scale societies, and it might be appropriate to speak of an inherent resistance to fashion in these instances. If the act of setting oneself apart threatened the identity of everyone that conformed, the result would generally be a negative impression for the non-conformist (e.g. Gell 1986). Only an extremely charismatic individual could succeed in creating an enhanced self-image through nonconformity.

But if conservatism and conformity are the norms in traditional societies, extraordinary circumstances can initiate or exaggerate the fashion process in almost any social setting. Virtually any situation that creates social uncertainty can lead to the elaboration, diversification and emulation of distinctive forms of expression. This association between social change and material variation is well-recognized in archaeology and anthropology (e.g.

Cannon 1989; Conkey 1985; Hays 1993; Martin, Lloyd and Spoehr 1938; Richardson and Kroeber 1940; Sapir 1931), and though the association is rarely explained explicitly in these terms, social change can clearly affect an individual's psychological desire to present an enhanced self-image. Change in the basis of prestige or status can undermine one's sense of position in relation to others, or create new means or new opportunities for achieving enhanced recognition. Either circumstance could lead individuals to seek new means of visible distinction. This, in turn, could initiate a cycle of emulation and differentiation capable of generating its own momentum, though the fashion process would normally be expected to slow or stop altogether as disruptive circumstances eased and social conditions stabilized.

Many circumstances that disrupt established patterns of social reckoning also lead to the self-doubt or opportunities for advancement that are at the heart of fashion (see Table 2.1), and most are applicable to all social contexts. The balance of status perceptions and power relations can be upset by an uncontrolled influx of resources, for example. These might translate directly into wealth or status or provide new means of display. Separating the two effects in prehistoric or even more recent social contexts, however, might not be possible since material wealth is often measured in terms of prestige goods mainly destined for conspicuous display (Renfrew 1986).

Table 2.1. Forces and Circumstances Conducive to Fashion.

Force or Circumstance	Relevant Social Contexts
Personal Charisma	All
Uncontrolled Influx of Resources	All
Rapid Population Growth or Aggregation	All
Rapid Depopulation	All
Political Power Shift	Chiefdom, Early and Modern State
Industrial Production	Capitalist, Industrial
Image Distribution	Post-industrial

Rapid population increase or sudden aggregation can also create the opportunity for developing new social roles, and has the further potential of weakening communication through existing media of visual display because of the scalar increase in information involved (Conkey 1985; Hays 1993). Larger population aggregates may require new visual media to signal individual identity, while the management of information and interaction creates new demands and opportunities for positions of enhanced status and authority, which must also be signalled through new forms of visual distinction. Associations of stylistic diversity and population growth are clearly evident in the archaeological record, and recent data increasingly show that local, rapid population increase was a common occurrence in the prehistoric past (e.g. Culbert and Rice 1990; Warrick 1990).

Rapid depopulation would have a similar effect on existing systems of social reckoning. The death of ranking individuals and major social reorganization resulting from massive population decline would open social roles to intense competition. The potlatch on the Northwest Coast of North America is one particularly well-documented example of the material effects of social reorganization resulting from population decline. In this case, competition to fill vacant social ranks and titles resulted in intense efforts to attain and legitimize status rights through feasting and material presentation (Codere 1950). The combination of rapid depopulation and social restructuring coupled with an influx of European trade goods resulted in unprecedented levels of material consumption and conspicuous display.

Population and resource fluctuations such as these have occurred throughout history, but other circumstances have also emerged over time to add new and more intense impetus to the fashion process. With the increased social complexity found in emergent and small-scale states, for example, the potential for shifts in the balance of political power created new opportunities for increased uncertainty in status reckoning, at least among members of political elites. The inherent instability of chiefdoms and early states, which were subject to ever-shifting alliances and tests of political power and will, provided increased incentive for maintaining symbolic visual distinctions of status and office. The very creation of sumptuary rules in these contexts is clear evidence of the pervading impetus toward fashion emulation, and the potential threat to status recognition this represented. The result was the elaboration and continuing differentiation of dress and adornment, which is as evident in the elaborate headdress and regalia of the Aztec nobility (Anawalt 1981) as it is in the costumes of the Elizabethan court (McCracken 1988).

The development of industrial economies introduced a new power to disrupt social reckoning on a mass scale, brought about in this case by the production and distribution of material fashions themselves. Easier access to styles that carried status associations meant that recognition of social position was in a much more constant state of flux. This, in turn, encouraged the continuous production of new styles (McKendrick et al. 1982; Mukerji 1983). Finally, in the contemporary post-industrial era, all of the existing forces affecting fashion continue to operate, but uncertainty now is almost perpetually created by the distribution of mere images of fashion. The result is a sense that styles and social associations are constantly changing.

These are at least some of the conditions that help to create the impetus for fashion, but their identification does not reveal anything about how they operate or their consequences in particular circumstances. The way that styles emerge and become acceptable or fashionable images for a particular time and place is still a question that can be answered only through specific historical analysis. Only the process of fashion is universal. It may be activated or enhanced in general circumstances that create social uncertainty, but the process results in the coming and going of particular styles as the result of unique historical trajectories of design comparison. New styles can develop through minor modification of earlier forms (Lowe and Lowe 1982) or through the reversal or amalgamation of opposing forms. Styles may also alternate between the poles of simple and complex (Cannon 1989; Clarke 1978:182–6), or be determined by the intrinsic rules of a particular design grammar (Washburn 1983) or simple inherent limits to design variation, such as those imposed on dress length (Richardson and Kroeber 1940). The emergence of new styles is part of the unique histories of fashion. The essential driving force is an ever-shifting scale of social values associated with existing and new designs.

But if unique fashion histories remain the subject of individual investigation, then what is gained in thinking about fashion as a universal process? A general benefit may be in seeing all culture change and diversity as the result of common processes, unique histories and conscious human agency. The artificial dichotomies of traditional and non-traditional societies, production and consumption, supply and demand, and status and display could be set aside in favour of analysis that recognized a range of variability and influence in the common process of materially-mediated social interaction. Simple explanations of fashion based on attribution to a particular culture or historical trajectory, such as recent industrial Europe, would give way to more specific and more detailed readings of how and why the fashion process becomes engaged. In more specific cases, the seemingly impractical drive to acquire new and varied styles of adornment and display can be made intelligible in terms applicable to all cultures. Thinking of this behaviour as fashion opens the door to more detailed examination of how and why the process developed, without having to invoke extraordinary explanation for each case.

The North American fur trade, for example, is a particularly well-documented case study, where the explanatory emphasis for Native-European interaction has largely neglected the role of indigenous fashion in favour of the exploitative and dependency relationships predicated on European technology and alcohol. The demand for cloth, beads and other items of adornment, however, illustrates that fashion concerns were a far from trivial component of trade relations. The example illustrates the applicability of fashion in non-Western settings and its importance in understanding the dynamics of the fur trade.

Fashion and the Fur Trade

Fashion's place in the North American fur trade is clearly evident in the European demand for furs, but its role in indigenous trade is also apparent according to several criteria commonly accepted as characteristic of fashion. Demand for adornment and apparel was substantial, subject to the control and particular tastes of Native consumers, prone to frequent change, and part of a process of status display and social comparison. Although these criteria must be established on the basis of information that is often anecdotal and drawn from a broad range of temporal and cultural contexts, they show that fashion in some form was an indigenous phenomenon, which played an important and often determining role in fur trade relations.

Early discussions of the North American fur trade emphasized Native dependency on superior European technology (Rich 1967:102–3), which suggested that European traders were able to maintain considerable control over the terms of exchange. Recent research, in contrast, has placed much greater emphasis on the independent role of Native consumers (Eccles 1988; Lohse 1988; Ray and Freeman 1978), illustrated, for example, by their frequently-exercised ability to dictate the type and quality of goods for which they were willing to trade. European traders also recognized that demand for practical necessities was inherently limited, which led to fears that lower prices would simply lessen the number of furs traded, and to efforts to encourage trade by increasing supplies of alcohol, tobacco and a wide array of luxury consumer goods (Ray and Freeman 1978:129,222,225).

Although recent explanations of fur trade dynamics have tended to neglect the significance of adornment, the consistent demand for glass beads and coloured cloth was a major element in exchange relationships from initial European contact on the East Coast to the later Hudson's Bay Company trade in western Canada. Sources also indicate that Native traders were consistently particular in their demands for goods of specific form and colour. A seventeenth-century trader in Virginia, for example, noted that his Native customers preferred 'sad' colours of cloth in mostly deep blues and reds, and might refuse to hunt furs at all if the colours of cloth did not please them (Axtell 1981:254). Sixteenth-century Narragansett on the coast of New

England specifically indicated their desire for blue beads and dark woolen blankets, and a seventeenth-century English trader could still lament that his stock of beads was not held in much esteem by the Narragansett, who preferred the cloth and other goods they could obtain from the Dutch (Turnbaugh 1993:141). Archaeological evidence indicates that Iroquoian peoples of southern Ontario also had very particular preferences for bead colours and styles (Kenyon and Kenyon 1983). The wide variety exhibited in early bead assemblages gave way to a predominance of simple dark blue and white beads, which later changed to red and turquoise blue beads as French traders became aware of their customers' desires. The more detailed documentary records of the Hudson's Bay Company also indicate that traders in the Canadian subarctic were faced with the same problem of meeting very specific desires for different sizes and colours of beads and cloth (Davies and Johnson 1965:100,157,178–9; Krech 1987). Demand for coloured apparel and beads was substantial and widespread throughout North America, and European traders were forced to respond to indigenous demands, however much they were in control of the actual supply of goods.

Despite the very specific demands for beads and other items of apparel and adornment, early traders were generally unconcerned with the role of these goods in Native society. Until recently the prevailing assumption has been that a fascination with colour and the glimmer of metal and glass was sufficient explanation for their continuing demand. Contemporaneous accounts dismissed beads as trifles and trash, and more recent commentary continues to describe trade beads in disparaging terms as gewgaws and worthless baubles (Lohse 1988:396; Woodward 1970:1). The Indian trade for trinkets has become part of American folklore, as exemplified by the often-repeated story of how Manhattan Island was traded for a handful of beads (Thomas 1991:83). Beyond their role as archaeological time markers, beads had been, until recently, accorded little interpretative value. Recent studies, however, have attempted to address the question of why beads and other particular items of adornment were so highly valued and widely sought after. Hammel (1983), for example, has outlined what he sees as the cosmological significance of coloured metal and glass, and has attempted to explain their intrinsic value and meaning in Native perception. The role of beads as gifts in the mediation of gender relations is cited as another reason for their continuing demand (Cannon 1991; Ray 1974:156), but, with rare exceptions (e.g. Krech 1987), little attention has been given to the role of fashion in creating a demand for beads and different bead styles.

Records of the early fur trade in the Northeast unfortunately give little direct indication of changing fashions. Beads, however, did become less valuable and subsequently less popular once their distribution had become widespread (Bradley 1983:36; Miller, Pogue and Smolek 1983:127), and this is consistent with change in demand in the face of market saturation that is also characteristic of modern fashion (Sproles 1985). Archaeological evidence also indicates that preferences for particular bead styles, as in the southern Ontario example, could change dramatically within as few as five years (Fitzgerald, Knight and Bain 1995). Later Hudson's Bay Company records, however, are the most detailed source of references to the very particular and changing demands of Native traders. Company traders recognized that Native tastes were highly volatile and subject to change at any time (Davies and Johnson 1965:325), and often had to request that particular sizes and colours of beads no longer be sent because there was no interest in trading for them. In one particular example, the Earl of Southesk, writing in 1859 from Carlton House, a trading post on the North Saskatchewan River, remarked with some amusement that fashion reigned there as imperiously as in 'more civilized lands' (Southesk 1969 [1875]:124). He noted that one variety of large, fine and richly coloured bead, which he considered his best, and which had been generally admired a year or two before, had become despised and out of date. In its place, tiny, white 'trashy' beads had become highly appreciated. A similar change in fashion was recorded by traders with the American Fur Company. In 1833 they ordered a shipment of 'agate beads', which were not delivered on time, but had gone out of fashion by the time of their arrival in January 1835 (Woodward 1970:22). Although the evidence for fashion is sporadic and largely anecdotal, it strongly suggests that Europeans were forced to respond to the changing demands of Native fashion throughout the course of the North American fur trade.

European traders, however, were no more content to respond passively to Native demand than Native traders were content to accept whatever Europeans supplied. From the beginning, European traders actively sought to increase demand for their goods. English traders in eighteenth-century New England, for example, were encouraged to multiply the desires of their trading partners by introducing them to 'a thousand things they had never dreamt of before' (Axtell 1981:52). Similar strategies were encouraged by the Hudson's Bay Company, as new lines of commodities were introduced in an effort to increase the total number of furs traded (Ray and Freeman 1978:225). Generally these efforts resulted in little success, though letters from trading posts suggest that Company traders were engaged in an almost continual process of trial and error in hopes of supplying local desires. In 1739, for example, a trader from Fort Albany expressed the belief that brass collars would be pleasing to the Indians and would allure them from the French. A letter later that same year noted that Natives were unwilling to pay the price of four beaver pelts per collar, though the hope was expressed that they might yet prove attractive to Indians from further inland. By the next year it was reported that the entire inventory of brass collars still remained and could not be traded for more than a single beaver pelt each (Davies and Johnson 1965:289,302,327). Untraded inventories and falling prices in this case and others make it clear that efforts to encourage demand were as likely to fail as succeed.

The selection of European items of adornment was governed by considerations that went well beyond their simple aesthetic value. Arguably, even the value of utilitarian goods went beyond their practical usefulness. In many cases, their true worth was probably social, and their demand also largely dictated by prestige value and fashion comparison. Although the precise social contexts and meanings of fashionable display during the fur trade era are not generally recorded, trade goods clearly were a means of social display and a measure of status distinction and wealth (Krech 1987, Lohse 1988). Illustrative examples are common in the documentary record. The Narragansett of New England, for example, avidly sought after English coats with rich trim for their value as status markers (Turnbaugh 1993:142), and a Hudson's Bay Company letter records a local leader's desire for a lace hat to distinguish himself from his common companions (Davies and Johnson 1965:71). European traders also deliberately sought to create demand by asserting that certain goods were especially appropriate for chiefs. An account by Captain John Smith, in 1607–1608, records a transaction in colonial Virginia in which he convinced two important local chiefs that some blue beads, which they admired, were to be worn only by the highest chiefs. As a result, he obtained up to 600 bushels of corn in exchange for a mere four pounds of beads (Miller et al. 1983:127). The value of the beads declined rapidly however, and by 1624, 20,000 blue beads were recorded as payment for some mats.

The Hudson's Bay Company's understanding of the importance of fashion in Native status display is evident in their creation of 'trading captains', who were chosen to act as leading representatives in trade relationships. (Fig. 2.1) These leaders were appointed in part because Europeans were frustrated by a lack of predictable leadership among indigenous groups (Ray 1974:137–9), but their creation was also an effort to encourage increased trade by rewarding individuals who led followers to trade at Company posts (Krech 1984:112–13; Ray and Freeman 1978:70). Captains were outfitted in bright red or blue laced suits, and given fancy items of adornment to symbolize their importance and unique role in trade (Ray and Freeman 1978:56). Company traders realized that status recognition was a primary incentive for individuals to act as trading captains, and this was one of the reasons that leaders were given the 'captain's outfit' prior to trade. By

SIR JOS JEBB.

Figure 2.1. Two Odawa chiefs, painted in the early nineteenth century. (National Archives of Canada/D114384).

outfitting captains in such elaborate garb, traders were also perhaps inadvertently working to create fashion leaders as well as social and economic leaders. Although members of trading gangs shared in the gifts of alcohol and tobacco given to their captain, the position of captain was apparently itself a focus of desire and emulation. Records show a proliferation of captains in the later eighteenth century, with many former lieutenants being promoted to the position of captain (Morantz 1983:136–9). The reason was the increased competition from Northwest Company traders, but demand for the title and clothing distinctions of the trading captains was obviously pervasive. In this sense, the example follows a pattern typical of the fashion process, in which leading individuals set the example in dress that others desire to follow (Sproles 1985). The result of this proliferation of captain's outfits was an outcome also typical of fashion, in that it contributed to the eventual end of trading captain distinctions. Although the practice of outfitting trading captains probably never had a major impact on overall Native consumer demand, it illustrates the pattern of social comparison that probably underlay all changes in Native demand for distinctive clothing and adornment.

The fur trade is just one example of the fashion-driven demand for goods that can develop among small-scale, non-industrial societies. Although the supporting evidence is sparse even in this relatively well-documented example, Native demand for beads, cloth and other items of apparel exhibits all the criteria of fashion. Consumption of these goods was substantial and clearly subject to the tastes and desires of consumers rather than suppliers. Tastes also changed, sometimes in as little as a year or two, and demands for particular styles shifted according to market saturation and the choices of fashion leaders. Although the precise social contexts that shaped the demand for trade good fashions were almost never recorded, the essential element of fashion, which is the expression of individual identity, shaped and modified through social comparison, is clearly evident in Native desires and European marketing strategies.

Fashion is recognizable in this case in part because the fur trade exaggerated the pace and profile of a latent process of material display and social comparison which already existed. The social disruptions created and exacerbated by European contact and the fur trade were also precisely the conditions most conducive to fashion. The influx of new material and informational resources, massive population decline and major social restructuring, and the development of new power relations based on alliances and relationships with Europeans disrupted existing systems of social reckoning and increased the demand for new material expressions of social distinction and affiliation. European traders willingly supplied the demand, but the fashion process and the particular demands of Native traders were beyond their control.

Discussion

In the end, as much as fur traders sought to shape and dictate Native consumer trends, there is no evidence they were any more successful in this effort than the contemporary fashion and retail industries are in dictating consumer choices for their own convenience and profit. Fashion suppliers may try to generate opportunities for change, and seek to identify or even create fashion leaders. They certainly try to maintain supply when trends become apparent. But whatever their success in manipulating circumstances and engaging the fashion process, they are ultimately incapable of controlling outcomes.

In part this is because fashion is an inherent part of human social interaction and not the creation of an elite group of designers, producers, or marketers. Because of its basis in individual social comparison, fashion cannot be controlled without undermining its ultimate purpose, which is the expression of individual identity. If self-identity were never in doubt and social comparison never took place, there would be no demand for fashion, and there would be no need or opportunity for style change. All cultures would be bound in the same manner as commonly envisioned for 'traditional' societies. In contrast, the reality is that style change and periods of fashionable display and emulation are evident in a broad range of cultural contexts and are pronounced under circumstances of social disruption and transition. In these circumstances, fashions past and present have developed and gained acceptance through individual choice and conscious effort to present a favourable social image. This is the common linkage that makes fashion a defining characteristic of humanity and allows us insight into the past through the processes we can see so much more clearly in the present.

Bibliography

Anawalt, P.R. (1981), *Indian Clothing before Cortez: Mesoamerican Costumes from the Codices*. Norman: University of Oklahoma Press.

Appadurai, A. (1986), 'Introduction: Commodities and the Politics of Value.' In A. Appadurai (ed.) *The Social Life of Things: Commodities in Cultural Perspective*. Cambridge: Cambridge University Press.

Axtell, J. (1981), *The European and the Indian: Essays in the Ethnohistory of Colonial North America*. Oxford: Oxford University Press.

Blumer, H.G. (1968), 'Fashion.' In C.F. Sills (ed.), *International Encyclopedia of the Social Sciences*, vol. 5. New York: MacMillan.

Bradley, J.W. (1983), 'Blue Crystals and other Trinkets: Glass Beads from 16th and Early 17th Century New England.' In C.F. Hayes (ed.), *Proceedings of the 1982 Glass Trade Bead Conference*. Rochester: Rochester Museum and Science Center Research Records No. 16.

Cannon, A. (1989), 'The Historical Dimension in Mortuary Expressions of Status and Sentiment,' *Current Anthropology*, 30:437–58.

—— (1991), 'Gender, Status, and the Focus of Material Display.' In D. Walde and N.D.Willows (eds), *The Archaeology of Gender: Proceedings of the Twenty-Second Annual Chacmool Conference.* Calgary: Archaeological Association, University of Calgary.

Clarke, D.L. (1978), *Analytical Archaeology.* Sec. ed. New York: Columbia University Press.

Codere, H. (1950), *Fighting with Property: A Study of Kwakiutl Potlatching and Warfare, 1792–1930.* Monographs of the American Ethnological Society No. 18. Seattle: University of Washington Press.

Conkey, M.W. (1985), 'Ritual Communication, Social Elaboration, and the Variable Trajectories of Palaeolithic Material Culture.' In T.D. Price and J.A. Brown (eds), *Prehistoric Hunter-Gatherers: The Emergence of Cultural Complexity.* Orlando: Academic Press.

Culbert, T.P. and D.S. Rice (eds) (1990), *Precolumbian Population History in the Maya Lowlands.* Albuquerque: University of New Mexico Press.

Davies, K.G. and A.M. Johnson (eds) (1965), *Letters from Hudson Bay, 1703–1740.* London: Hudson's Bay Record Society.

Eccles, W.J. (1988), 'The Fur Trade in the Colonial Northeast.' In W.E. Washburn (ed.), *History of Indian-White Relations.* Handbook of North American Indians, vol. 4, W. Sturtevant, general editor. Washington, D.C.: Smithsonian Institution.

Fitzgerald, W.R., D.H. Knight, and A. Bain (1995), 'Untanglers of Matters Temporal and Cultural: Glass Beads and the Early Contact Period Huron Ball Site,' *Canadian Journal of Archaeology,* 19:117–38.

Gell, A. (1986), 'Newcomers to the World of Goods: Consumption among the Muria Gonds.' In A. Appadurai (ed.), *The Social Life of Things: Commodities in Cultural Perspective.* Cambridge: Cambridge University Press.

Hamell, G.R. (1983), 'Trading in Metaphors: The Magic of Beads.' In C.F. Hayes (ed.), *Proceedings of the 1982 Glass Trade Bead Conference.* Rochester: Rochester Museum and Science Center Research Records No. 16.

Hays, K.A. (1993), 'When is a Symbol Archaeologically Meaningful? Meaning, Function, and Prehistoric Visual Arts.' In N. Yoffee and A. Sheratt (eds), *Archaeological Theory: Who Sets the Agenda?* Cambridge: Cambridge University Press.

Kenyon, I.T. and T. Kenyon (1983), 'Comments on 17th Century Glass Trade Beads from Ontario.' In C.F. Hayes (ed.), *Proceedings of the 1982 Glass Trade Bead Conference.* Rochester: Rochester Museum and Science Center Research Records No. 16.

Krech, S. (1984), 'The Trade of the Slavey and Dogrib at Fort Simpson in the Early Nineteenth Century.' In S. Krech (ed.), *The Subarctic Fur Trade: Native Social and Economic Adaptations.* Vancouver: University of British Columbia Press.

—— (1987), 'The Early Fur Trade in the Northwestern Subarctic: The Kutchin and the Trade in Beads.' In B.G. Trigger, T. Morantz, and L. Dechêne (eds), *Le Castor Fait Tout: Selected Papers of the Fifth North American Fur Trade Conference, 1985.* Montreal: Lake St. Louis Historical Society.

Lohse, E.S. (1988), 'Trade Goods.' In W.E. Washburn (ed.), *History of Indian-White*

Relations. Handbook of North American Indians, vol. 4, W. Sturtevant, general editor. Washington, D.C.: Smithsonian Institution.

Lowe, J.W.G. and E.D. Lowe (1982), 'Cultural Pattern and Process: A Study of Stylistic Change in Women's Dress,' *American Anthropologist,* 84:521–44.

Martin, P.S., C. Lloyd, and A. Spoehr (1938), 'Archaeological Work in the Ackmen-Lowry Area, Southwestern Colorado, 1937,' *Anthropological Series, Field Museum of Natural History,* 23:219–304.

McCracken, G. (1988), *Culture and Consumption: New Approaches to the Symbolic Character of Consumer Goods and Activities.* Bloomington: Indiana University Press.

McKendrick, N., J. Brewer, and J.H. Plumb (1982), *The Birth of a Consumer Society: The Commercialization of Eighteenth Century England.* Bloomington: Indiana University Press.

Miller, H.M., D.J. Pogue, and M.A. Smolek (1983), 'Beads from the Seventeenth Century Chesapeake.' In C.F. Hayes (ed.), *Proceedings of the 1982 Glass Trade Bead Conference.* Rochester: Rochester Museum and Science Center Research Records No. 16.

Morantz, T. (1983), *An Ethnohistoric Study of Eastern James Bay Cree Social Organization, 1700–1850.* Canadian Ethnology Service Paper No. 88. Ottawa: National Museum of Man.

Mukerji, C. (1983), *From Graven Images: Patterns of Modern Materialism.* New York: Columbia University Press.

O'Brien, M. and T.D. Holland (1990), 'Variation, Selection, and the Archaeological Record.' In M.B. Schiffer (ed.), *Archaeological Method and Theory,* vol. 2. Tucson: University of Arizona Press.

Quimby, G.I. and A. Spoehr (1951), 'Acculturation and Material Culture,' *Anthropological Series, Field Museum of Natural History,* 36:107–47.

Ray, A.J. (1974), *Indians in the Fur Trade: Their Role as Trappers, Hunters, and Middlemen in the Lands Southwest of Hudson Bay, 1660–1870.* Toronto: University of Toronto Press.

—— and D. Freeman (1978), *Give Us Good Measure: An Economic Analysis of Relations Between the Indians and the Hudson's Bay Company before 1763.* Toronto: University of Toronto Press.

Renfrew, C. (1986), 'Varna and the Emergence of Wealth in Prehistoric Europe.' In A. Appadurai (ed.), *The Social Life of Things: Commodities in Cultural Perspective.* Cambridge: Cambridge University Press.

Rich, E.E. (1967), *The Fur Trade and the Northwest to 1857.* Toronto: McClelland and Stewart.

Richardson, J. and A.L. Kroeber (1940), 'Three Centuries of Women's Dress Fashions: A Quantitative Analysis,' *University of California Anthropological Record,* 5,2:111–54.

Sapir, E. (1931), 'Fashion.' In E.R.A. Seligman and A. Johnson (eds), *International Encyclopedia of the Social Sciences,* vol. 6. New York: MacMillan.

Simmel, G. (1904), 'Fashion.' *International Quarterly,* 10:130–55.

Sombart, W. (1967), *Luxury and Capitalism*. Ann Arbor: University of Michigan Press.

Southesk, Carnegie, J., Earl of (1969), *Saskatchewan and the Rocky Mountains: A Diary and Narrative of Travel, Sport, and Adventure, During a Journey Through the Hudson's Bay Company's Territories, in 1859 and 1860*. Edmonton: M.G. Hurtig.

Sproles, G.B. (1985), 'Behavioral Science Theories of Fashion.' In M.R. Solomon (ed.), *The Psychology of Fashion*. Lexington, Massachusetts: Lexington Books.

Thomas, N. (1991), *Entangled Objects: Exchange, Material Culture, and Colonialism in the Pacific*. Cambridge: Harvard University Press.

Turnbaugh, W.A. (1993), 'Assessing the Significance of European Goods in Seventeenth-Century Narragansett Society.' In J.D. Rogers and S.M. Wilson (eds), *Ethnohistory and Archaeology: Approaches to Postcontact Change in the Americas*. New York: Plenum Press.

Warrick, G.A. (1990), *A Population History of the Huron-Petun, A.D. 900–1600*. Ann Arbor: University Microfilms.

Washburn, D.K. (1983), 'Toward a Theory of Structural Style in Art.' In D.K. Washburn (ed.), *Structure and Cognition in Art*. Cambridge: Cambridge University Press.

White, R. (1989), 'Production Complexity and Standardization in Early Aurignacian Bead and Pendant Manufacture: Evolutionary Implications.' In P. Mellars and C. Stringer (eds), *The Human Revolution: Behavioural and Biological Perspectives on the Origins of Modern Humans*. Edinburgh: Edinburgh University Press.

Wiessner, P. (1983), 'Style and Social Information in Kalahari San Projectile Points,' *American Antiquity*, 48:253–76.

—— (1989), 'Style and the Changing Relations Between the Individual and Society.' In I. Hodder (ed.), *The Meaning of Things: Material Culture and Symbolic Expression*. London: Unwin Hyman.

Woodward, A. (1970), *The Denominators of the Fur Trade: An Anthology of Writings on the Material Culture of the Fur Trade*. Pasadena: Soci-Technical Publications.

3

Transformations in the Use of Traditional Textiles of Ngada (Western Flores, Eastern Indonesia): Commercialization, Fashion and Ethnicity

Andrea K. Molnar

Introduction

During an international trade fair in Jakarta in mid-July 1994, the eastern Indonesian Province of Nusa Tenggara Timur (N.T.T.) was represented by a booth containing a display that was almost completely dedicated to the exhibition of handicrafts, especially of local textiles in the form of interior decoration, fashion and accessories. Eastern Indonesian *ikat* and other textiles have come a long way from their traditional use as *sarong* and are now used for such varied purposes as designer furniture and cushion upholstery. This paper considers how the use and valuation of 'traditional' textiles have changed in the Ngada regency and also in other parts of the province of Nusa Tenggara Timur, particularly in Kupang, where small groups of people from this regency can be found. This transformation in the uses of local *ikat* textiles is an aspect of wider cultural changes of modernization and development efforts occurring in this eastern province of Indonesia. Before proceeding with the discussion of these various changes relating to textiles, however, it is prudent to provide a very brief description of Ngada and Nusa Tenggara Timur in order to contextualize the cultural changes occurring. It is also essential that such salient concepts of this paper as 'fashion', 'traditional' and 'modern' be first defined.

The eastern Indonesian province of Nusa Tenggara Timur consists of five major islands (Sumba, Flores, Solor, Alor, Timor) and numerous smaller islands (such as Roti, Sawu and so on) in the eastern part of what once used to be known as the Lesser Sundas. The islands are part of a greater volcanic mountain chain in Indonesia. Ecologically there also are differences between the islands. While the western part of Flores is fertile and lush with tropical forests, most other islands are dry and not as fertile. Economically most people are occupied in agriculture (mainly dry field cultivation) and animal husbandry with coastal fishing. The province is very diverse culturally and possesses many different cultural or ethnic groups and languages. Historically, Nusa Tenggara Timur was influenced by both the Portuguese (fifteenth to early seventeenth century) and Dutch (seventeenth to twentieth century) colonial powers. However, the degrees of influence vary from island to island, and even within an island, in direct relations to when colonial interests extended to particular regions.[1] This differential interest in the people and region of present day Nusa Tenggara Timur has also been mirrored in the development efforts of the Indonesian government since the nation's independence. This part of Indonesia is still very underdeveloped from the perspective of economics, health, education and infrastructures.[2]

The Ngada regency is the second from the west on the island of Flores. It consists of numerous cultural groups and traditions, although the local government agencies only recognize three major groups (Ngadha, Nage-Keo and Riung). Geographically and ecologically this region is mountainous with several volcanic peaks and is mostly covered in tropical forest. People are mainly swidden cultivators with only certain areas suitable for wet-rice cultivation. Colonial interest in the region and Catholic missionizing did not touch most of the regency until 1907 onward. Results of economic development efforts in this regency are far below that of the averages of the province of Nusa Tenggara Timur. Cultural changes and transformations as a result of such modernizing efforts vary greatly within the regency. However, the majority of the population is still strongly adhering to traditional ways of life and values.

1. For example, while the eastern part of Flores was under Portuguese dominion during the fifteenth and sixteenth centuries, the western part of Flores did not experience the influence of either Portuguese or Dutch colonization until the early decades of the twentieth century – both Manggarai and Ngada regencies came under direct Dutch control as late as 1907.

2. For example, the per capita income in Nusa Tenggara Timur in 1991 was only about a third of that for the nation. The per capita income for N.T.T. was Rp. 345,234 in contrast to per capita income of the nation which was Rp. 924,743 (see Kantor Statistik Kabupaten Ngada 1991).

The terms 'modern' and 'traditional' in this paper are used in the senses of 'Westernized' and 'local and customary', respectively. In contrast to the sense of 'modern' as being something foreign, the term 'traditional' is used in the sense of local, indigenous and customary. This concept of the 'traditional' does not imply something that is static and unchanging. Local traditions are dynamic systems and have always accommodated changes by incorporating and localizing cultural elements adopted from other (or) neighbouring groups. The notion of 'modern' initially has been associated by the Ngada population with Dutch goods. Such goods obtained a high valuation and often became the symbols of status and prestige.[3] In former times, Dutch goods were given to approved local rulers and nobility in the context of indirect colonial rule. The status of these local rulers was already high within the local social-political systems and the goods only complemented such status. These prestige goods consisted of Western-style clothing, china dishes, cars, houses built from brick or concrete block, and so on. The possession of material aspects of 'Western' culture, including many of the kinds of items just mentioned as well as electronics and other types of technology, are nowadays still associated with 'modernity'. An aspect of this popular association of Western goods with 'modernity' is the higher valuation of these goods over more traditional ones. This valuation is, however, contextually specific and may be a function of the type of goods in question. Thus, in the context of clothing, Western-style clothing is valued more over local *sarongs* when visiting places of authority that require respect, such as when going to church or when visiting a government office. However, western-style clothing would not be the preferred garment for local ritual and ceremonial occasions. Although this kind of valuation is found both among peasant villagers and civil servants of towns, it is usually the latter that would readily make such a distinction.

'Fashion' is a difficult concept to define. The difficulty derives from the fact that there might be many different ways of viewing and understanding fashion. From the perspective of local populations of Ngada and their customary lives, there does not seem to have been a concept similar to Western ideas of 'fashion'. However, if 'fashion' is taken to refer to bodily adornment and the aesthetic and social valuation of traditional textiles and jewellery used in this context, then the possession of the concept of 'fashion' may be attributed to local cultures of Ngada. However, a Western popular notion of 'fashion' seems to be a relatively recent one among the Ngada of

3. For example, most villagers aspire to accumulate enough wealth to be able to build a brick or concrete house which has become a status marker. Moreover, any surplus cash income, most often becomes converted into a 'modern' item of wealth, such as a tape player or television or even a generator for electricity.

Flores and appears to be closely linked with social change and the processes of modernization (or 'Westernization'). Thus, 'fashion' in this sense refers to being 'in style' where 'style' is dictated by forces of 'modernity'. As Blumer (1995[1969]:385) points out in connection with fashion and modernity, to be modern is to be 'sensitive to the movement of current developments as they take place . . . in the larger social world'. . . . . Robert and Jeanette Lauer (1995:410) incorporate Blumer's formulations about fashion and provide a more broadly applicable definition for the analysis of fashion:

> . . . fashion is a process of collective definition in which a particular alternative in a set of possibilities is selected as appropriate. A particular way is selected and becomes the fashion as the result of collective definition. The definition is the outcome of ideological evaluation. . . . Thus if a proposed style is defined as having a meaning that is congruent with existing ideology, the style is likely to become fashion.

These interpretations of 'fashion' seem applicable, as the paper will show, to the transformed and modernized uses of traditional textiles in the Ngada regency and among people deriving from this region of Flores but currently residing in the provincial capital of Kupang. Thus, fashion in these places is manifest in Western-style clothing and accessories, as well as in interior decoration and modern furniture upholstery, all of which are made of traditional textiles.

Traditional Textiles and Their Customary Use

Textiles in Indonesia always had a complex and multi-levelled role in the lives of local populations. In the framework of the local political organization of domains and their clans, textiles often 'served to indicate rank and status, particularly membership of a ruling elite' (Maxwell and Maxwell 1989:131). Thus, textiles in Indonesia had and still have a prominent place in 'expressing identity, both ethnically and in the social hierarchy' (Geirnaert 1989:77). Traditional *ikat* cloths also served as economic goods on Flores island, especially in the sense of bartering for food (Hamilton 1994:48). In her discussion about traditional textiles, Gittinger (1979:13) particularly notes 'the role that textiles play as a symbolic medium, functioning on many levels of understanding and communication. They enter into all phases of social custom and religion, assuming unusual properties and attributes.' Textiles are media of communication within the context of local religious and ritual systems as well. As Therik (1989:23) observes, 'Particular motifs on the textile have spiritual/mystical value in accordance with the local culture and belief.' In an 'engendered' system of valuables (McKinnon 1989:27), textiles tend to be symbolically valued as 'feminine' or 'female' goods.

Many of these distinctive features of traditional Indonesian textiles are readily applicable to the local cloths found in the Ngada regency of Flores island. Here textiles serve both as garments and as items of exchange. As in other Indonesian societies, textiles in the Ngada regency are worn as clothes protecting the body from the elements. They also indicate social status and serve as items in gift exchange in various social contexts. Textiles also served in the past as items of economic exchange, particularly between weaving and non-weaving regions where clothes were exchanged for food. There are ordinary and special ceremonial textiles that are hand-made – formerly, hand-spun cotton, after being dyed with natural plant colours, was woven on a back-strap loom.

There are at least four different weaving styles or traditions in the Ngada regency. These include the styles found in Riung, Bajawa, Nagé and Mbai.[4] The Bajawa and Nagé weaving traditions produce *ikat* textiles. Whereas the Bajawa textiles look like the drawings of a school child with large angular motifs of horses, chickens and houses on them, the Nagé cloths boast of more intricate and colourful patterns. Although the supplementary weft technique is similar in both Riung and Mbai, their motifs and colour arrangements differ. These latter styles of textiles look rather like floral patterns embroidered onto a black background. Since the region I am most familiar with used Bajawanese[5] textiles extensively, I shall focus on this weaving tradition in the following discussion.

Among the Bajawanese of the Ngada regency there were a number of different kinds of *ikat* textiles in use, but all possess a basic pattern. On a black surface, white motifs in the form of large horses (*jara mézé*) or small horses (*jara kèdhi*), chickens (*manu*) or chicken feet (*wai manu*) and a so-called elephant (*gaja*) motif decorate the textile. These motifs were usually associated with cloths worn on festive and ritual occasions and were

4. In the Sara Sedu area of the Ngada regency, where I have conducted field research, the Hoga Sara originally were not familiar with weaving but they did exchange things for textiles with other regions of Ngada – with Nagé, Mbai and with the Jere Bu'u people of the Bajawa group. Only during the Dutch occupation (during the 1920s) did one of the traditional villages of Sara Sedu start weaving. They produced plain black textiles that were coloured by soaking the threads in mud and trampling them. These textiles were referred to as *lawo pisa* or *lué pisa* (*lawo* refers to a woman's dress, *lué* is a man's *sarong*, while *pisa* means mud). It is said that other regions once referred to Sara Sedu sometimes as *pisa* – after the textiles they produced (Molnar 1994).

5. The group I am referring to as Bajawanese were called the Ngadha by the missionary, Paul Arndt, in his volumes of cultural descriptions about this region and its peoples.

considered to be indicators of social status. The chicken feet or plain cloth signified a member of the slave (*ho'o*) class. Chicken motifs usually identified someone of the commoner class (*ga'é kisa*), while the small horse motif occurred on the clothing of a person of noble rank (*ga'é mézé*) who was still young and had not yet fulfilled all social and ritual obligations. The large horse or the 'elephant' motif occurred on textiles worn by an elderly noble who had a greater social status, having sponsored several ritual feasts.

Besides serving to indicate one's social status within a group, in a regional context, textiles also functioned as ethnic or regional identity markers. When people attended ceremonies as guests of another ethnic group, they usually displayed their own ethnicity by the type of textile they wore. For example, at a Nagé ceremony, invited guests from Bajawa could clearly be identified by their region, simply from the type of textile they wore.

Textiles are also used in the Ngada regency as items of exchange in special social contexts. As among many other Indonesian groups, here as well, textiles are given by the woman's family in exchange for various kinds of livestock provided by the husband's family on the occasion of life-cycle rites – birth, puberty, marriage and death. In these exchange contexts, like in other eastern Indonesian societies (e.g. McKinnon 1989:27–42), the textiles are symbolically valued as 'feminine' or 'female' goods.

Textiles continue to be worn usually on ceremonial occasions, which nowadays include attending Sunday mass. Certain textiles are particularly valued, such as those that were formerly traded from other regions (Mbai) or those which possess stone bead work decorations (those formerly used to receive a new infant among the Bajawanese). Highly valued cloths were often treated as heirlooms and passed down from generation to generation. These textiles were wrapped and kept in the attic of the traditional houses and could only be worn during a ritual occasion. To take such a textile outside the house in any other context required special rites – namely the sacrifice of a chicken, smearing its blood on the textile and asking for ancestral protection – otherwise the people taking the textile from the attic would meet an untimely death.

As everyday clothing, most people wore plain black textiles or cloths with large checkers formed by intersecting lines. There are also regions in Ngada where people claim to have been wearing clothing made out of tree bark for everyday clothing up to the Japanese invasion (1943).[6] Nowadays, although

6. The Japanese, after requiring the creation of cotton plantations, also forced the populace to weave plain white textiles. In some parts of western Flores, such as in parts of Manggarai, the people claim that the original cotton species was replaced with a new one introduced by the Japanese. They found the new species more difficult to process and this also contributed to the recent disappearance of the desire for making home-spun textiles.

plain black cloths are still preferred, on a daily basis people usually wear factory-made, checkered *sarong* or *sarong* made from textiles of any eastern Indonesian and Javanese region.

Traditional textiles are produced on a back-strap loom. It is claimed that the processing of cotton, making thread, counting out the length of yarn for a particular textile, as well as the colouring process take at least one and a half months. The colouring is extracted from plants, indigo being one of these.[7] The weaving itself is thought to take no longer than an additional month, and is usually done in the weaver's spare time – in the evenings after all other chores are finished, or during the day by some young women. Formerly, hands were never still, as girls and young women went about with their drop spindles while attending to other chores.

Transformation in the Production and Use of Traditional Textiles

With recent economic changes accompanying modernization, the production, use and valuation of textiles are being transformed. Whereas formerly all women spun and wove textiles to clothe their families, for trade and ceremonial occasions, nowadays places where home-spun and naturally coloured textiles are still produced are few. There are several factors influencing this change. For one thing, a market economy was introduced by the Dutch a little more than seventy years ago. Western-style clothing initially became prestige items that were available to high-ranking natives who were working together with colonial government and church officials. Many native peoples however, aspired to have Western clothes. With Indonesian independence it became easier and less costly to buy shirts and blouses and factory-made Javanese sarong in the market or in stores in the regency's capital. Factory-produced thread, some already coloured, also appeared among produce in the markets and stores, as did chemical dyes for dyeing the threads.

In most textile producing regions the growing of cotton, and spinning and colouring of threads practically disappeared. The time spent on textile production was significantly reduced by eliminating these early tedious steps. Most traditional textiles – that is textiles with their regional colours and motifs – can be completed more rapidly by using commercial thread and

7. The plants whose extract is used for the natural colours include: *sepa* (*Caesalpinia sappan*) for red; *pisa* = mud for black, or more commonly *taru* (*Indigofera*); *kuné manu* (*kuné=Curcuma viridiflora*) for yellow but also *kebo* (*Morinda*) for the same colour (Verheijen 1990).

dyes. In addition, not all women are weavers any longer, since skills have also rapidly disappeared with the option of buying ready-to-wear clothing. There has also been a loss of knowledge among present day weavers with regard to the repertory of motifs and their combinations. This is often reflected in a decrease in the number and intricacy of motifs and the enlargement of certain motifs in order to speed up the weaving process. The commercialization of local textiles also influenced this latter development, since with fewer or larger motifs to tie, more textiles can be produced in a shorter time to meet demands.

Before discussing the effects of commercialization, a few things need to be said about the changes in valuation of textiles. With the national drive for a democratic society, there is no longer official recognition of traditional ranks or social classes, such as nobles, commoners and slaves, even though some middle-aged to elderly people still recognize such distinctions in subtle ways. Therefore, who wears a textile with what motif is no longer any indication of their social standing or age in a community. Motifs that have indicated commoner or slave ranks have disappeared from currently prod-uced textiles. Now, when wearing traditional textiles, everybody wears the horse motif among the Bajawanese group. Thus all Bajawanese textiles are produced with this motif. Furthermore, the size of the horse is no longer associated with age, at least not among the younger to middle-aged generation.

Whereas formerly, one's ethnicity was indicated by the textile one was wearing as a guest during a ceremonial occasion in another ethnic region, nowadays anybody can wear a textile from any weaving tradition. More specifically, one may find Bajawanese wearing the Nagé or Mbai style of textiles at various functions. However, people wearing textiles corresponding to their own region's traditions still occur. The type of cloth that is chosen for the ceremonial attire is linked with a variety of factors, including economic, individual aesthetic choice and the context in which ethnicity may be emphasized or de-emphasized. Although textiles were always highly valued for their aesthetics and intricate designs, currently they may be even more so. Even though the Ngada regency has at least four different weaving traditions, when the Indonesian minister of information, Harmoko, came for an official visit to the regency capital, he was only presented with Mbai textiles. The fact that ethnicity is not always clearly displayed in the textiles worn for ceremonial occasions may also be linked with the efforts of the local government to give more emphasis to ethnic unity rather than to ethnic distinctions within the Ngada regency.[8]

8. The Indonesian motto, Unity in Diversity = Bhineka Tunggal Ika, is alluded to here. As will be argued below, it is important to duly consider the degree of inclusivity of the ethnic group that is being emphasized and symbolized within a local political context during these festive occasions.

A further issue related both to the valuation and commercialization of traditional textiles in the Ngada regency is a recent development in local fashion. This development can be linked with the work of the wives of officials in the context of certain government projects. The spouses of the officials from the village level government up to the district and regency level of government have recently become involved in an awareness campaign aimed at women for increasing family income. In an effort to increase the livelihood of families through various activities, women are encouraged and sometimes trained in different economic activities. Among these are the programmes that encourage women to weave and sell their wares. Women's groups in the regency capital and district capitals then produce other items from these home-made textiles. These new products usually take the form of skirts, vests, blouses, shirts and jackets, that is to say modern or Western-style clothing, that are only available to those who can afford to buy them. It is generally the officials and their spouses who don such attire for official or ceremonial occasions, for example, when attending formal receptions of government guests, church and parties. Each new fashion creation from traditional textiles is greatly admired and discussed among the wives.[9] This fashion trend has also been followed by some members of the general populace, who may want to imitate those whom they consider as being of a higher social standing. Thus whoever can afford the services of a tailor or seamstress will order special clothing to be made from traditional textiles.

Another occasion when one can see new clothing creations is wedding festivities. At several weddings I attended, the bride usually changes into a dress or suit made from a local textile (which is often decorated with other sheer fabrics) as the evening progresses. It is quite fashionable to do so, and such outfits are greatly valued. At the village level, one also finds traditional and church weddings taking place in outfits sewn from traditional textiles. Since the sewing of these outfits requires an expenditure which is considered quite high and unaffordable by ordinary people, wearing such an outfit is also a sign or display of the economic ability of the bride and/or groom's family. When marriage takes place between partners of different ethnicity, their regional origins are usually indicated by the type of textile they wear or from which they make outfits.

9. The expression 'fashion creations' is quite applicable to these outfits, not only because that is the way the officials' wives talk about them, but also because they are not simple clothing items made from traditional textiles. One may find a combination of other (often store bought) textiles with the traditional textiles as well as accessorization with elaborate buttons in the creation of these outfits. The texture of textiles combined are also sometimes of different kinds (e.g. sheer crepe material combined with traditional textile).

Traditional textiles serving as fashion items have also contributed to the use of new colours. Whereas formerly Bajawanese textiles had white motifs on black background, nowadays the motifs are often a greenish-blue or shocking-pink colour. Similarly, in Nagé textiles the formerly dark and deep reds (closer to brownish red thus more earthy colours) recently have become a brighter red. The appearance of new colours is also associated with the easy availability of coloured yarn straight from the shelf in local stores.

It is not only Western-style outfits that are made from traditional textiles. There is a growing local market for handbags, wallets and other accessories made from local textiles. These serve both as fashion items for the civil servants and their wives, and also as souvenirs and gifts for visiting officials, and when acquired by sale, they are mainly bought and sold by the wives of the officials. Although tourism in the regency's capital has been rapidly increasing in the past ten years, most tourists are still unaware of where such items can be purchased. This trend is likely to change, however. During my last visit to Bajawa in November 1994, there were at least two stands set up in the local market place with the sole purpose of attracting foreign souvenir hunters.

A further extension of the utilization of traditional textiles as fashion and accessory items is their use as interior decoration. Although a hundred years ago the Dutch were importing eastern Indonesian textiles which made their way into European homes as curtains and bedspreads (see Gittinger 1979:157), in a local Indonesian context this is a very recent development which began only about three years ago. The house of the regent in Ngada serves as a good example in this regard. Although I myself have not recently seen the interior of this house, it was described to me by one of the regent's friends. The house is decorated with textiles from all the different textile producing places of the Ngada. The textiles are used as curtains, tablecloths and serve as the upholstery for the couches and chairs (Figs 3.1 and 3.2).

The use of regional *ikat* and other hand-made textiles from the various regions of the province as fashion creations and interior decoration reached its height in the provincial capital of Kupang. However, here the use of textiles, at least the use of textiles from Ngada, has a definite character of an ethnic identity and pride marker.

Four years ago government officials still had to wear *batik* to their place of work at least once a week and on all formal occasions.[10] This practice, however, has been changing the past two years. Instead of *batik*, now regional

---

10. The wearing of *batik* shirts is a western Indonesian, more specifically Javanese, tradition. *Batik* are textiles that are patterned by the wax-resistant technique (Maxwell and Maxwell 1989:131).

Figure 3.1. Traditional textiles worn during ceremonial occasions among the Hoga Sara cf the Ngada regency in West-Central Flores.

Figure 3.2. Examples of the modern usage of traditional textiles.

textiles are made into safari jackets that are worn for these functions. Each official usually wears a jacket made from the textile of his or her place of origin. The present governor of the province, who was born in the Ngada regency of western Flores, usually wears jackets made from textiles from his place of derivation. On most occasions he chooses shirts and jackets from the Mbai region of the Ngada, although he himself is from the Bajawanese weaving region. In the home of the governor, all reception furniture is also upholstered from the same kind of textile (bamboo furniture with Mbai textile cushions) and textiles from other regions are used as tablecloths and curtains. Carved statues (*ana deo*) of ritual significance from the Nagé region complement his home's decor and clearly proclaim his ethnic identity.[11] Other people of the Ngada regency who live in the provincial capital Kupang usually wear fashion items and accessories from Ngada textiles for various official and ceremonial occasions.

In Kupang, clothing and accessories made from regional *ikat* and other textiles have become a fashion for civil servants and their families for several reasons. Wearing Western-style clothing, deemed to be more suitable than *sarong* by most urban dwellers, yet being able to identify and be proud of one's ethnicity in a heterogeneous cultural environment is just one complex reason. As an up and coming government and cultural centre of the province, there has been an increase in the number of people belonging to the upper middle class. They are economically prosperous, and seek social, recreational and entertainment activities. Each year since 1991 a cultural festival is held, replete with regional fashion shows, ethnic cooking contests and also ethnic beauty queen contests. The fashion shows and beauty contests proudly display the fashion creation of local designers who all work with the medium of regional textiles from all over the province. Those who attend these events often wear their own fashion items made from the same kind of textiles.

The tourist trade is also booming in Kupang. Numerous gift shops have sprung up that sell not only local handicrafts from sandalwood or Rotinese hats and *Sasando* (a musical instrument), but also local *ikat* and other textiles from all the regencies of the province. Not only are the textiles for sale in the form of *sarong*, but increasingly jackets, pants, vests and even dresses whet the tourists' appetites. Furthermore, the production of accessories (handbags, briefcases, purses, neckties, and so on) has achieved high quality in these shops. But not only international tourists frequent such souvenir or gift shops. Local tourists and visiting officials who have heard so much about the rich weaving traditions of this province also include on their list of 'things to do while in Kupang', a short stop in such shops.

Obviously the use of traditional regional textiles for fashion, accessories and interior decoration is becoming a booming business in eastern Indonesia. However, this trend also brings with it a lot of changes in the weaving traditions and creates several problems in the context of new businesses. The changes not only concern the use of textiles, but also their valuation, method of production and cultural significance. While fashions made of traditional *ikat* and other textiles are still used as an indicator of membership in a particular ethnic group or of one's origins from a particular region, increasingly such clothing items are not just simple ethnicity markers but

---

11. Although Governor Mosa Kabé has lived for a long period away from Flores in Java, according to photographs and accounts he always tended to openly and proudly identify his origins by such means (through regional textiles).

are used in a way that strongly reflects the political context or inclusivity of the region in which ethnicity is being signified.

A major problem for the small businesses that make their livelihood from the selling of fashion, accessories and interior decoration items is marketing and sometimes supply. At present, at the level of the regency, at least in Ngada, the supply of textiles woven on traditional back-strap looms does meet the demand. However, in the provincial capital, where the demand is the greatest, supply of regional textiles is sometimes short, and this is especially the case for traditional textiles from the Ngada regency. There are several factors involved here. Usually there is no broker or buyer who will go between the regional weaving districts and the small businesses of Kupang. Most small business people cannot afford to go in search of textiles in the various regencies of the province. On the other hand, most weavers cannot afford to take their products to the Kupang market. Thus, the major issue here is marketing.

A further problem is that, as the demand increases in Kupang, the regional production of traditional textiles will also need to increase. From the perspective of textile production in the Ngada regency, this is rather difficult to achieve due to the manual nature of production and also for the fact that, by and large, textiles are still produced by individual weavers and not by weaving groups. Some weaving groups have already been established in Ngada, but these groups often break up and reassemble with a different membership each time. Making a weaving group work involves several difficulties. First among these is the fact that women cannot specialize in weaving alone, as culturally they are expected to fulfill several other work obligations around the household. Second, there are often disputes about the division of profits made from the selling of textiles produced in a group. Thirdly, most women in such groups do not want to wait for monetary rewards, but require payment as soon as a textile is completed. Related to this, many women are financially unable to invest in the purchase of raw materials, such as yarn and dyes. Other studies done on the issues of development in eastern Indonesia have also identified similar problems elsewhere (cf. Barlow, Bellis and Andrews 1991).

Producing textiles with regional characteristics could easily be done in textile factories and is done in both Kupang and the island of Java. However, part of the attraction of regional textiles is that they are hand-made. An *ikat* textile with authentic regional designs, woven on a back-strap loom from hand-spun cotton and with a dyeing process utilizing local plant extracts, tends to obtain a very high monetary value both from local and foreign (tourist) customers. Only this type of textile would be considered by most local consumers (and by more knowledgeable foreigners) as *asli* or original and authentic. Some less knowledgeable tourists are quite happy with and willingly pay a relatively high price for textiles produced from commercially available raw materials *as long as these were woven on a back-strap loom*. Thus the technique of production may be an important aspect of the valuation of traditional textiles – whether aesthetic or monetary. Therefore, some of the representatives of small businesses also feel that factory production would drive the prices down. In such an event the prestige associated with owning hand-made textiles would also be reduced or disappear.

It is hard to predict how regional textile production will change in the near future. It is obvious, however, that the government's rural development section favours and promotes the production of traditional textiles produced on back-strap looms and to some degree supports women's weaving groups. Many tourists visiting the Ngada regency also search for such 'authentic' regional textiles as souvenirs. Thus, in the short term, the work of women's weaving cooperatives producing hand-made textiles is most likely to prosper.

Conclusion

Among the people of the Ngada regency and those who represent this region in the provincial capital of Kupang, the transformation in the use of traditional textiles can be closely linked with processes of rapid cultural change. Local textiles, however, still possess many meanings and functions. Two ideas are particularly significant in the altered utilization of *ikat* clothes: (1) traditional textiles are still indicators of ethnic identity, albeit, in a changing form which is directly related to historical transformations in local political relations between cultural groups; and (2) they came to be used as items of fashion within a framework of modernity and modernization.

As noted earlier, formerly (and to some degree at present) traditional textiles in the Ngada region of Flores not only signified status and rank of individuals but also their membership in a particular cultural group – Ngadha, Nage-Keo and Riung. Thus, textiles reflected an individual's standing within his/her social group and also ethnic affiliation in the context of inter-group relations within the region. Inter-group relations were (and in respects still are) important aspects of the traditional political organization in Ngada. During Dutch colonialism as part of the indirect rule policy – rule through the local leaders and nobility – these relationships were not interfered with.

Nowadays, traditional textiles no longer indicate an individual's rank since such ranks as nobles, commoners and slaves were abolished or no longer recognized after Indonesian Independence which is a direct consequence of the 'democratic' ideology promoted by the state. A person's status is still indicated however by the type of textiles used either in traditional or modernized context. As pointed out earlier, nowadays people may wear textiles from cultural regions other than their own from within the Ngada regency during ritual occasions. Often the textile of choice is one with currently high monetary value, such as textiles from the Mbai region. Wealth traditionally has been an indicator of status and by donning a valuable textile (e.g. Mbai cloth) the person still signifies and emphasizes more his social status than his regional cultural affiliation.

Another explanation for the seemingly indiscriminate use of cloth from any textile traditions in the regency within a ceremonial context is that ethnic diversity is de-emphasized in favour of unity. This emphasis on unity can be viewed as an aspect of national policies and propaganda that aim to strengthen and reaffirm the unity of the diverse cultural groups of thousands of islands within the framework of a nation-state. This emphasis on artificial cultural homogeneity is replicated at the provincial and regional levels as well, thereby reflecting various degrees of unity and diversity. In this context the people of the Ngada regency express their unity when they symbolize their ethnic identity with a culturally non-specific textile derived from any of the various traditions present in their region. Thus, in this case ethnic identity is defined in terms of a contrast to that of other regencies on Flores. This interpretation is particularly applicable to the culturally heterogeneous environment in the capital of Nusa Tenggara Timur province, in Kupang.

The transformed use of traditional textiles in the context of modernity and modernization is particularly relevant in viewing these developments in terms of fashion. Indonesian people often view modernity in contrast to tradition. Especially among young people, traditional ways tend to be considered as *kuno* (out-moded or old-fashioned). To be modern often implies the possession of Western technology, including clothing, electronics, brick houses and so on. The contrast between urban and rural spheres is important within this framework of modernity. The use of Western-style clothing, furniture and housing among other things is characteristic of town and city life. These are all markers of modernity as opposed to 'backwardness' of rural ways of life. The possession of these facades of modernity furthermore signifies social mobility. Therefore, the fact that the use of traditional textiles in the creation of a new style of clothing and interior decorating fashion has emerged within the context of city and town life, and that those most influential in the selection of this new style are in the civil service, are significant and congruent with the currently existing ideologies of modernity.

As pointed out earlier, people in the villages also aspire to obtain new fashion creations, namely Western-style clothing and accessories made from local traditional *ikat* textiles. The possession of such pieces by certain villagers is an expression of their desire to be perceived as modern and progressive (in contrast to traditional in the sense of 'old-fashioned'). Perhaps, an even more important function of owning such a fashion item is the expression of social-economic mobility. The villager who wears it outwardly indicates his/her wealth and status to the other members of his/her group, thus he or she shows an ability to afford not only the purchase of a valuable traditional textile but also the hiring of a seamstress to create the fashion item.

The historical and political context in which these developments of fashion occurred needs one last mention. During the Dutch colonial period foreign goods, such as Western-style clothing, furniture and housing were political emblems of power and authority which were invested on local rulers and nobility who participated in the indirect rule of the colonial powers. Therefore, foreign goods were signifiers of power relations within the colonial political contexts. However, since in the framework of traditional social organization and values these items were bestowed upon individuals who held particular wealth, status and prestige in Ngada, these Western types of material goods quickly became markers of these customary qualities. Thus, many villagers still aspire to express their economic prosperity by erecting a house made of brick or concrete blocks, although currently very few are able to do so.

After Indonesian Independence, however, Western-style goods came to acquire a different meaning, more specifically, they became associated with modernity, development and progressiveness. The fashion trend described in this paper – the use of traditional Ngada textiles in the creation of Western-style clothing, accessories, furniture and interior decor – may be interpreted as the generation of a style that is at the same time both modern and Indonesian and reflects both cultural diversity and unity. Thus, the prevalent ideology of modernity, that tends to be expressed in terms of foreign media, is being recast in newly emerging forms that more firmly identify regional as well as national identities and loyalties. Therefore, this emerging style in the transformed use of traditional textiles can be defined 'as having meaning that is congruent with existing ideologies' (Lauer and Lauer 1995:410). The case study of new Ngada textile trends appears to be consistent with Blumer's interpretation of fashion as 'a form of control in a changing society . . . [that] prevents change from becoming chaos by identifying those new directions which are collectively defined as appropriate' (Blumer, as cited in Lauer and Lauer 1995:385).

Bibliography

Barlow, Colin, Alex Bellis, and Kate Andrews (1991), *Nusa Tenggara Timur: The Challenges of Development*. Political and Social Change Monograph 12. Department of Political and Social Change, Research School of Pacific Studies, The Australian National University. Canberra: Panther Publishing.

Blumer, Herbert (1995), 'Fashion From Class Differentiation to Collective Selection.' In Mary Ellen Roach-Higgins, Joanne B. Eicher, and Kim K. P. Johnson (eds), *Dress and Identity*. New York: Fairchild Publications.

Geirnaert, Danielle (1989), 'Textiles of West Sumba: Lively Renaissance of an Old Tradition.' In Mattiebelle Gittinger (ed.), *To Speak With Cloth: Studies in Indonesian Textiles*. Los Angeles: Museum of Cultural History, University of California.

Gittinger, Mattiebelle (1979), *Splendid Symbols: Textile and Tradition in Indonesia*. Washington, D.C.: The Textile Museum.

—— (ed.) (1989), *To Speak With Cloth: Studies in Indonesian Textiles*. Los Angeles: Museum of Cultural History, University of California.

Hamilton, Roy W. (1994), *Gift of the Cotton Maiden: Textiles of Flores and the Solor Islands*. Los Angeles, California: Fowler Museum of Cultural History, University of California.

Kantor Statistik Kabupaten Ngada (1991), *Ngada Dalam Angka 1991*, Publication of the Indonesian government. The Statistics Bureau of the Ngada Regency.

Lauer, Robert H. and Jeanette C. Lauer (1995), 'A Case Study: The Bloomer Costume.' In Mary Ellen Roach-Higgins, Joanne B. Eicher, and Kim K. P. Johnson (eds), *Dress and Identity*. New York: Fairchild Publications.

Maxwell, Robyn J. and John R. Maxwell (1989), 'Political Motives: the Batiks of Mohamad Hadi of Solo.' In Mattiebelle Gittinger (ed.), *To Speak With Cloth: Studies in Indonesian Textiles*. Los Angeles: Museum of Cultural History, University of California.

McKinnon, Susan (1989), 'Flags and Half-Moons: Tanimbarese Textiles in an "Engendered" System of Valuables.' In Mattiebelle Gittinger (ed.), *To Speak With Cloth: Studies in Indonesian Textiles*. Los Angeles: Museum of Cultural History, University of California.

Molnar, Andrea K. (1994), 'The Grandchildren Of The Ga'é Ancestors: The Hoga Sara Of Ngada In West-Central Flores.' Unpublished PhD, the Australian National University, Canberra.

Sungkoro, Ruzwar, Jes Therik (1993), *35 Tahun Nusa Tenggara Timur*. Kupang: Pemerintah Propinsi Daerah Tingkat I. Nusa Tenggara Timur.

Therik, Jes A. (1989), *Tenun Ikat Dari Timur: Keindahan Anggun Warisan Leluhur. Ikat in Eastern Archipelago: An Esoteric Beauty of Ancestral Entity*. Jakarta: Pustaka Sinar Harapan.

Verheijen, Jilis A.J., SVD. (1990), *Dictionary of Plant Names in the Lesser Sunda Islands*, Pacific Linguistics Series D – No. 83. Canberra: Department of Linguistics, Research School of Pacific Studies, The Australian National University.

4

Transnational Commodity Flows and the Global Phenomenon of the Brand

Ian Skoggard

The advent of the atomic age brought with it dire warnings about technology outstripping our imagination, and rendering obsolete former geopolitical arrangements and practices. One could make a similar warning regarding the recent globalization of manufacturing, markets and finances, which has marked the so-called postmodern period. A new circuitry has been laid over the globe – the true legacy of the modern era – and we, its inhabitants, are reeling in its effects, unable to conceptualize and understand all its ramifications, precipitating a crisis of representation (Jameson 1991). Although both capital accumulation and social reproduction now occur on a global scale (Wallerstein 1980), people still focus on local effects and regard them as constituting an autonomous, or near-autonomous, system. The reality is that these local effects, like sub-atomic particles, have long tails connecting them to worlds beyond our perception and even imagination. In today's global economy, commodity flows link consumers, in a city like Montreal, to peasant household manufacturers deep in rural China, a realm many North Americans know little about or think has little relevance for their everyday lives. Nevertheless, the recognition and understanding of such transnational commodity flows are necessary in order to bring into relief our postmodern culture. Like Flatlanders who confused circles for spheres, it is difficult from any one spot to perceive the full dimension of the global economy with its transnational stroke of production and consumption. In one part of the world, people are driven to work long hours to supply the commodities which people in another part of the world are driven to consume. Their respective worlds of all work and all play are indeed one dimensional. The reluctance to engage the scope and depth of this global system of cyclic capital flows gives an additional twist to commodity fetishism, one in which the brand name now stands for the commodity that stood for social relations (Baudrillard 1988).

In this chapter, I examine the disarticulated discourses that one finds as one follows the flow of athletic shoes from their site of production in Taiwan to their marketing and consumption in North America. In this divided world of transnational commodity flows, the dominant discourse at each end of the flow promotes either production or consumption. At one end state ideologies stress the urgency of nation-building in order to inculcate a hard work ethic that spurs production. Their over-production of commodities has flooded the world's affluent markets where private corporations dazzle consumers with a vast array of goods that has transformed the 'real' world. Beyond the utilitarian, many commodities now take on the cachet of fashion, including running shoes and sweat suits. This is possible, I would argue, because in the global division of labour, the commodity can stand for everything and anything savvy marketers wish to make of it.[1] For example, the athletic cult which surrounds the marketing of Nike shoes and apparel is only possible because the actual making of Nike merchandise occurs out of view, a half-world away. Obscured by distance and culture, the problem of labour and class is easily effaced by marketing campaigns which confer on the product an authenticity all of its own. Nike can weave its myth how it chooses, and purvey a false notion of agency as an individual athletic act which has its only real referent in the singular purchasing transaction of consumers, and not in the social relations and organization of production. The only way most people can really 'just do it' is to consume, which, although a facile act, nevertheless serves the global machine of production and consumption, and the accumulation of capital on a global scale. To consume becomes a consummate act, and to slip on a pair of Nikes becomes a complete, and therefore winning act, such as those performed by the hundreds of professional athletes Nike sponsors.

Commodity Flows and Mythologies

The modern global communications grid has allowed transnational firms such as Nike to exploit the cost differentials found among countries with unequal standards of living. In addition to seeking out cheap labour, some

---

1. One could generalize and argue that the successful marketing of fashion lies in divorcing the product from any referent to its actual production and the class relations involved in its manufacturing. See Anne Brydon's article in this volume.

transnational corporations have divested themselves entirely of all fixed capital costs by subcontracting out the manufacture of their brand-name products to local firms in an arrangement referred to as 'flexible specialization' (Priore and Sabel 1984). Nike is an example of a marketing firm which owns no factories to speak of and instead concentrates solely on design and marketing. Almost all (99 per cent) of Nike shoes are manufactured in Asia by independent firms. In 1980, nearly 90 per cent of Nikes were made in Taiwan or South Korea. Ten years later, half of this production shifted to China, Indonesia and Thailand. Most recently, Nike-producing Taiwanese shoe companies have opened factories in Vietnam. Nike's primary market, on the other hand, is the United States where it sells 60 per cent of its shoes in what had become in 1991 a $12 billion (US) athletic shoe market (Korzeniewicz 1994:248–60).

Flexible specialization represents a qualitative shift in the method of capital accumulation from one in which profit is based on volume production to one based on the quick turnover of capital (Harvey 1989).[2] Shoes are an ideal commodity for the fast consumption favoured by flexible specialization. From 1971, when Nike sold its first shoe, to 1989, the average life of its shoe designs decreased from seven years to ten months. Constant innovation in shoe design compels consumers to keep up with fashion and buy shoes more frequently. Nike's most important distributor, the Foot Locker, promotes itself as being the first store to have the latest Nike models in stock. Innovation also keeps Nike ahead of the competition, especially East Asian manufacturers who might want to cash in on Nike's fame and produce Nike-look-a-likes.

Because commodity flows span different cultures and incorporate different kinds of work, they generate a diversity of opinion as to their nature. Arjun Appadurai refers to these different perspectives as mythologies:

> Culturally constructed stories and ideologies about commodity flows are commonplace in all societies. But such stories acquire especially intense, new, and striking qualities when the spatial, cognitive, or institutional distances between production, distribution, and consumption are great. Such distancing either can be institutionalized within a single complex economy or can be a function of new kinds of links between hitherto separated societies and economies. The institutionalized divorce (in knowledge, interest, and role) between persons involved in various aspects of the flow of commodities generates specialized mythologies (Appadurai 1986:48).

2. The term Harvey uses is 'flexible accumulation'.

Appadurai considers three variations of 'specialized mythologies':

> (1) Mythologies produced by traders and speculators who are largely indifferent to both the production origins and the consumption destination of commodities [he gives the Chicago grain exchange as an example].
>
> (2) Mythologies produced by consumers alienated from production and distribution processes of key commodities [e.g. cargo cults of Melanesia].
>
> (3) Mythologies produced by workers in the production process who are completely divorced from the distribution and consumption logics of the commodities they produce [e.g. the Bolivian tin miners described by Michael Taussig in his book, *The Devil and Commodity Fetishism*]. (ibid)

In the athletic shoe industry, all three types of mythologizing operate, constituting different perspectives of the flow of that particular commodity from the different locations of production, distribution and consumption. In this chapter, I will examine three different discourses associated with:

1. A popular new Taiwanese religion which depicts the postwar period of rapid industrialization in the mythical language of catastrophes and miracles.
2. The idea of the commodity chain which reifies the flow of commodities between sites of consumption and production.
3. The aura of the brand which confers on basic commodities a fashion-like status.

Worker Mythologies

Anyone who has travelled recently in the East cannot but be impressed by the level of economic dynamism found there. In the new global economy, these are the lands of opportunity, the new engines of world history. The township where I carried out research on Taiwan's shoe industry was a quintessential postmodern landscape with bowling alleys, stock brokerages and factories, juxtaposed alongside paddy, ancestral halls and shrines to the earth god.[3] There I saw a spirit medium in trance with a three-foot metal rod pierced through his cheek, lead a religious procession past a coffee shop where customers were watching the daily stock quotations on a bank of colour TVs. Shoe factories surrounded the town and workshops could be found on almost every block. In addition there were housewives sitting in

---

3. The research was carried out in 1989–90 and funded by the Wenner Gren Foundation for Anthropological Research.

their living rooms or outside their homes doing piecework, such as trimming shoe uppers or silk screening on the logos: New Balance, Saucony, Puma and Avia. According to government labour statistics, by 1971, everyone in Taiwan was fully-employed, forcing the labour-hungry export-industry to go into the countryside to tap the 'underutilized' and 'flexible' labour of farmers and housewives. Rural towns became new centres of capital accumulation evident in the rise of palatial-looking homes of entrepreneurs, Japanese restaurants, and foreign car dealerships selling BMWs, Mercedes, Volvos, Saabs, Astin Martins and other world-famous brands.

Although historical Taiwan was largely an agrarian society, an image which conjures up a land-bound peasantry, the organization of rural Taiwan was actually more complex, comprised of temple networks which encompassed the island and provided island-wide communications for commercial activities. This system was dormant under the Japanese occupation (1895–1945), but was reactivated in the postwar period when an emerging international subcontracting system brought new opportunities for local entrepreneurs. The religious system provided a cultural substrate and medium of trust, along which local subcontracting networks could flow. In the shoe industry, the labour-intensive manufacturing process was broken down into the smallest technologically-viable units and claimed by entrepreneurs intent on enjoying a greater share of the industry's profits. The incentive of ownership and a culture of cooperation partly accounted for the quick spread of rural industry which contributed to Taiwan's phenomenal postwar expansion. Long worshipped for their efficacy in helping people to get things done, the local gods continued to be useful in the postwar period (Skoggard 1996).

At the production end of the shoe industry, there appears to be no mystery: hardworking families making a living, creating prosperity for themselves and a patrimony for their descendants. However, they are working at an accelerated pace, late into the night, seven days a week, pushing the limits of manufacturing capacity as they endeavour to supply a bottomless North American market. During the peak season and when deadlines loom, Taiwanese labourers work weekdays, 8 am to 9 pm, with an hour off for lunch and a half hour off for dinner, and 8 am to 6 pm on Saturdays and alternate Sundays (Hsiung 1996:113).[4] They are the sorcerer's apprentices caught between highly capitalized corporations that spew out the raw material at one end and those that buy their finished product at the other end. Opposite to buyers such as Nike are Taiwan's large petrochemical corporations. Nanya Plastics is Taiwan's largest corporation and one of the

---

4. When I asked a manager at a Taiwanese auto parts manufacturing company how long his workers have been working overtime, he responded 'three years!'

largest petrochemical companies in the world. In 1988, the combined sales of Nike and Nanya Plastics (US$3.1 billion) was more than three-quarters the sales of the entire Taiwanese shoe manufacturing industry (US$3.7 billion), with its 5,600 independent factories and workshops, employing 350,000 workers.[5] Taiwan's hardworking shoe-making families have contributed to the accumulation of capital on a grand scale by corporations and individuals outside the shoe manufacturing sector.

Taiwan's sudden prosperity is seen by some as a blessing from heaven, a reward for their filial piety, hard work and frugality. One popular new religion, Yiguan Dao, claims that the Eternal Mother, Laomu, has sent the Buddhist Messiah, Milefo, to disseminate the Dao among the people of the world in order to save them and spare the world from imminent destruction.[6] This image of the Dao as seed cast across Taiwan and then throughout the world, is an apt metaphor of Taiwan's postwar experience as first a recipient of capital through export manufacturing, and then an exporter of capital to China and Southeast Asia. Yiguan Dao followers speak of an impending apocalypse which underlies an urgency to cultivate the Dao, but also reflects the profound disruption wrought by Taiwan's rapid industrialization. They give testimony to everyday miracles, which are evidence of the truth and efficacy of the Dao, but also reflect the tremendous surge of capital that has entered Taiwan in the postwar period, bringing fortune to some, while disrupting the lives of nearly everyone. Seeing the world in terms of disasters and miracles underscores the strain Taiwan's export-driven industrialization has had on workers and entrepreneurs alike, and the ambivalence in which they regard Taiwan's modernization.

The daily rituals of Yiguan Dao involve precise, syncopated movements of bowing, praying and kowtowing that mimic the motions of machines and give meaning to a manufacturing discipline already inculcated by Taiwanese workers under industrialization. In the Yiguan Dao induction ceremony, the Dao is reified, associated with a point on the initiate's body, which becomes the basis for a new identity. The objectification of both the Dao and self in Yiguan Dao ritual also helps to validate Taiwan's increasingly commodified society (cf. Skoggard 1996).

Yiguan Dao is an example of Appadurai's workers' mythology, one divorced from the distribution and consumption segments of the commodity

---

5. *Business Groups in Taiwan 1988/1989*, Taipei: China Credit and Information Service Ltd, p. 287; Hoover Business Directory, America On Line; Skoggard (1996), *Indigenous Dynamic*, p. 61.

6. Yiguan Dao had an estimated following of 1,000,000 adherents in the 1980s.

flow. The Taiwanese do not design, market or consume the products they make, but just labour in their manufacture, a practice which has brought general and unprecedented prosperity to the island. Although Taiwan's entrepreneurs have a clear understanding of their place in the world economy and the reasons for their success, they are nevertheless overwhelmed by the success and the urgency to reconstitute the moral order of local society, which their newly won wealth has partly undermined. Taiwan's new religions address this need.

Trader Mythologies

A visit to the Taipei World Trade Center, Taiwan's wholesale emporium for export commodities leaves behind the realm of manufacturing and miracles. Here, the global division between production and consumption is made strikingly apparent. Built in 1986 on the edge of the city and surrounded by empty, undeveloped space, the World Trade Center is a huge triangular edifice of glass and pink and gray granite, a monument to Taiwanese modernity. This is the place where foreign trade missions and importers come to shop. Inside is a seven-storey-high gallery space surrounded by tiers of floors which hold the offices and show rooms of hundreds of trading and manufacturing companies. Wandering through the floors one sees every object of the modern lifestyle from coffee makers to desk top computers, from scuba gear to yachts, from footwear to office chairs and desks. Here are the commodities which comprise the 'standard package' defining North American middle-class identity and standing (Baudrillard 1988), but which one rarely finds in the homes of local Taiwanese.

A visit to the World Trade Center is like stepping into some Wellsian dimension where the world is divided between two societies, one making real the fantasies of the other. One society has become reduced to grazing, stimulating appetites and desires, which drives the engines of industry and capital accumulation in the other society. The former have become lotus-eaters in a pleasure dome, whose slightest whims and fancies materialize before them, with little effort on our part but a thought and word, creating the conditions for a postmodern aesthetic (Harvey 1989). In North America, a voracious 'culture of consumption' has emerged unchecked by productive constraints and spurred by easy credit, which Cornel West sees as eroding the local foundations of community and identity (West 1994). It is another Opium War, although this time the sides are reversed.

While wealth is once again flowing back to the East, it is also flowing into the hands of international brokers like the American Phillip Knight, the head of Nike, who is now a billionaire.[7] Although the popular labels 'post-industrial' and 'information age' deny the obviously continued need for manufacturing in the global economy, they nevertheless point to where the power lies in the system. In the international division between production and consumption, the corporations which dominate the system are those which occupy the nodes lying between these two realms, developing the product ideas which can be sold in the West and made in the East. Nike owns no shoe factories and until recently, no retail stores, and subcontracts out all manufacturing to independent firms (Barnet and Cavanagh 1994:376). Phillip Knight saw early on the implications of the laying of a modern communications grid over the global topography of uneven development. His Stanford Business School thesis project was an analysis of importing cheap running shoes from Japan for the local west coast market (Strasser and Becklund 1991:13). Nike's legacy will not be shoes, but its leading role in developing flexible specialization, and establishing transnational networks of production, marketing and consumption, which has restructured the global economy. Nike is a corporation built on the historical anomaly of uneven development. Who can explain uneven development in purely economic terms? It is not possible. And yet this 'impossibility' gave Nike its advantage in underselling its major competitors, Adidas, Puma and Converse, and contributing to its overall success.

Nike's power and wealth are based on transnational processes which until recently have all but been hidden from view, all we see are the shoes and the advertisements. It is easy to hide processes that occur halfway around the world. Furthermore the cultural distance that separates producers from consumers in the global economy obscures any sense of their entwined fate. Most significant is the distance created by racism, specifically the notion that the East lacks a modern spirit – a mind of its own – and is merely replicating Western capitalist development. In this view the East assumes a subordinate and less significant role in the global capitalist development and accumulation, when in fact it is a key link in a recently transformed global system, one that makes it all possible.

Appadurai's traders' mythology is found in the middle of the commodity flow, where the myth of the 'commodity chain' reifies the connection between production and consumption. Commodity chains have a 'density', 'centrality', 'depth' and 'length' (Gereffi, Korzeniewicz and Korzeniewicz 1994:7). They crisscross the globe, holding the new world order together. They articulate a corporate strategy about where to situate oneself in a commodity flow

7. *New York Post*, 19 September 1995. (Phillip Knight owns 48.54 million shares of Nike stock, at the time worth $4.83 billion.)

and product cycle to extract the greatest profit. According to Korzeniewicz, 'Nike's rise to prominence has been based on its ability to capture a succession of nodes along the commodity chain, increasing its expertise and control over the critical areas of design, distribution, markets and advertising' (Korzeniewicz 1994:257). In this strategy, brand ownership is crucial. We have entered Baudrillard's political economy of signs, where the brand name means everything with regard to profit, wealth and status. We even wear brand names to validate our social status and identity, inscribing the new world order onto ourselves and reducing ourselves to the status of commodity. As Baudrillard writes: 'In an environment of commodities and exchange value, man is no more himself than he is exchange value and commodity. Encompassed by objects that function and serve, man is not so much himself as the most beautiful of these functional and servile objects' (Baudrillard 1988:69).

At this point in the commodity flow the slogan 'Just Do It' is as meaningless and arbitrary as the Nike 'swoosh' logo, a sign that grins at consumers from the bottom of copy-less advertisements. This campaign strategy, called 'whispering loudly' – that is, massive but understated advertising – is only possible by a corporation whose dominance in the market is such that one out of every three purchases of athletic shoes is a Nike.[8] The 'swoosh' reflects the minimalist stance Nike takes in the global economy, where it assumes as little risk as possible, borrowing credit from Japanese shipping companies, obtaining cash in advance for large orders, called 'future contracts', from distributors and retailers, and subcontracting out all production. As a Nike lawyer and major shareholder put it, 'we will be better off if we can build this company on no guarantees' (Strasser and Becklund 1991:256).

The modern system of communications has allowed first-world nations to pass risk onto a third world intent on development. Nike occupies as little space as possible on the thin surface of the production-distribution-consumption interface. A space complemented by Phillip Knight's own Warhol-like personality: secretive, unassuming, tagged the least likely to succeed by his graduating class at business school. The true entrepreneur is a cipher. According to Schumpeter, 'entrepreneurial leadership consists in fulfilling a very special task which only in some rare cases appeals to the imagination of the public. For its success, keenness and vigor are not more essential than a certain narrowness which seizes the immediate chance and *nothing else*' (Schumpeter 1934:89; italics in original).

---

8. *New York Post*, 19 September 1995.

Consumer Mythologies

The last stop on this transnational commodity flow is Nike Town, New York, which opened on 1 November 1996, just in time for the New York City marathon. Nike Town, NY is part of Nike's new marketing strategy to locate their own retail outlets in high-traffic international cross-roads, such as Orlando, Las Vegas, Los Angeles and Chicago. The object is not just to sell shoes – the New York store is a money loser[9] – but to establish an 'authenticity of presence' in the world's consumer capitals. Nike Town, NY is located in Manhattan's exclusive shopping district, 57th Street, just off Fifth Avenue, next door to Tiffany, Co. and across the street from Burberry's, Hermes and Chanel. Nike has entered the high world of fashion and Phillip Knight has become another fashion designer, putting his shoes on sport celebrities.

The store itself is nothing less than a shrine for athletes and athleticism. The building's facade has an arched glass entryway that rises its full five storeys. On either side are Greek columns in relief with the words 'victory,' 'honor,' 'teamwork' and 'courage' inscribed above and below them. Inside the entrance is a gallery displaying 200 different styles of Nike shoes, an array only made possible by flexible specialization. Inlaid in the terracotta floor is a map of the world with a Nike Town-'swoosh' anagram super-imposed over it. One enters another set of doors into the main lobby, a five-storey atrium, encircled by five floors of merchandise. Behind the information counter is a bank of eight colour televisions broadcasting current sport events, on this day, football, baseball and golf. In the floor in a recessed chamber, at least six feet across and covered by thick Plexiglas, is a stencilled knight's helmet and a basketball, representing the mythical team Bowerman-Knight, the founders of Nike and inventors of the waffle sole. On the back wall of each floor are photographs – altogether 320 – of some of the athletes Nike sponsors. Each picture is set in a glass-covered niche with the athlete's name printed on the cover. On an upper floor is another recessed Plexiglass-covered chamber with Michael Jordan's number 23 basketball jersey. Michael Johnson's gold-coloured track shoes are also on display with a label that reads: 'If you wear these shoes you run the 200 meters in 19.32 seconds.' The meaning is intentionally ambiguous. Nike custom-made the shoes just for Michael Johnson and only he can wear them. However, the other message is one of seduction, allowing the consumer to fantasize and identify them-selves with one of the world's fastest runners.

---

9. This information was related to me by a New York retail consultant.

Throughout the store are television monitors showing fast-edited videos of Nike-sponsored athletes and teams. Muzak fills the store with a driving beat. Leaning over the railing from the upper floors one sees at the top of the building a large stopwatch ticking off the seconds and tenths of a second. Next to it is another large digital clock that counts down from 30 minutes. At zero, the house lights dim, strobe lights flash, the music changes to something more emphatic, and a three-storey screen drops down the back wall, led by the swoosh logo in lights. A one-and-a-half-minute video follows of various athletic feats, including a mountain biker careering down a hillside trail, a snow boarder jumping off a sun-silhouetted cliff, a kayaker racing through rapids. Superimposed over the images, individual words of the text fade in and out: 'You,' 'are,' 'what,' 'you,' 'do,' 'do gravity,' 'do adrenaline,' 'do speed,' 'do altitude,' 'do snow.' Nike Town, NY is theatre, a universe unto itself. The whole effect of the multimedia presentation, including the architectural space, is to weld seamlessly together a cult of athleticism with consumption and Nike merchandise. I asked a fellow spectator what he thought. 'Its awesome,' he replied. However I was not as impressed, because I have seen the other half of team Bowerman-Knight's success story: Taiwanese housewives stitching together the shoe uppers for pennies a shoe.[10]

With the North American athletic shoe market near saturation and having secured a cheap and plentiful source of quality merchandise, Nike has begun to move into women's apparel, and overseas markets. A March 1995 ad in Vogue magazine marked Nike's entrance into the women's apparel market. The three-page spread depicts two very tired women runners with their arms around each other. There are no men in the ad, nor any shoes, rather, the ad is a tribute to female bonding: women competing against women, women being friends with women, women liking women. The text shockingly explodes conventional gender stereotypes: 'Pursue pleasure. [N]o matter how damn hard it may be. We are hedonists and we want what feels good . . . If it feels good then just do it.' The ad validates women's identity and solidarity, and challenges women to be indulgent in this regard and to make their claim through Nike fashions.

At this end of the commodity flow, the slogan 'Just Do It' has come to take on many meanings, as many as there are markets to exploit. Its evocation of agency and will has a hollow ring. In the age of welfare reform and the New Federalism, of Wal-Marts, Home Depots and Shop Rites, of globalization and the over accumulation of capital, the odds of 'just doing it' and

10. In stitching workshops, each worker performs a single stitching task. In the twenty different shoe orders the workshop filled in 1989, the number of different stitching tasks for each shoe upper ranged from 14 to 28. The average piece rate for each task ranged from US$.02 to US$.035. The unit cost of each shoe upper was below US$1.00 (Skoggard 1996:81–9).

getting somewhere are stacked way against the ordinary person. The ladder as a metaphor for social mobility has been replaced by a wall or cliff, which requires technical aides to surmount. Nike is as technological as a shoe can get, promising us the leaping ability to carry us over seemingly insurmountable obstacles or at least to dunk the ball, an emblematic act of triumph and dominance. One Nike shoe model, the $130-a-pair Air Max2 Light, looks like a bionic appendage in which plastic, rubber and leather replicate overlapping muscle, ligaments and cartilage, seeming to offer extra power in a shoe that weighs next to nothing. Whether or not the shoe lives up to its billing, we nevertheless embody the promise. It is magic and fantasy, but with a realist gloss.

A Nike ad broadcast during the 1995 NCAA Final Four shows a quick montage of shaky black and white shots of ball players in an urban playground. With no sound the copy reads:

> There is a time
> when all that is [best]
> is before us.
>
> A time of hope
> Hope [forever tied] to a game
> Hope not so much to be the best that there is to be
> but struggle to stay in the game
> and ride it
> wherever it goes.
>
> Just do it.

The message is an evocation of agency, but agency without any direction, or consequences, not like that of Taiwan's entrepreneurs who have transformed their society, or Phillip Knight, who established international subcontracting networks and made a fortune exploiting the differences of uneven development. One could argue that the ad copy is an example of Baudrillard's 'nostalgic resurrection of the real', in this case, labour; a 'third-order simulation' of the real labour that is going on half-way across the world (Baudrillard 1988:121–2). The viewer is asked to hang in there and ride it out, which is exactly what unemployed and underemployed workers, and workers with dead-end service sector jobs are doing. Although appearing proactive, Nike is merely putting its stamp on the new status quo, the global division of production and consumption, and transnational class relations, while at the same time concealing them.

What is most remarkable about the above television commercial is how Nike turns the real-life inner-city conditions of unemployment and violence – conditions worsened by globalization – into a game, effacing altogether the issues of labour and class.[11] Production, craftsmanship and community do not enter into Nike's marketing campaign. Nike shoes are not built tough like Ford trucks, nor are the products of skilled craftsmen like Coach bags; Nikes are worn on the feet of great athletes. In Nike Town, NY, there is a display representing the making of the first waffle sole: Pipes, tubing, pressure gauges, a waffle iron, and a small flickering black and white TV give verisimilitude to this totemic act. However, there are no similar displays acknowledging the genius of Taiwan's local entrepreneurs and the diligence of their workers, or the spirit of cooperation which underlies Nike's historical ties with Asian manufacturers, traders and shipping companies, and has contributed enormously to Nike's success.

Only recently have Nike's international subcontracting relationships been made public, and the company criticized for taking advantage of oppressive patriarchal social relations in third world factories and workshops.[12] This and other revelations have the power to dispel the aura of the brand, and the fashion-like status of Nike merchandise. In light of these revelations, the slogan 'Just Do It' takes on a callousness associated with economic expedience and capitalist exploitation. Perhaps now consumers will no longer feel the lift and bounce they once sensed in a new pair of brand-name running shoes, and instead they will see their world for what it is: a bigger place.

Bibliography

Appadurai, Arjun (1986), 'Introduction: Commodities and the Politics of Value.' In A. Appadurai (ed.), *The Social Life of Things: Commodities in Cultural Perspective.* New York: Cambridge.

Barnet, Richard and John Cavanagh (1994), *Global Dreams: Imperial Corporations and the New World Order.* New York: Simon & Schuster.

Baudrillard, Jean (1988), *Selected Writings.* Stanford: Stanford University Press.

11. Twenty per cent of Nike's shoes are sold in the inner cities, and worn by members of youth gangs whom Cheryl Cole, in her article, 'P.L.A.Y., Nike, and Michael Jordan: National Fantasy and the Racialization of Crime and Punishment' (unpublished manuscript), sees as the alterity of celebrated black sports figures. According to Cole, our adulation of the latter casts the former as deviants, thus masking in racist terms the downside of global restructuring.

12. *Time*, 17 June 1996; *Women's Wear Daily*, 11 June 1996; also, see the reports by Charles Kernaghan, Executive Director of the National Labor Committee: 'Paying to Lose our Jobs' (1992) and 'Free Trade's Hidden Secrets' (1993).

Cole, Cheryl L. (1996), 'P.L.A.Y., Nike, and Michael Jordan: National Fantasy and the Racialization of Crime and Punishment.' Unpublished manuscript.

Gereffi, Gary, Miguel Korzeniewicz and Roberto P. Korzeniewicz (1994), 'Introduction: Global Commodity Chains.' In Gary Gereffi and Miguel Korzeniewicz (eds), *Commodity Chains and Global Capitalism*. Westport, Conn.: Greenwood Press.

Harvey, David (1989), *Condition of Postmodernity*. Cambridge, Mass.: Blackwell.

Hsiung, Ping-Chun (1996), *Living Rooms as Factories: Class, Gender, and the Satellite Factory System in Taiwan*. Philadelphia: Temple University Press.

Jameson, Frederic (1991), *Postmodernism, or The Cultural Logic of Late Capitalism*. Durham, N.C.: Duke University Press.

Korzeniewicz, Miguel (1994), 'Commodity Chains and Marketing Strategies: Nike and the Global Athletic Footwear Industry.' In Gary Gereffi and Miguel Korzeniewicz (eds), *Commodity Chains and Global Capitalism*. Westport, Conn.: Greenwood Press.

Phillips, Kevin (1994), *Arrogant Capital: Washington, Wall Street, and the Frustration of American Politics*. New York: Little, Brown and Co.

Priore, Michael J. and Charles F. Sabel (1984), *The Second Industrial Divide: Possibilities for Prosperity*. New York: Basic Books.

Schumpeter, Joseph A. (1934), *The Theory of Economic Development: An Inquiry into Profits, Capital, Credit, Interest, and the Business Cycle*. Cambridge, Mass.: Harvard University Press.

Skoggard, Ian A. (1996), *The Indigenous Dynamic in Taiwan's Postwar Development: The Religious and Historical Roots of Entrepreneurship*. Armonk, N.Y.: M.E. Sharpe, Inc.

Strasser, J.B. and Laurie Becklund (1991), *Swoosh: The Unauthorized Story of Nike and the Men Who Played There*. New York: Harcourt, Brace, Jovanovich.

Wallerstein, Immanuel (1980), *The Capitalist World System*. New York: Cambridge University Press.

West, Cornel (1994), *Race Matters*. New York: Vintage.

5

Fashioning the Body in Post-Mao China

Xiaoping Li

Since modernization became the Chinese government's key agenda in 1976, China's economic reforms and integration into the world system have had complex implications. Travelling through the country in the summer of 1994, I noticed the penetration of Western fashion, and the prolific styles which my friends and I had longed for in the late 1970s and 1980s. Modernization had reinscribed the Chinese body just as it had changed many women's lives. In southern China, relatives took me to some of the 'world market factories' and the dormitories for the employees – primarily country girls from remote, poverty-driven villages. Their participation in the global economy lent itself to official rhetoric. In the mass media, the peasant-turned-working girl has been represented as the Chinese Cinderella. Together with a whole set of new female roles (e.g. Avon-ladies, fashion models, female entrepreneurs, and so on), they signify the advent of modernity as well as the advancement of Chinese women.

As a woman who grew up in communist China, I was hardly surprised about this new fascination with women. From the very beginning, modernization in China has involved the construction of the 'new' or 'modern woman'. Current economic reforms and globalization, however, have permitted new forces to play a significant role in re-fashioning the 'modern woman'.[1] I

---

1. Feminist scholars have argued that the category of woman has long been exploited by the communist state, which has subsumed women's liberation under the nationalist agenda. See Barlow (1993); Gilmartin et al (1994); Barlow and Zito (1994). I argue, however, that a better understanding of the 'woman question' in China today necessitates a shift away from a viewpoint that the All-China-Women's-Federation (ACWF) dominates inscriptions of womanhood in China.

want to call particular attention to the newly-emerged beauty industry (e.g. fashion and cosmetics) and cultural industry. Both fashion and popular culture constitute a major arena of femininity by offering new forms of bodily adornment and new female role models. The re-fashioned 'modern woman' reveals how aesthetic values and body techniques have been reshaped by global consumer capitalism. It also conjures up and adds a new dimension to a historical truth: the female body is now a site on which party politics, consumer capitalism and patriarchy are played out.

To develop a critical perspective on the practice of bodily adornment in post-Mao China, I shall go briefly through a Western theoretical trajectory of fashion and trace the development of fashion in post-Mao China. Then I shall analyse fashion's role in reconstructing the 'modern woman' and the interplay of global and local forces manifested in the use of fashion.

The Many Faces of Fashion

'Fashion', like many other terms and cultural systems, is polysemic, due to its relationship with all clothing systems and stylistic conventions, and the prolific discourses to which it gives rise. Writings on fashion in the mid-twentieth century relegated fashion largely to the realm of the feminine, linking it to pleasure, leisure and aesthetics. Art history, the pioneer location for serious studies of fashion, routinely treats fashion primarily as *haute couture* in its attempt to preserve the elitist distinction between high art and popular art (Wilson 1985:48). This approach has been filtered into the prevailing perceptions of fashion today. The face of fashion in the syndicated television programme *Fashion Television* and fashion magazines is essentially that of high fashion. Fashion is then often seen going hand in hand with the exercise of power. It is 'an authoritarian process driven by a recognized elite core of designers dictating the fashion behaviour of the majority' (Craik 1994:v).

The connection of fashion with centres of power in capitalist systems makes fashion a target of criticism. Critics of consumer culture relate fashion, style and bodily adornment to capitalist operation and capital accumulation. Capitalist expansion depends on perpetual consumption and there seems to be nothing more alluring than fashion's ever-changing yet glamorous face.[2] Fashion, as part of consumer culture that manufactures 'false consciousness', is then ideologically obfuscating.

2. This is the position taken by Christopher Lasch (1979); Stuart and Elizabeth Ewen (1982); Jean Baudrillard (1981).

Feminist critiques of fashion are more ambivalent. Wilson observes that fashion provoked 'intense irritation and confusion' from the beginning of the women's movement in the 1970s (ibid.:230). Nonetheless, a whole-hearted condemnation of consumer culture and fashion stemmed from the contours of Simone de Beauvoir's thoughts about women, and developed into two recurring charges against a culture of femininity that reproduces sexist ideas and images of women. As Gaines (1990:2) describes: first, 'fashion is enslavement; women are bound by the drudgery of keeping up their appearance and by the impediments of the styles which prohibit them from acting in the world'. Second, fashion may 'disguise the body, deform it, or follow its curves; but ultimately puts it on display'. In all these critical accounts, fashion is a hegemonic instrument serving the interests of capitalism and patriarchy.

Liberal feminist and culturalist approaches purport a more affirming attitude towards fashion and the adornment of the body. Wilson's important book advocates a move beyond the feminist ambivalence and 'a most conspiratorial of Marxist critiques of capitalism', calling for a recognition of human autonomy and the rights for pleasure and fantasy. Her tone has a clear postmodernist nuance: 'we can use and play with fashion' to 'express and explore our more daring aspirations' (Wilson 1985:245–6). This high-lights not only individual agency, but also fashion's rich political and cultural meanings.

Recent theoretical movements have expanded the concept of fashion to allow for a broad range of bodily displays to be recognized as fashion behaviours. Scholars have taken fashion out of the elitist realm of high fashion and relocated it within that of popular culture and everyday life. The implicit notion that fashion is a Western phenomenon is also contested by accounts of changing clothing codes and stylistic registers in non-Western societies (cf. Cannon, this volume). Take for instance Craik's (1994:5) attempt to blur the conventional binaries between traditional/modern, fashion/costume, and Western/non-Western by conceptualizing fashion as 'a technology of civility'. Researchers on clothing in Africa also argue that 'Africa and the West are mutually engaged in a semiotic web', and challenge conceptions that 'divide too clearly "first" and "third" worlds, colonizer and colonized' (Hendrickson et al. 1996).

The culturalist approach has shifted the inquiry and opened up new spaces. As an important component of our current critical investigation of contemporary society and culture, studies of fashion, however, cannot be limited to the analysis of signification and individual/group practice of self-representation. Fashion's intricate links with other dimensions of society necessitate the semiotics of fashion to be addressed in relation to political and economic issues. The process of globalization has placed bodily adornment and fashion in the global and local nexus. Investigations of fashion in this context cannot avoid questions of imperialism and colonialism, nor can they be detached from analyses of the dynamics of globalization and localization.[3]

A negotiation of Western understandings of fashion is essential to analysing clothing behaviours and fashion in contemporary China, where styles are often associated with hegemonic operations by authorities and dominant ideologies. The clash between bodily inscription from above and self-formation/self-presentation allows the 'body surface' (Hendrickson 1996) to become rich testimonies of political struggle. Furthermore, fashion's entanglement in China's current capitalist transformation under the name of modernization demands us to consider the conjunction between fashion, global capitalism and modernity. The operation of global capitalism and China's modernization has allowed the formation of a conjunction between local and global centres of power. In this context, fashion has expressed itself in multiple ways. This study reads fashion closely in its local manifestations rather than through Western theoretical premises.

Modernizing the Chinese Nation/Body

Shizhuang, the Chinese word for fashion, soon resurfaced in the public discursive space in the wake of the Cultural Revolution.[4] Since then, both the meaning of 'fashion' and clothing styles have undergone considerable transformation in accordance with larger societal changes. As the country has further turned to capitalism, a high fashion discourse modelled on elite fashion in capitalist consumer culture has come to dominate. The order of fashion spells out the nature of China's modernization.

Fashion resurfaced in response to both the official modernization project launched in 1976 and popular aesthetic needs. In 1979, the Chinese media began to address the emerging 'fashion consciousness' among the populace, signified by the return of skirts, dresses and shoes with high or medium heels. Meanwhile, the state economic plan made a decisive shift from heavy industries to light industries, prioritizing textile and garment industries. Increases in textile products and popular demands pushed the garment

3. See Brodman's (1994) discussion on the impact of Western imperialism on Latin American Indian dress and culture.

4. The Cultural Revolution lasted for ten years (1966–1976) and was a major upheaval that deeply politicized communist China and brought the national economy to the edge of bankruptcy.

industry to manufacture new styles (Chen 1981; Wen 1981). However, it is clear that in the early 1980s the lexicon of the new Chinese fashion shared little with fashions in the West. Fashion meant brighter colours, moderately altered uniforms that were popular in the 1960s and 1970s, and skirts and dresses modelled on the patterns of the 1950s. After decades of state surveillance over bodily practices, neither state-run garment industries nor private tailors had the experiences and imagination to produce something fresh. Individual experimentation with techniques of selection and combination suggests greater ingenuity in the general climate of post-Mao freedom, yet this was substantially curtailed by the lack of aesthetic and material resources. Like the blue and green uniform of the Cultural Revolution, the new fashion was a classless and homogeneous style. This remained largely unchanged in the first half of the 1980s despite the arrival of Western high fashion.

In 1981, the French designer Pierre Cardin went to China with twelve models from Paris and staged shows in Beijing and Shanghai. It was a little-publicized mission, revealing both the underdeveloped mass communications system and Chinese authorities' reservations about Western fashion. A Chinese reporter recalled an anecdote during a Pierre Cardin show at the Cultural Palace of Nationalities in Beijing:

> The spectators, mostly officials from the foreign trade department clad in sober greys and blues, were bowled over: The models, as lithe and graceful as cats, were in total contrast to their own quiet selves. Suddenly one model with blond hair and bright blue eyes stopped in the middle of the stage. She whirled towards the audience, and with one swift motion spread her long, flowing skirt out into a fan. The movement and its spectacular result were so alien to the watchers, they reared back in unison, as if from the lash of a whip. (Li 1993:34)

A party newspaper expressed its disapproval by ridiculing Cardin and his Chinese sponsor with the headline 'Foreign Fart is Fragrant' (Wei 1989). The xenophobic writer/editor had little idea that the same headline could be re-used, without any satirical sense, for China's zeal for Western commodities in the near future.

Modernization became the major driving force behind the development of new fashion systems in China. In fact, the Chinese term *shizhuang* (fashion) has always signified the modern, as it is clearly contrasted to *fushi* (costume), which refers to clothing styles in Imperial China and of ethnic minorities. It is *shizhuan* (fashion), not *fushi* (costume), that links China to the outside world. If *fushi* always points to tradition and past, *shizhuang* is closely associated with internationalization and modernization.

Indeed, a chain of internationally-related activities went hand in hand with the development of new fashion. One year before Pierre Cardin's arrival, China started publishing its first fashion magazine to pronounce the country's entry into international competition. In the same year the country's first clothing research institute was established and began to standardize sizes for China as a member of the International Clothing Standards Association. That summer at the Shanghai Clothing Export Fair, China's first modelling team presented its first show. It was reported to have won 'high praise' from the forty or so members of a delegation from an international clothing buyers' association, securing an order of US$15 million. Then the first national fashion show was held in 1981 in Beijing (Tie 1983). Two years later the city hosted the first national fashion design competition, assisted by a number of Japanese and American fashion designers and writers (Qi 1983). Increases in garment production and foreign trade prompted in 1984 the first privately-organized fashion show and modelling training schools in a number of cities. Meanwhile, the Yves Saint Laurent exhibition went to Beijing and became an 'enormous success'. The curator, Di Pietre, recalled:

> Thousands and thousands of people came to see it. I don't know what they thought of all these things . . .They didn't have a historical perspective to understand how fashion changes or any background of European fashion, especially the young people who were brought up during the Cultural Revolution. Still they poured in, quietly, respectfully and almost every person with a sketchbook and pencil.
>
> A year after the exhibition they were in the Beijing streets in YSL copies, in everything from the Mondrian dress to the Ballet Russes (cited in Craik 1994:26).

Fashion came to assume a much more prominent role in national development and public life around the mid 1980s. The state's seventh Five-Year Economic Plan (1986–90) included setting fashion trends. To connect the Chinese fashion industry closely with the global fashion market, state-run designing institutes started to announce twice a year, in line with international practices, fashion trends to guide production and consumption. Efforts were made to penetrate international fashion extravaganzas and the potential domestic market. In 1987, Chinese models made their first appearance at the International Fashion Festival in Paris. At home, garment factories organized fashion shows and clothes affairs in big cities, small towns and even villages. Another national design contest was held in Beijing in conjunction with a clothing exhibition and sales fair. The China Clothing Industry Corporation announced proudly that China's clothing industry had experienced rapid growth in both production and export (Wei 1989; Wen 1987).

Corresponding to these events was a gradual shift in the meaning of fashion. During the 1980s, both fashion design and practices of fashioning the body in everyday life fluctuated with the political climate and official attitudes towards the foreign, particularly the West. Until the mid 1980s, fashion design was not only a new terminology but remained 'pretty much a hit-or-miss affair' (Wen 1987). True, both old and new fashion centres produced a greater variety of styles. Shanghai, the major fashion centre in China, regained its reputation as having the best designs in the country, whereas new garment industries in Canton and Fujian provinces attracted private vendors from all over the country. There remained, however, a considerable disjuncture between the new Chinese styles and Western fashion trends. Unlike visual arts which thrived on extensive borrowing from Western discourses, fashion designing was confined to reworking existing local styles. Foreign or Western references were scarce – most Western references came from images in foreign films, magazines, television (international news) and international trade affairs. It was not until January 1985 that the first group of Chinese garment designers paid a visit to Paris (ibid.).

This 'pilgrimage' to the West reflected a decided change in official attitudes. Although Western-style suits, sport jackets and women's ready-to-wear had appeared at national sales exhibitions, explicit official affirmation of Western dress codes did not come until 1984, when the younger generation of China's top leaders suddenly appeared in suits and ties at the 35th anniversary celebration of the People's Republic of China.[5] If this was meant to boost modernization and the new leadership through image-making, it practically encouraged the 'modernization' of the body at a time when a large number of the masses were still clothed in the blue Mao jacket. The Western-style suit has become the trendiest men's wear since the mid 1980s.

Nonetheless, official acceptance of both Western and new styles was selective. Local authorities in particular continued overseeing individual clothing styles; the latter continued to diverge outside the state-governed domain of fashion. Unsatisfied with styles provided by the national garment industry, young urban Chinese searched for clothes with individuality. Conjuring up styles from the early fifties and copying (and altering) occasionally-available images of Japanese and Western fashion were common practices of fashion lovers. The desire for more stylish self-representation also made second-hand clothes smuggled into China from Hong Kong and Macao popular items on sidewalk stands in the major cities. A small number of young urban males declared a sub-cultural identity through trousers modelled on jeans and bell-bottoms (Fig. 5.1).

The liberating/subverting role of clothes/fashion seemed to be equally

5. The then Party-Secretary-in-General Hu Yaobang was particularly a trend-setter and advocate of new styles.

noticed by the followers of fashion and Chinese authorities. For the former, dressing up differently was a badge of individualism and a breakaway from the manufactured uniformity that authorities still tried to maintain. For the authorities, alternative styles always gestured towards defiance. The official campaigns of 'anti bourgeois-liberalization' in the 1980s were in part fought over clothes and hair styles. Local authorities condemned 'peculiar styles', and on some occasions, publicly destroyed those trousers bearing traits of 'Western bourgeois decadence'.

Westernization

This battle over styles was closely related to the issue of national identity. Tensions between the Western/global and the Chinese/local were obvious. Consistent with the intellectual debate over culture and concerns about national identity, for much of the 1980s China's emerging fashion industry was oriented towards a combination of national culture and Western styles. The former was epitomized by the *qipao* and costumes of China's ethnic minorities.[6] In particular, the *qipao* was favoured for its ability to enhance 'oriental femininity'. It became a major topic of fashion writing; its modified forms appeared on the domestic market and represented Chinese fashion on international occasions. In 1988, Chinese designer Ma Ling participated in fashion shows in Hong Kong and France, and her designs were praised for the 'combination of oriental charm with Western culture'. The Chinese media were especially thrilled by the Paris show, citing enthusiastically Western responses towards the Chinese fashion team. In this regard, China's new fashion designers seem to share with Hong Kong and Taiwanese designers the same strategy of creation, since all use the *qipao* as an element of conscious orientalizing. Nonetheless, mainland Chinese designers were motivated by a sense of nationalism. It was a shared hope that by drawing from Chinese tradition they would be able to catch up with the rest of the world, and even influence world fashion trends in the future (Wei 1989; Wen 1987). This national pride suggests the lingering schizophrenia that originated from China's defeat by the West in the nineteenth century.

'Foreign fart' did turn fragrant in the late 1980s. Western 'fashion experts'

---

6. At the first national fashion show, Western-style wedding gowns and evening dresses already appeared, but it was the *qipao* that dominated the event. The new styles displayed at the first national fashion competition were much based on appropriations of ethnic minority costumes. Combining current international trends with a national style was also a major theme at the first national symposium on the art of clothing design held in 1987.

were hired to coach models, and Chinese models travelled to France, Italy, Germany, Japan, Hong Kong, Thailand and the former Soviet Union. When Chinese model Peng Li won the first prize in the International New Models Competition in Italy in 1988, it was hailed as a sign that China's new beauty industry finally could match international/Western standards. More joint ventures of clothing production appeared; fashion shows and national/ international model contests were held annually (Li 1993). Western fashion dominated a televised, grand fashion show titled the *Wind of the Century* in the early 1990s, which displayed costumes of Imperial China and contemporary high fashion with over 2,000 Chinese and Western models (including a number of super models). The *haute couture* by Chinese designers and evening dresses by Pierre Cardin and Valentino were the climax of the occasion and defined glamour. Meanwhile, Hong Kong and Western clothing retail industries have moved into the country, setting up stores to 'take advantage of China's growing affluence'. Boutique fashion catering to the neo-rich has appeared in the cities and taken over the upper end of the market. As of 1994, the big attractions were reportedly European designs (Blanchi 1993; Blass 1993; Bow 1993).[7]

The gradual centralization of Western high fashion suggests the emergence of a hierarchical order of fashion. The indigenous has been retained as one of the sources of creation; mass-produced women's ready-to-wear fashion hybridizes Western styles with conventional Chinese aesthetics. Nonetheless, global and Western fashion trends now serve as the framework of fashion designing. Western-style high fashion occupies a predominant place in the economy of representation, operating as the major discourse that acts on the public imagination. Westernization is furthered by the shift of the global 'needle trade'. In attracting foreign investment, China has turned itself into the world's largest cheap labour pool. Joint ventures and foreign investment allow garment industries in China to become part of the world-scale putting-out system of Western fashion industry. By producing clothes designed by designers from outside of the country, these factories help sustain the Western fashion world and lead the production of new styles at the domestic market.

The transformation of fashion is accompanied by a shift in the ideology of beauty and the import of other techniques of femininity.[8] The fashion

---

7. Western fashion is also centralized in the *Style Weekly*, a national publication on fashion and beauty trends that aims at reaching ordinary Chinese. Its pages are dominated by photographs of Western and Chinese fashion models and reports on major Western fashion houses and fashion trends.

8. The term 'techniques of femininity' is borrowed from Craik (1994:44). It refers to the techniques of display and projection of the female body. The new model of femininity recycles

model has become the ultimate archetype of beauty, dominating the iconography of women. She has established a new model of the female body and beauty, and spawned a cosmetic industry, beauty salons and plastic surgery. In popular culture, fashion and fashion models are essential to the manufacturing of both modern women and modern lifestyles.

(Re)inventing the 'Modern Woman'

In recent years a large number of television dramas and films produced in China concentrate on female experiences. This new fascination with women indicates the commodification of cultural production. Moreover, it is part of a larger promotional discourse that utilizes the narratives of modern women as testimonies of modernization. The new female images advanced by the media sharply contrast with conventional female prototypes. These are the female stars rising out of the market economy, namely, the newly emergent upper-middle class women in the corporate world and the world of spectacle. Dressed in high-style clothes, the entrepreneurs, managers, lawyers, fashion designers and models, pop stars, and journalists occupy a central place in the China rejuvenated by global capital. This is, however, the latest chapter in a long history of (re)inventing 'modern women'.

There has been an intricate relationship between Chinese modernity and women, since the 'woman question' was long viewed as an integral part of nation-building. The meaning of 'modern' or 'new woman' seems to be redefined at each major historical moment; in most cases masculine constructions prevailed. Early male modernizers promoted a 'modern woman' whose female biological function is complemented by literacy.[9] The nationalist construction of 'new woman' in literature and films between the 1920s and 1930s offers a role model engaged in a nationalist or class struggle rather

typical ingredients of dominant Western femininity, which Craik identifies as the importance of appearance, fetishization of body, manipulation and moulding of the body, the discipline and labour associated with beauty and body, the equation of youth with femininity, and feminine lifestyles (1994:70). With regard to 'beauty', appearances embellished by fashion and beauty products have replaced the 'spiritual beauty' cherished in communist China. Beauty contests have been held since 1993 to select 'Miss China', 'Miss Factory' and 'Miss School'. The contests are described by a reporter as a 'fever' for 'watching half-clad pretty young women pose in public' (Liu 1994).

9. See Yue's 'Gendering the Origins of Modern Chinese Fiction' (1992).

than the miniature world of subjective desire.[10] In the 1960s and 1970s the discourse of the Cultural Revolution promoted the 'iron girls' – masculinized women – by obliterating not only gender but also sex differences.

The 'new woman' and women's entry into the public sphere via new social roles have been signified in part by changed styles. Styles drawn from the West were essential to the early constructions of 'new women'; they replaced traditional women's wear and highlighted the coming of a modern age.[11] A small group of urban upper-middle class women was active in the dress reform brought by the establishment of the Republic of China. Cross-dressing, for example, was favoured in some cases as a sign of new female subjectivity. The *qipao* was altered to fulfil nationalist sentiment at one time or to imitate new style trends in the West at other times. For instance, following the 1920s vogue for short skirts in the West, the *qipao*'s hemline was shortened to just below knee-length. It became the standard outfit, matched with a short haircut, for China's first generations of formally educated women (Zhu 1984).

Under communism, women were said to 'hold half of the sky'. But their desire and self-formation were largely prescribed by the state. Masculinization of clothes came to achieve a brief moment of hegemony during the Cultural Revolution. The green army uniform was popularized by the party leaders and consequently by the Red Guards, and became an important instrument in maximizing political and ideological uniformity.[12] It was adopted by young urban women as a fashion in order to relocate themselves within the new revolutionary crusade. In the middle of the 1970s, an attempt to rescue femininity was made by the wife of then-paramount leader Mao, Jiang Qin. Motivated by political ambition, Jiang introduced to the masses a plain dress with a V-shaped collar, derived from women's costume in the Tang and Ming Dynasty. The body was loose, square cut, but moderately curved in at the waist to feminize the look. Its formality as a national female dress was endorsed by the few high-ranking female communist cadres, who wore the

10. The masculine construction of 'new women' was initially constituted by heroic female roles in literature. Later she came to assume a high profile in the film entitled *New Woman* produced by leftist filmmakers in the 1930s, in which a female activist engaged in the class struggle was presented as a role model. See script by Sun Shiyi in *Collection of Modern Chinese Literature* (1968). By contrast, the 'modern girl' in feminist writings during the period is marked by a distinctive female subjectivity. See Ding Ling's short stories 'The Diary of Miss Sophy' and 'Spring in Shanghai – 1930,' in *Collection of Modern Chinese Short-stories* (1980).

11. The founding of the Republic of China fostered dress reforms. Western-educated leaders introduced men's wear modelled on a Western-style suit (later called *Zhongshan Fu* in China) and short hair to construct a new identity compatible with a new age.

12. The Red Guards were organized students who claimed to be the defenders of revolution during the Cultural Revolution.

dress when receiving foreign guests. The so-called *Jiang Qin Fu* (Fig. 5.2) was reproduced by state garment industries and sold nationwide.

With its capitalist orientation, the current stage of modernization requires new female role models, stylized by fashion and careers compatible to modernity. In popular culture, fashion intersects with the remaking of the 'modern woman' through the translation of the *mise-en-scène* into items of clothes. The fashion industry frequently supplies the wardrobe for film and television production; fashion and fashion shows are often incorporated into film and television narratives. Film and television screens then serve as a sort of clothes fair to display an elaborate array of new designs, whereas the vibrant colours and rhythms of the fashion world help project sensations of a 'modern' China. The fashion tie-up is involved in the manufacturing of national dreams.

The 'modern woman' in the 1990s is embodied in the protagonist of the popular, award-winning television serial *Woman Is Not the Moon*, aired in 1993. By claiming that a woman is not the moon, the tele serial appears to subvert a traditional, gendered allegory derived from the ancient Chinese metaphysical framework of masculinity/femininity – yin and yang, the two fundamental ethereal forces that create and perfect the cosmic mode of existence. Equated in the Chinese consciousness with the moon/woman and the sun/man, yin-yang functions as a cosmic principle to regulate behaviours and social orders in which women are positioned as the subordinate, obedient and self-sacrificing.[13]

What is intriguing is that the narrative pertains to a particular link between fashion and women's emancipation. It centres around the transformation of a country girl who ran away from an arranged marriage – an archetypal theme in modern Chinese literature and popular cultural texts produced after the 1949 revolution. Like previous tales of female emancipation, the protagonist suffers from repressions of various kinds and is in need of rescue. Unlike previous tales, her saviour is not a communist cadre, but a fashion designer who notices her 'oriental beauty' and recruits her as a model. Instead of taking the standard female rites of passage by converting to the communist revolution, then, the country girl answers modernity's call by going into a big city to pursue a career as a fashion model.

While this re-invokes the Western theme of going to the big city to be modern, the country girl's transformation is an allegory of the reinvention

13. Yin-yang has a set of gender connotations: yang is warmth, light, daylight, masculinity, ascent, strength, power and action. Yin means coldness, darkness, night, femininity, descent, gentleness, smoothness, and inaction. Along with other social and political arrangements, yin-yang constitutes a cultural system that sustained Chinese society and identity. See Wang Yuejing's 'Mixing Memories and Desire' (1989).

Figure 5.1. Characteristic style of a male member of a subculture during the late 1960s and early 1970s.

of China through modernization. Taking on the celebration of modernity as its mission, the serial polarizes the countryside and the city, the traditional and the modern. The former denotes repression and tradition, whereas the latter liberation and modernity. Fashion, implied as an agent of transformation, acquires larger social meanings.

Between the Global and Local

Fashion has become a major aesthetic medium for the expression of new desires and values in post-socialist China. But to say that the above phenomena suggest China is being Westernized/colonized, we would overlook the dynamics of globalization. In recent years, theorization of the globalization of culture has shifted from the 'cultural imperialism' thesis to a postmodernist global mapping that emphasizes global pluralism, contingent structures and local resurgence (Sreberny-Mohammadi 1991). The local is seen as being capable of 'corrupting' the centre's 'high ideas' (Hannerz 1991) by turning the 'instruments of homogenization' into 'heterogeneous dialogues' (Appadurai 1990). This attempt to re-evaluate the global situation may have some unfortunate results, if representations of local realities privilege theoretical premises rather than substantial investigations of local heterogeneity – including acknowledging the political, social or cultural divisions among the populace in a given local society. The complex manifestations of globalization and localization, it seems, have led to Jameson's (1994) cautious remark that the outcomes of globalization are too ambivalent to be easily evaluated.

China's on-going transformation further complicates the adoption of Western styles and the use of fashion. The 'theory of articulation' initially formulated by Meillassoux (1981) is useful in this regard as a 'model of cultural change', allowing one to explore the richly unintended consequences of the localization of global cultural flows (Gupta and Ferguson 1992).[14] 'Articulation' spells out conjunctures: for instance, in reshaping Chinese life, global capitalism has come to be intertwined with communist party politics and Chinese feudalism. No doubt, Chinese endorsement of styles invented by Western fashion industries and the new 'modern woman' speak volumes about a West-dominated globalization and a colonial mentality. Fashion's

---

14. Gupta and Ferguson (1992:8) write: 'articulation models . . . posit a primeval state of autonomy (usually labelled "pre-capitalist"), which is then violated by global capitalism. The result is that both local and larger spatial arenas are transformed, the local more than the global to be sure, but not necessarily in a predetermined direction.'

intersection with popular culture, for instance, reiterates a Western commercial strategy which dates back to the early twentieth century (Herzog 1990). The new standard of beauty and new femininity indicate the arrival of modern forms of patriarchy embodied in the market economy and consumer capitalism – two major components of Western modernity. Finally, the fact that fashion is utilized to embellish a collective modern Chinese identity reveals Chinese embracing of a 'universal modernity' based on European Enlightenment thought. In this light, the adoption of Western styles resembles the characteristic behaviour and mentality of a local elite class in a colonial society, who adopted Western dress to comply with the colonial order, and more importantly, to accomplish an identity transmutation via the exteriorization of the self-as-other. It is as if 'the acquisition of a new visible identity worn on the body ensures the acquisition of a new "modern" cultural identity' (Craik 1994:27).[15]

Nonetheless, Chinese uses of fashion have multiple registrations for two major reasons: one, global and Western forces offer local groups a broad range of possibilities; two, different actors utilize Western styles to respond to particular local situations and to meet their own needs. In contemporary China, the plurality of styles brought by global cultural flows provides individuals with unprecedented opportunities for self-representation and self-formation. Western styles have been used for a wide range of purposes, and in some cases, they disrupt local repressive practices. The construction of subculture identity (e.g. China's first generation of rock musicians and their fans) is enabled by appropriating the styles of their Western counterparts. Similarly, fashion annihilates the suffocation of feminine beauty and desire in the Mao regime, and it may open up space for the rejuvenation of female subjectivity.

What also needs to be noted is the operation of a constellation of power through fashion and the image of the 'modern woman'. Ironically, global economic and cultural flows have enlivened local, traditional forms of patriarchy. While the 'modern woman' is constructed by iconizing Western/capitalist cultural symbols, she is a reincarnation of the characteristic allure of 'oriental femaleness' sedimented in conventional, male expectation, desire and pleasure. While fashion is largely Westernized, its use can be highly localized. At times it is not Western styles but the very word 'fashion' and its association with the female body that matter. For instance, it has become

---

15. Clothes allow us to trace the operation of colonialism and local insurgency. Colonialism's symbolic violence is partially achieved by suppressing local dress in order to enhance the authority of 'Western ways'. Local resistance then includes wearing indigenous clothes. Shifting dress codes and the modification of indigenous clothes in colonial societies are registrations of such contestations. See Craik (1994:26–36) and Brodman (1994).

Figure 5.2. Jiang Qin Fu.

a familiar sight that in private restaurants and night clubs teenage girls, half-clad in clothes made of low quality materials, awkwardly imitate the mass-mediated images in front of a primarily male crowd. In this case, fashion operates as Chinese patriarchy's instrument of subjugation and exploitation.

Moreover, fashioning the body in post-Mao China is a national event orchestrated by the state. Fashion is implicated in the state project of modernization precisely because of its signification of change, and its identification with Western fashion centres, high lifestyles, and most importantly, an exuberant modern society that China is striving to become. It satiates a genuine desire for annihilating China's status as a 'Third World' country. It has, therefore, effects of elevation and concealment. It elevates China by giving it a modern and cosmopolitan look. It conceals the collective body of the Chinese nation by operating to resolve, at the imaginary level, real contradictions and problems that have not been solved but rather amplified in some cases by the amalgamation of local systems and global capitalism. The re-fashioned 'modern woman', for instance, masquerades the disparity between women's social roles today and the female roles portrayed in popular cultural texts. By clothing the grotesque faces of Chinese communism and patriarchy in Western-style clothes, fashion allows both to coalesce within modernity.

Conclusion

Post-Mao China saw the development of new fashion systems and plurality of styles as a response to both individual needs of self-representation/ formation, and more importantly, the national need for modernization. In the process, fashion has come to be associated with the world of spectacle and defined primarily by Western fashion trends. Western styles now adorn the Chinese body in accordance with a vision of modernity modelled on consumer capitalism. Fashion in post-Mao China, then, has ambiguous effects. It undercuts the politicized codes of masculinity and femininity prevalent in Maoist socialism, but at the same time subjects the body, especially the female body, to another set of bodily inscriptions and prescriptions. Moreover, fashion and the re-fashioned female roles have created the illusion of an affluent modern China and women's emancipation. The political content of change in dress codes is consequently undermined.

Fashion's transformation and the recodification of the 'modern woman' reveals how global and local forces converge in the domains of discursive and bodily representation. It is this mesh that turns the female body into a site on which patriarchy, party politics and consumer capitalism are played out. This joint act crystallizes the paradox of Chinese modernity. It strives, on the one hand, to achieve a modernity largely based on the model of the West. On the other hand, the 'simulation' is always complicated by local forces.[16]

Bibliography

Appadurai, A. (1990), 'Disjuncture and Difference in the Global Cultural Economy,' *Public Culture*, 2(2):1–24.

Barlow, T.E. et al (eds) (1993), *Gender Politics in Modern China*. Durham: Duke University Press.

Barlow, T.E. and A. Zito (eds) (1994), *Body, Subject & Power in China*. Chicago: University of Chicago Press.

Baudrillard, Jean (1981), *For a Critique of the Political Economy of the Sign*, Charles Levin (trans). St. Louis, Mo.: Telos Press.

Blanchi, G. (1993), 'Mao's Out,' *China Trade Report*, July:11.

Blass, A. (1993), 'No Mao Jackets Please,' *China Trade Report*, December:6.

Bow, J. (1993), 'Fashion's In,' *China Trade Report*, July:10.

Brodman, B. (1994), 'Paris or Perish: The Plight of the Latin American Indian in a Westernized World.' In S. Benstock and S. Ferriss, (eds), *On Fashion*. New Brunswick: Rutgers University Press.

Chen, Yifang (1981), 'Clothing a Billion People,' *China Reconstructs*, May:5–7.

Craik, J. (1994), *The Face of Fashion*. London: Routledge.

Ding, Ling (1980), 'The Diary of Miss Sophy' and 'Spring in Shanghai – 1930,' In *Selected Works of Modern Chinese Short-stories*. Beijing: People's Publishing House.

Ewen, Stuart and Elizabeth Ewen (1982), *Channels of Desire: Mass Image and the Shaping of the American Consciousness*. New York: McGraw Hill.

Gaines, J. (1990), 'Introduction: Fabricating the Female Body.' In J. Gaines and C. Herzog (eds), *Fabrications: Costume and the Female Body*. London: Routledge.

Gilmartin, C. et al (eds) (1994), *Engendering China*. Cambridge, Mass: Harvard University Press.

Gupta, A. and J. Ferguson (1992), 'Beyond "Culture": Space, Identity, and the Politics of Difference,' *Cultural Anthropology*, 7,1,:6–23.

---

16. Raymond Lee (1994) uses 'simulated modernity' to describe modernities in Third World countries. Local forces include the subjectivity of the people who use fashion. For instance, the pleasure gained through fashion may come to form a new female subjectivity. Self-adornment may give men and women a sense of potency to act in the world. Fashion and other body techniques enable the Chinese to join modernity symbolically; can that symbolic entry (or the gap between manufactured dreams and material existence) prompt any substantive actions? My point is that bodily inscription by the state and global capitalism could only be partially successful.

Hannerz, U. (1991), 'Scenarios for Peripheral Cultures.' In A. King (ed.) *Culture, Globalization and The World System: Contemporary Conditions for the Representation of Identity.* Binghamton: State University of New York at Binghamton, Dept. of Art and Art History.

Hendrickson, H. et al.(1996), *Clothing and Difference: Embodied Identities in Colonial and Post-colonial Africa.* Durham: Duke University Press.

Herzog, C. (1990), '"Power Puff" Promotion: The Fashion Show-in-the-Film.' In J. Gaines and C. Herzog (eds), *Fabrications: Costume and the Female Body.* London: Routledge.

Jameson, F. (1994), 'Conference Themes,' *Globalization and Culture: Conference Reader.* Durham: Duke Center for Critical Theory.

Lasch, Christopher (1979), *The Culture of Narcissism.* New York: Warner Books.

Lee, Raymond (1994), 'Modernization, Postmodernism and the Third World,' *Current Sociology* 42(2):1–63.

Li, Anding (1993), 'The Fashion Industry: Cash Rewards and Growing Pains,' *China Reconstructs,* xlii,6:34–6.

Liu, H. (1994), '"Miss China": A Thing Of Beauty,' *China Today,* February:41–3.

Meillassoux, C. (1981), *Maidens, Means and Money: Capitalism and the Domestic Community.* Cambridge: Cambridge University Press.

Qi, L. (1983), 'First National Fashion Design Competition,' *China Reconstructs,* December:58–61.

Sun, Shiyi (1968), 'New Women. In *Selected Works of Modern Chinese Literature.* Hongkong: Hong Kong Institute of Literary Studies.

Sreberny-Mohammadi, A. (1991), 'The Global and the Local in International Communications.' In J. Curran and M. Gurevitch (eds), *Mass Media and Society.* London: Edward Arnold.

Tie, Y. (1983), 'First National Fashion Show,' *China Reconstructs,* October:4–7.

Wei, Liming (1989), 'Chinese Clothing Catches Up With World Trend,' *Beijing Review,* 27:20–4

Wen, Tianshen (1981), 'What They're Wearing in Beijing,' *China Reconstructs,* May:8–9.

—— (1987), 'New Fashion Trends,' *China Reconstructs,* October:66–8

Wilson, E. (1985), Adorned in Dreams: Fashion and Modernity. London: Virago Press.

Yue, Mingbao (1992), 'Gendering the Origins of Modern Chinese Fiction.' In Tonglin Lu (ed.), *Gender and Sexuality in Twentieth-century Chinese Literary and Society.* Albany: State University of New York Press.

Zhu, Jinghui (1984), 'The Checkered Career of the *Qipao*,' *China Reconstructs,* May:28–9.

6

The Body of Art and the Mantle of Authority[1]

Gordon Roe

This paper is the result of my ethnographic research on the lives of 'professional' artist's models. Professional models are those who have consciously chosen modelling as a job, and make all or a substantial part of their income as an artist's model. I myself am a model and began modelling when I was a student seeking a source of on-campus work. Because I lacked formal training in art history and practice, my point of view was always from the podium, looking out on artists and art. I have come to see the peculiar position I occupied in the studio as an anthropologist would: by doing the work and observing the studio as an outsider; by asking questions of instructors, art students and models; and from reading about the role and history of modelling in Western art. Through this exploration, I discovered that we models were at the centre of an intense debate over the ethics of representation in the figurative arts, a debate in which models neither had a voice, nor were considered to have any reason to speak. This is attributable to the terms of legitimacy in the art field, and to the idea of 'text'. To be a legitimate producer or interpreter of art-texts, one must possess what Bourdieu (1984, 1993) calls 'cultural capital': acknowledged expertise in the art field. In both 'modernist' and 'postmodernist' arguments, models are defined as what the artist has made of them in the art work, and these art-works become the texts both use to further their arguments. These textual constructions and deconstructions are reflected back onto the model, and result in the model becoming an appropriated object even by those who claim to be acting in the interests of those marginalized by patriarchal tradition.

It was this glaring absence of the model's voice that my research was focused on. I interviewed a total of nine female and four male professional

1. The drawings accompanying the text are by marilyn lemon.

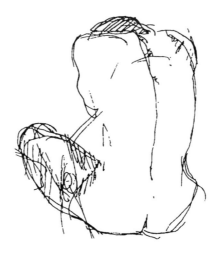

models in Edmonton, Toronto, London, Ontario and Vancouver, as well as model schedulers for art schools in Edmonton, Toronto and London. Although some of these models were also artists, it was their thoughts on modelling I was most interested in. In this chapter, I have concentrated on these models' work in instructional life classes rather than their work with individual artists. These classes are important because they provide the bulk of the professional model's income, and because they expose the pattern of socialization that defines the model in the context of art. The topic I will be presenting in this paper is how the artist's model constructs herself as an aesthetic object in the studio. The metaphor for this construction is the model's gown, which I will examine as exemplary of the 'naked and nude' (Clark 1960) distinction so important to figurative art. I will show that, although models are regarded as pure creations of art, models are actually self-constructed artists in their own way.

It all begins with the studio and the life class. There the student is confronted with the ambiguity of the model's nudity for the first time. The initial response of most new students is discomfort, because they have not yet unlearned societal interpretations of the naked body. The professional model in the life class has the job of teaching them a new attitude. The signifying practices of the model are the aestheticized simulations of eroticism, activity, nudity and violence, detached from the social reality of these acts and emotions by the carefully constructed, ritualized conduct of the life class. They are performance, spectacle. Nothing about the life class is 'real', and all of those engaged in the act of representation conspire in the staging of the performance of 'life'. The act of modelling and the act of artistic representation come together in each performance of the model, contained within the instructional studio and bounded by the history of figurative art. The life model performs a valuable role in maintaining and transmitting artistic practice.

The model of fact and fiction is female: fact, because the ratio of working models today is three or four females to every male; and fiction, because both popular and art history accounts of 'the model' almost invariably represent the model as female and the artist as male. Roles in the visual arts are profoundly gendered, so a model who is male will still be occupying the role of a female, and the female artist that of the male. The source of this gendering is found in assumptions about the ownership of the image, gained through the act of artistic appropriation: those who actively take and use images are male, and those who 'give' them away, who cannot 'use' them as cultural capital, must be female. This 'nature/culture' (Ortner 1973; Saunders 1989) division operates at a level below discourse and structures the studio 'habitus' (Bourdieu 1984,1993) physically and psychologically.

The model's role is that of intelligent object, some-*thing* that can both take and give instruction, a still life that arranges itself. This role is well established in art history and art practice as that of the professional model, one skilled in becoming an object for the comfort and convenience of artistic appropriation, and for the pleasure of her studio and gallery audiences. The model as icon and role is created through a combination of factors: her discursively constructed history, as propagated through popular and art history literature; by the physical and ritual construction of the studio; and by her own practices, designed to create a body to enclose her interior self and to protect the latter from, while making the former available to, the appropriating gaze.

The instructional studio is a mythological space reinvented by each class that uses it, and its physical structure reflects this. The life class requires its own arrangement of people and objects. The model's podium (or platform, or stage) is a special place reserved for the model and no other. Its placement is generally in the centre of the studio, and students take position around it. With easels and drawing boards surrounding it, the podium is clearly visible from all angles to the students, but the model sees little of them from it. This arrangement implies that the student-artist has the right to look in by virtue of their physical position on the outside. The model in the centre cannot look out because of the obstructing easels and boards: she does not because 'the gaze' (Berger 1980) is the artist's prerogative. Her role is passive. She must clothe her 'self' in a body which becomes a singular iconic, fetishized, commodified 'other' – 'the model', 'the figure', 'the nude' – of artistic representation (Cormack 1976; Parker and Pollick 1981; Pointon 1990).

Gordon Roe

Creating the Fine-Art Nude

In the popular imagination, the presence of a nude model in the studio and the artist's ability to look at her are examples of 'artistic licence', the freedom from social constraints that artists enjoy. The obvious next step is to conclude that the model grants the artist complete licence, including sexual, in the studio. The studio, the artist and the model together form the Bohemian myth of the artist. But this assumes that the absence of one set of social conventions rules out social convention altogether. The studio is actually governed by very clear – if unwritten – rules and roles for its occupants. Professional models are experts at using and even manipulating these conventions (Steer 1993).

Becoming 'the model' for the life class requires the model to make a carefully staged transition from socially-inscribed individual to aesthetically-inscribed object through a series of ritualized stages. The first stage is the preparation of the studio for her arrival: the reorientation of all of the objects in the room towards the podium. In a dramaturgical metaphor, the students act as stage hands, creating the space for a performance, preparing the places for the audience and performer. When this is done, the students take their places and become the audience, waiting for the curtain to go up and the model to appear on stage.

The individual, prior to becoming the model, is 'matter out of place' (Douglas 1967), someone for whom there is no role in the studio. In order to be an unproblematic object of appropriation, she must shed her social individuality before she formally enters the studio and steps onto the podium. For this reason, the unwritten protocols of the life class require the individual model to undress out of sight of the class, so as not to interfere with the performance of the life class. This is 'backstage', in the dramaturgical sense (Goffman 1963), where the actor gets into the appropriate role and costume out of the audience's sight. This helps introduce the distinction between 'nude' in the studio and 'naked' in other contexts. This is most overtly enforced for beginner classes, and less so in the conduct of advanced classes when students have internalized the distinction. Most studios have a changing room, or at least a screened off area, for this purpose. In the absence of either, the model may leave the room and change somewhere else – an empty studio or a washroom. The removal of her street clothes is the removal of the visual signifier of the society outside of the studio, and her identity as a person. The model then dons her dressing gown (or robe, or wrap), and takes one step away from social identity, one step closer to becoming the model.

The model re-enters the studio dressed in her robe, and will remain in it

until she actually begins her first pose. She is now on stage, but the performance has not begun. The gown becomes the curtain, the cue for the beginning of class. Most of the models I have interviewed were aware of the symbolic importance of the robe. They had been instructed in its importance by the numerous images of models and robes in the canon, and had it confirmed by their own experience. They could describe their favourite robes and the role they play in mediating the ambiguous, 'liminal' (Turner1970) state between one status and another. The robe is the trademark costume of 'the model', whose only two wardrobe choices are robe or skin. Since there is little interaction between the students and the model, the robe functions as a communication, symbolizing her general status as 'the model' and, in some ways, what type of model the individual is. Models who were introspective, or felt threatened by the attention of the students, described large and long robes in subdued colors. Models who were more confident, more physical or more sexual in their style of modelling favoured shorter, brighter or thinner robes. Most had a single robe, but one model took advantage of symbolism of the robe to create different modelling personae. She had several: a plain one for introductory classes – 'reassurance'; a 'slinky' one for an artists' group that she bantered with from the podium – 'one of the guys'; a flowered feminine one for a weekend artists' watercolour group – 'nice girl'. For all of the models, their robes were important props for their consciously constructed personae as models and aided their 'professional' need to control their audience's perceptions of, and interactions with, them. The model's robe gives the wearer the historical authority as the artist's inspiration and muse, and gives the individual model the means to project a particular tone of 'high' culture. The robe is not the sexual undress of the artist's mistress, or 'bedroom' wear: it is the practical uniform of the working model. It is a tool.

The life class begins when the model on the podium removes her robe and takes her first pose. This is the moment when the individual model becomes, not naked, but 'nude', when she becomes fully an aesthetic object. After the model begins a pose, she is generally only referred to as a role ('the model') or an anatomical feature ('the model's hip'). Words and phrases that personalize the model or the pose are absent, which has the effect of making the model's body and the pose ownerless, available and useable. The language reveals this in other ways. The model is 'in pose' or 'takes a pose' or 'holds a pose', as if the arrangement of the body is not connected with the actual individual, as if the body is something 'put on', like clothing. The models themselves fall in line with this practice of separating self from body. In the interviews, when discussing the act of modelling, of posing, all models began referring to their bodies in the third person. There was a clear separation between the physical body and a protected, controlling self, as if their bodies had become a troublesome machine which the 'I' operates. One said, 'When you take a pose, a certain amount of pain happens – it's called your body!' The physical circumstances of modelling work encourage this separation. Models are skilled body workers, who have trained themselves to 'hold' or 'sustain' poses despite aches and pains, and the natural inclination of their bodies to move.

But this separation of self and body also protects models from personalizing the intense scrutiny of the students, and being personalized by them. The model's gaze from the podium is directed up or down or at some vague middle distance, but never at the students – as if the students were not there, or the model was indifferent to their presence. In the studio, the gaze becomes the exclusive property of the students and, for models, there is no concealment from it. All features of their bodies are seen, reproduced and distorted in the resulting art work. Models overcome the inevitable self-consciousness by regarding their body as an 'as-is' tool of their work, with the real skill lying in how they present it in pose. By emphasizing their skill over their bodies' appearance, models can move beyond the societal judgements they endure outside of the studio. By maintaining and projecting this attitude they cause their audience of students to move beyond these attitudes towards the body as well.

The Teaching Studio

Most of the popular literature on art and the model has dealt with the studio as an individual male artist's work space, and the female model as existing through her personal relationship – business and/or pleasure – with him. In this mythology, the artist defines the studio, and it is often portrayed as a place where he lives as well as works, reinforcing the 'art as life', biographical perspective on the artist's product (Kluver and Martin 1991; Kris and Kurz 1979; Mulvey 1975; Nead 1992). Such 'romantic' imagery has concealed what models actually do with artists, and is a source of humour and irritation to models, since many students have this bohemian image of the sensual model and the sexual artist firmly fixed in their minds (Borzello 1982; Hollander 1986,1991a and b; Steer 1993). As I have shown in the preceding descriptions, the actual working model of today approaches modelling as a profession, and regards herself as a professional whose employers are artists. Most of her work will come from instructional classes composed of groups of students and instructors who are both male and female, not from posing for individual male artists. Her posing is not motivated by a personal relationship with a particular artist, nor even an interest in art in many cases. For a professional model, sex with artists is a less effective means of getting work than being a good model, and the latter is much easier to keep under control. This is not to say that models and artists don't have relationships, but these are neither the inevitable outcome, nor the point, of modelling. Professionalism requires that the model's physical and social boundaries with her employers are constantly reinforced.

There are many lessons taught in the studio, some designed to give the student a sense of historic continuity with art and artists of the past. In addition to the practice of drawing from the figure, students are shown slides and colour plates, and given lectures, in order to illustrate how their art and their work in the studio is part of a continuous history – 'the canon'. Models in the studio find themselves learning a great deal about their role from these lessons. Students are taught that, in order to maintain what Bourdieu calls the 'symbolic capital' of artistic representation, the distinction between the artistic and the voyeuristic gaze is fundamental. Thus the act of modelling is constituted in the studio as a reflection of the pure aesthetic of the nude, sexuality at a distance – as opposed to the 'in your face' sexuality of the mundane and popular pornographic representation. The individual model embodies the Western tradition of the nude by properly conveying its historic significance to the artist. Models agree with this distinction, and regard themselves as heirs to an honourable profession. Oddly, the image that appears in the art work based on their poses is not really relevant to the

models I spoke with. One male model criticized another who was upset about distortions of his body in student drawings by saying: 'He thought it was about him.' The art produced by the artist is none of the model's business: the art of providing images worthy of being appropriated is. What models emphasized, particularly the female models, was that the act of modelling was their art, and was in many ways a resistance to objectification. A number mentioned that objectification was an integral part of their lives in all circumstances:

> I feel like, people are looking at me all the time . . . I don't like it. But in the studio I know they are, I know why, I know how, I know everything. It's just such a relief (female model).
> I was working as a lifeguard before and I got tired of guys playing 'pick up the lifeguard'. The first few times I modelled, I wore my swimsuit, but it was like I had something to hide (female model).

Sexuality in modelling is denied by most of the models I spoke with. The standard comment was 'that's not what it's about, that's not why I'm there'. 'Sensuality' was the word applied to poses that could be interpreted as sexual by the artist. A model described the difference in this way:

> The most potent aspect of the presented self is the visual. Modelling is singularly pure in this respect, for where actors and prostitutes and statesmen make use of their looks, the model's sole end is the image she makes of herself. (Hollander 1991a:133)

For reasons of personal reputation and professional conduct, sexual display is something they avoid. Male models have a particularly fine line to walk in the studio. Stereotypical sexuality is either male and female, with attributions of 'nature' attached to them (Levy 1968; Walters 1979). Male models report working harder to ensure that they contain any suggestion of their sexuality, because it is the expectation that the 'nature' of their sexuality is to make things happen, to take action, and students have to be protected from them. Male sexuality is a threat; it must be restrained. 'Natural' female sexuality is expected to be passive, and so women are expected to repel the sexuality of the class passively, by denying it, by an assertion of physical and psychological distance. In the stereotype, female sexuality is not considered threatening – it is attractive, and so the students must be kept away from her.

There is also an expectation that harassment will be something that a male will do to a female (Coward and WAVAW 1987). But in the sometimes sexually charged life class, anybody can step out of line. A female model was harassed by a female student in a situation which pointed up differences in gendered expectations: 'I had to tell this student off . . . I said "Y'know, it's really interesting that, if you were a male talking about a female model that way, you would be looked down on, you'd be in a lot of trouble".'
A male model recounted an example of harassment he'd had to deal with:

> This one student, she was whispering to her friends about my penis, about how well hung I was and what I was getting out of this – y'know, dumb stuff. She was really loud, I wasn't the only one to hear her and I was getting mad, other people [in the class] were getting uncomfortable . . . It still makes me mad though, she was so rude.

Models and the work they do cannot be defined entirely by dichotomous categories: male/female; artist/model; active/passive; victim/agent. The position of the model in the studio is a paradoxical one. The life class is dependent on her body being present and available, and is created and uncreated by her presence alone: but the studio and the art field themselves exist independently of the model. By performing as a skilled object, models may seem to the observer to be reducing themselves to objects, or even victims, of artistic appropriation. But in the studio the removal of the dressing gown and the suspension of normal social protection from the gaze of others actually frees the model from that gaze. In return for granting others the use of her image, she gains control over and freedom from her image. The critiques of the ethics of representation neglect to take the possibility of a distinctly separate motivation and meaning for models into account. Both

the studio and the model are embedded in societal values which are fundamentally patriarchal: for many models, the explicit gaze of studio is a release
from the implicit, sexist judgement that is part of their lives outside of it.
They chose this work, they have a good idea of what they are doing. They
could even explain it, if asked.

Similarly, there is no formal recognition that studio practices designed to
produce artists also produce models, or that models are active participants
in maintaining them – and could be as active in reforming them.

Bringing the Political into the Studio

Deconstruction of artistic practice and tradition has been undertaken to
unseat patriarchal attitudes which have prevented the inclusion of female
artists and subjects in the canon. This has been most critically examined in
relation to the female nude. These representations have been extensively
analysed as a patriarchal exploitation: male artists appropriating, exploiting
and (mis)representing the helpless female object (Duncan 1982; Mulvey 1975;
Nead 1992; Wolff 1984). Such images have perpetuated stereotypical, popular
images of the bohemian artist, and have implicitly reduced female artists
and models to secondary, generally sexual, roles in the lives of male artists.
Because of the rigidly patriarchal basis of this mythology, female artists and
male models are rarely mentioned in the modernist accounts of art. This
analysis leads many critics to conclude that figurative art is intrinsically
structured on a gender-based inequality, and so the life class must be reconsti-
tuted on a more ethical, less exploitative basis. This new life class would:

> . . . introduce feminist concerns into the life class situation. Theoretical sessions
> are run alongside the practical classes so that at every stage the students are aware
> of the meanings of the images they are producing. Rather than the question of
> power being ignored, the relationships between teacher, student and model and
> the power of the image are constantly addressed (Nead 1992:54).

This is an admirable agenda. But is the question of power 'ignored'
currently? And will this new programme actually alter the existing structures
of power in the studio? My interviews with models and my own experience
indicate that Lynda Nead's programme may have its flaws.

Her first assumption is that power in the studio is only a question of the
artist's power over the model. Models are adamant that they have power as
well, and all recounted instances when they used it.

[Y]our body has a little clock in it and if you tell them five minutes, it starts ticking. If [instructor] keeps me over, I've been suffering for part of that . . . then I'll give [instructor] a lecture in class about how models appreciate punctuality. Or, if he goes out, I'll tell the students that this isn't a polite way to treat a model, this is cruel. I did that once, I turned this class against him – he'd already given them a bad attitude – and . . . he started being nice to everyone after that. (female model)

While the instructor had a great deal of power in this instance, the model had power in her traditional, professional role which gave her the right and the means to resist abuses. She taught the students how to treat not only her body and person, but also all bodies and people.

The next question is whether making a new awareness of power part of the curriculum would necessarily lead to a more equitable situation for the model. Again, models had experiences which contradict this assertion.

Oh yeah, I had an instructor at [institution] who did that. I came in at the beginning of the class . . . and she just told me hang in the studio while she delivered this big lecture about how I was the model, how I should be treated with respect and not objectified, and, well, on and on about it for the first half hour. It was an introductory class, I'm sure a lot of them had never had a model before and were already nervous . . . They just got more and more scared of me, you could see them looking at me out of the corner of their eye. I just wanted to talk to them, to tell them not to worry, that this was just my job and I wasn't – a monster. But she was making a big deal of it . . . Anyway, when she finally started the class everyone was nervous, they didn't even know how to look at me. I felt really self-conscious, they were awkward . . . It was awful. (female model)

What I found interesting in this incident was that the instructor took it upon herself to speak for the model, even though the model was present and able to speak for herself. Involving the model in a discussion that was about her was apparently not an option. A possible reason for why this was so may be found in examining who is to be empowered.

As this story indicates, there are contradictory agendas at work in the studio. There is a recognition of the need to empower the disempowered and replace patriarchal authority with a regime that brings the marginal subject to the centre. Critics of the packaging of the female nude in art aspire to a new treatment of the body, one in which ownership of the image is wrested from those who impose a patriarchal agenda on the bodies of women (Betterton 1987; Coward and WAVAW 1987; Currie and Raoul 1992; Curti 1992; Duncan 1982; Frascina and Harris 1992; Galler 1984; Hobhouse 1988; Mulvey 1975). But this assumes 'that on the one hand we have "women" and on the other hand we have (distorted, partial, inaccurate) "images" of them' (Wolff 1991:711).

These changes may threaten the security professional models now enjoy in the studio. The threat is contained in the uncritical (and politically useful) acceptance of the patriarchal 'image' of the model as a created object of desire, or reverence – whore or Madonna. These models are passive, plastic, silent bodies, wholly dominated by the representations of 'it' (the nude). These critics see the models' robes as allusions to the artist's bedroom, their nudity as a symbol of sexual availability, their silence as complicity. But what is at stake in current political debates of 'old vs. new' art history is the image and not the substance of the model. Many of the arguments simply repackage the same product (the nude) in new theoretical wrappings.

This new agenda aims to empower the female artist, who has been excluded from recognition on the basis of her gender. It also aims to change the way women have been valued only as objects in art. The female model is often used as a symbol of this exclusion, representing the sexual ghetto to which all women were exiled in the past. The logic by which the instructor in the preceding story was able to ignore the presence of the actual model is structured in the following way: (1) women have not been allowed to become artists because they weren't men; (2) female artists are finding their voice in the art field; (3) models are unable to speak because they are neither artists nor men; therefore, (4), female artists can now speak for models, because models remain both marginal and disempowered.

The unfortunate confusion between the image of the model and the lives and activities of the people who model is perpetuated. Once more, models become what others need them to be – voiceless, passive, empty vessels awaiting the content of interpretation.

Models undeniably benefited from the feminist revolution in the academy. Codes of conduct, sexual harassment policies, redress for abuses by instructors and students and the acknowledged right to make reasoned demands are just a few of the comparatively recent changes that have made models more aware and active. Models are learning more about their profession and its limitations from new instructional lectures based on feminist critiques of art. Many models reported being involved in the instruction of students and speaking about themselves as models in class. Some are gratified by this, some are threatened. There is no doubt that the role the model plays in the studio is changing, and the way models work must change as well. But will we be allowed the opportunity?

In the tradition of the visual arts, only the artist has something to say and the means to say it. In the private and instructional studio the professional models will 'play along' with this authority in order to appropriate from the artist what they wish for themselves. They avoid conflicts which may undermine the artists' or instructors' authority, and hence their own prospects for employment. Most models are casual workers without full-time work and no union or association for protection. The development and enforcement of codes of conduct and sexual harassment policies in institutions allow models something to appeal to, but the individual model must still deal with most problems alone, because they are alone in the studio. Every model I interviewed could describe quite clearly the limits of their compliance to the artist's or instructor's authority: all could describe situations where they publicly opposed abuses of this authority by artists and instructors. They were not passive, they did not see themselves as helpless. This was because they felt they had recourse to their position as models. A part of their confidence comes from the very iconic status so roundly criticized by reformers.

In the studio, the male model occupies the female role (as appropriated model), the female artist the male (as appropriating artist), and both inherit the gendered behaviours these roles are invested with. These roles are gendered, but are frequently independent of the sex or political position of those who occupy them, and tend to impose certain behaviours on them (Butler 1993). These are imposed by history and by practices, especially the practices of the studio. One model described the different attitude imposed on her by being both a model and an artist. The models' robes are a mantle of historic practice and a definition of a role that provide them with the right – the obligation – to resist abuse *in defence of the aesthetic*. Removing this politically problematic status without thought to its utility to the model has the consequence of making the model less of an acknowledged professional and less able to deal with these inevitable social abuses effectively. In the current efforts to address the undeniable abuses of the modernist tradition, there is a danger that these new practices will isolate and appropriate the model as much as those they replace. What appears in the artwork should not be reflected back on the model and used to arrive at the 'truth' of her situation. Models exist for themselves and for modelling, quite apart from the artist's image and artist's intent. The trademark attire of the model – the gown and their skin – are the most misinterpreted aspects of the role the model plays.

The Mantle of Authority

Making the body into a 'flesh dress' provides the model with an additional barrier between her self and her audience. One model said that 'when I'm in pose I can feel myself curling away from the edges of my body, I don't touch anywhere, isolated'. She (her self) is insulated by her body (the object), which is the subject of the gaze of the artist and, later, the audience. Far from being a victimization or an affront, this self-objectification is expressed by models as an advantage to their work and to themselves. In the latter case, they are able to distance themselves from the depictions of their body. In the former, it reinforces their authority as skilled body workers to themselves and their employers.

The role and status of a model is put on and taken off as clothing is taken off and put on. It is a pose, an illusion that serves to reinforce the authority of artistic licence. In the studio, models present images for appropriation by artists: outside of the studio they are represented in the resulting artwork.

The models' job is implicitly and explicitly an instructional one, in that they instruct the students how artists must view the person and the role of the model. They should not be regarded merely as self-arranging anatomical displays. Models know this and use their current status to emphasize respect in the studio. Models already occupy a strategic position in the studio. But critical analysis of the model's actual position in the studio through artwork which exploits her appropriated images in ideologically 'good or bad' ways misses this strategic positioning. Models function in a manner that is not reflected in the art work, they have a knowledge of their role which is quite different from that ascribed to them. Calls to reform studio practice and the treatment of the figure which do not take this into account run the risk of simply replicating the very exercise of power they seek to destroy. Reforms on the basis of authority, be it the authority of historical practice or postmodern theory, still rely on a hierarchal power relationship based on knowledge.

A model who was also an artist told me that when she was modelling and had to shift in pose, she responded to the annoyance of the students with the thought: 'Get over it, I haven't any choice.' But when she was drawing and the model moved, she felt the same irritation. She laughed at this and said it was a matter of being in a different mindset for each activity. This mindset separates the model and artist. Rather than artists telling models what they are, what they do and why they do it, a more fruitful approach would be to work with what the model knows and involve her in the project of reform. Through consciously educating models, and reinforcing the value of their practices in the studio through a new iconic status for 'the model', models would be very effective allies in unseating patriarchal attitudes.

I have not written this paper to oppose efforts to bring social theory into the studio. Rather, I am suggesting that models could be important allies in this very necessary struggle. But power is power; it needs to be watched closely. There is a risk that reforms which do not include the model will simply remove her mantle of authority, leaving her with no means to oppose abuses of authority from any source.

Bibliography

Berger, John (1980), *About Looking*. New York: Pantheon.

Betterton, Rosemary (ed.) (1987), *Looking On: Images of Femininity in the Visual Arts and Media*. London: Pandora.

Borzello, Frances (1982), *The Artist's Model*. London: Junction Books.

Bourdieu, Pierre (1984), *Distinction: A Social Critique of the Judgement of Taste*, London: Routledge & Kegan Paul (trans. R. Nice).

—— (1993), *The Field of Cultural Production*. New York: Columbia University Press (trans. R. Nice).

Butler, Judith (1987), *Subjects of Desire: Hegelian Reflections in Twentieth-Century France*. New York: Columbia University Press.

—— (1993), *Bodies That Matter: On the Discursive Limits of 'Sex'*. London: Routledge Press.

Clark, Kenneth (1960), *The Nude: A Study of Ideal Art*. London: John Murray.

Cormack, Malcolm (1976), *The Nude in Western Art*. Oxford: Phaidon.

Coward, Rosalind, and WAVAW (1987), 'What is Pornography? Two Opposing Feminist Viewpoints.' In R. Betterton (ed.), *Looking On: Images of Femininity in the Visual Arts and Media*. London: Pandora.

Currie, Dawn H., and Valerie Raoul (eds) (1992), *Anatomy of Gender: Women's Struggle for the Body*. Ottawa: Carleton University Press.

Curti, Lydia (1992), 'What is Real and What is Not: Female Fabulations in Cultural Analysis.' In Lawrence Grossberg, C. Nelson and P. Treichler (eds) *Cultural Studies*. New York: Routledge.

Douglas, Mary (1967), *Purity and Danger*. New York: Frederick A. Praeger.

Duncan, Carol (1982), 'Virility and Domination in Early Twentieth-Century Vanguard Painting.' In Norma Broude and M. D. Garrad (eds) *Feminism and Art History: Questioning the Litany*. New York: Praeger.

Frascina, Francis, and Jonathan Harris (1992), *Art in Modern Culture: an Anthology of Critical Texts*. New York: Icon/Harper Collins.

Galler, Roberta (1984), 'The Myth of the Perfect Body.' In Carol S. Vance (ed.), *Pleasure and Danger*. Boston: Routledge and Kegan Paul.

Goffman, Erving (1963), *Behavior in Public Places*. New York: Free Press.

Hobhouse, Janet (1988), *The Bride Stripped Bare: The Artist and the Nude in the Twentieth Century.* London: Jonathan Cape.

Grossberg, Lawrence, C. Nelson & P. Treichler (eds) (1992), *Cultural Studies.* New York: Routledge.

Hollander, Elizabeth (1986), 'On the Pedestal: Notes on Being an Artists' Model,' *Raritan,* 6(1): 27–37.

—— (1991a), 'Subject Matter: Models for Different Media,' *Representations,* 36:133–46.

—— (1991b), 'Working Models,' *Art in America,* 79(5):152–4.

Kluver, Billy, and J. Martin (1991), 'A Short History of Modelling,' *Art in America,* 79(5):156–83.

Kris, Ernst, and Otto Kurz (1979), *Legend, Myth, and Magic in the Image of the Artist.* New Haven: Yale University Press.

Levy, Merwyn (1968), *The Human Form in Art: The Appreciation and Practise of Figure Drawing and Painting.* London: Odhams Books.

Mulvey, Laura (1975), 'Visual Pleasure and Narrative Cinema.' In Brian Wallis (ed.), *Art after Modernism.* Boston: David R. Godine.

Nead, Lynda (1992), *The Female Nude: Art, Obscenity and Sexuality.* London: Routledge.

Ortner, Sherry (1973), 'Is Female to Male as Nature is to Culture?' In M. Rosaldo & L. Lamphere (eds) *Women, Culture, and Society.* Stanford: Stanford University Press.

Parker, Rozsika and Griselda Pollock (1981), *Old Mistresses: Women, Art and Ideology.* London: Pandora Press.

Pointon, Marcia (1990), *Naked Authority: The Body in Western Painting 1830–1908.* Cambridge: Cambridge University Press.

Saunders, Gill (1989), *The Nude: A New Perspective.* London: The Herbert Press.

Steer, Mary (1993), 'Looking at Nudity the Wrong Way,' *Globe and Mail,* 19 February:A22.

Turner, Victor (1970), *The Ritual Process.* Chicago: Aldine Publishing Co.

Walters, Margaret (1979), *The Nude Male: A New Perspective.* London: Penguin.

Wolff, Janet (1984), *The Social Production of Art.* New York: New York University Press.

—— (1991), 'Excess and Inhibition: Interdisciplinarity in the Study of Art.' In L. Grossberg, C. Nelson and P. Treichler (eds) *Cultural Studies.* New York: Routledge.

7

Breaking Habits: Gender, Class and the Sacred in the Dress of Women Religious

Rebecca Sullivan

Perhaps one of our most instantly recognizable examples of symbolic dress is the monastic habit for women religious.[1] Although it appears unchanging and rigidly conformist, the habit is, in fact, a compelling artefact of both temporal and spatial elements in the social construction of gender, class and the sacred. At first the habit seems to mask completely any bodily identifications or shapes but in actuality it acts upon the corporeal body to communicate at the most immediate levels of perception that this particular woman has joined both a social body and sacred body of women. Thus, the habit is not necessarily an anti-sexual, anti-sensual shield between the body of a woman religious and her environment but is the primary mediation of her carefully constructed identity to the world. In fact, it begins to make little sense to speak of 'the habit' as simply a material object of dress but instead the term denotes a discursive field of artefactual and structural articulations, embodying both desire and discipline, imagination and order. This chapter seeks to build a bridge between analyses of the role of the sacred and its material conditions, which is generally relegated to the discipline of religious studies; and studies of gender and class, which usually receive examination from secular viewpoints of political alliances and economic relations. The sacred is not a unique entity signalling the moral opposite of modern secularism but is intricately involved in the cycles of civilization building: the cultural, epistemological and economic systems

---

1. The term 'woman religious' refers to any woman who has taken perpetual vows to a spiritual community. The more common term, 'nun' is used in contemplative orders while 'sister' is used in apostolic congregations. Both nuns and sisters are 'religious', denoting a state of being rather than a value of piety.

which position the individual in relation to others and to social networks reaching out across time and space. This is particularly so with regard to research on social networks comprised of women since sacred living has often been a crucial force in many historically and geographically significant feminine collectives and women have traditionally been both the primary gatekeepers of popular religiosity and primary resisters of institutionalized Christian faith and morality.

Religion and religious living is as crucial an aspect to culture today as it was in pre-modern times. As Elizabeth Rapley has noted, by the early modern age, rather than a full-scale replacement of an economic-based social system over the preceding era of Christendom, '[r]eligion, the study of salvation, merged imperceptibly into *civilité*, the study of one's place in the world' (Rapley 1990:158). Throughout successive histories of Western civilizations women have grouped together to synthesize the possibilities of a life based upon sacred principles of piety, charity, poverty and chastity with the ceaseless opportunities for imaginative and productive labour provided by the increasing urbanization of social space. Inserted into these multi-levelled networks of relations, the figure of the woman religious as either nun or sister has been laced into a continual process of negotiation and opportunity and periodically subjected to systematic authority and structural limitations. Corporeal body, sacred body and social body shift and merge imperceptibly according to the stresses imposed upon the woman religious by these dual, duelling principles of civilization, the sacred and the social. Rather than signifying a static, unknowing and unknowable identity, the woman in habit is one of the most complex, dynamic and inter-contextual agents of creative living and feminine possibility. Before embarking on a specific analysis of habits and women religious, however, it is necessary to investigate how questions of religion and the sacred have entered into cultural analysis and been responsive to issues of gendered power and identity. From an interdisciplinary framework which combines social history, sociological investigation into the construction of life-styles and the material culture of social groups into gendered theories of the body as both actor and text, an analysis of the habit will extend beyond a simple description of order and representation. Instead, by determining the dynamic relationships between gender, class and the sacred which circulate through the bodies of women religious within both trans-national and trans-historical cultural systems, the habit can become an insignia of the power of imagination, the subtle transgressions in the name of individualization and the symbolic and material work of every woman who elects to wear it.

Fields of Possibilities

Research on aspects of the lives of women religious benefit from integrative, interdisciplinary theoretical frameworks because their histories and cultures have been marginalized from traditional academic disciplines. Most of the extant work on women religious derives from feminist social history, an offshoot of the Annales School.[2] An analysis of the culture of dress as social history would examine women's production and circulation of textiles and garments and weave in discussion of class distinctions around particular styles of dress. With the individual absent from the processes of determination, feminist social history ironically tends to reduce the role of the gendered body in culture, eschewing individuals and personalities in favour of roles and positions. This is particularly problematic when applied to the history of women. The unending feminist struggle for women to be recognized as agents of their own lives can be elided and large psychological and epistemological questions are often overlooked in the meticulous emphasis on a single social factor as fully determining cultural practice, rather than looking dynamically at how practice shapes structures and is, in turn, circumscribed by those very structures. It is necessary, therefore, to look beyond the history of religious dress to reveal the socializing and sacralizing properties of the habit upon the body. While social history focuses predominantly upon systems of production and circulation, other sociological methods can bring consumption into focus, making explicit the embodying practices of dress. Pierre Bourdieu suggests a model of analysis which uncovers implicit class orderings made explicit through consumption, defined by him as 'a stage in a process of communication, that is, an act of deciphering, decoding, which presupposes practical or explicit mastery of a cipher or code' (Bourdieu 1984:2). For Bourdieu, therefore, clothing is a most public and seeming expression of social identity. Interestingly, although he is resolutely discussing capital exchange and secular life-styles, his understanding of the relationship between gender and dress incorporates many sacred motifs. In discussions

---

2. Known also as the French historical method, the Annales approach inquires into one of any number of systems or structures of a society and surveys its integration into the totality of culture and civilization. Although much analysis of women religious and their daily life develops from social history, its dominance has lessened in recent years. Most notably, the work by Caroline Walker Bynum and new cultural history also work to reveal the strategies of hegemony but argue that women have historically appropriated those strategies and retooled them in subversive ways to afford them limited power. Working within the parameters of new cultural history allows for arguments not only against a dominant history but also the present dominant political forces which limit our potential to theorize today. See Caroline Walker Bynum, *Fragmentation and Redemption* (1991).

about women's dress and deportment, he writes, 'The chances of experiencing one's own body as a vessel of grace, a continuous miracle, are that much greater when bodily capacity is commensurate with recognition' (ibid.:207). Thus, to inscribe oneself as a 'religious' in part through the wearing of the habit acts as a *habitus* of the sacred; in other words, the habit signifies the totality of the practices, forms and structures which the individual woman undertakes to reproduce her body as that 'vessel of grace'. By re-integrating the body which wears the clothes with the body which produces the clothes, analysis need not stop at the level of material or symbolic currency but can seek a space of understanding for the spiritual profit earned through cognitive acts of self-presentation.

Looking at the habit's design, production, integration and interpretation at a number of different historical and cultural moments can reveal both structural and narrative issues for women vowed to a life in service to the Catholic Church; in particular, their place in systems of gender and class which pervade in multiple forms in all societies. However, it is important to not only look at the clothes but also to listen to the women who choose to put on this particular form of dress, what it means to them and how they see themselves in it (McDannell 1991:375). It means asking both what are the women saying about their dress and what is the dress saying about these women. Unlike other primary social categories of everyday life (like food and shelter) clothing is deeply implicated in the morality of the wearer and her society. It summons her to reveal some of the most intimate aspects of her self while simultaneously shrouding her in secrecy (Wilson 1990:28). In contradiction to the preconceived notion that a Christianized culture has internalized a division between outer physical appearance and inner spiritual truth, the habit marks its wearer, positions her in fields of both memory and forgetfulness: memory of the social body of women bound together regardless of distance or death as one in union with the sacred body of Christ; and, in order to maintain that memory, forgetfulness of the long history of urgent needs and spiritual longings which are invested into the habit. Thus, the habit not only decodes but also encodes distinct methods of communication, like a 'cultural fingerprint' left upon the matrix of belief systems which exist in any society (Gordon 1993:89). To analyse the habit as discursive field suggests that the wearer and the dress are both actor and text: the habit acts upon her body to bring her into the larger social and sacral bodies of religious community life and her body acts upon the seemingly impenetrable guise to articulate the person existing inside the living cloister of the habit. In this way, research on the habit can embrace the everyday needs of the individual body including hygiene, labour and environmental conditions; the symbolic ordering of the sacred body through selections in colours, dress cuts and accessories; and the historical changes to the social body imposed by institutional restructuring or personal or congregational redefinition.

It is important to note that much of this discussion shifts back and forth from the heights of Christian monasticism and the threshold of modernity in the twelfth century to the dramatic changes wrought by the Second Vatican Council from 1962 to 1965 and its aftermath, which often included the laying aside of the habit and a return to simple, secular dress. To do a linear history could undercut the scope of this study by requiring a limited set of examples and even possibly result in a deterministic approach to understanding the relations between the individual, the social and the sacred which are mediated by the habit. Similarly, a single case study approach might not reveal the diversity and complexity of choices women religious have had and also might not make important historical connections between women's practices across successive networks of history and culture. A more fluid, thematic framework facilitates analyses of the varying spaces of identity, community and religiosity available to women, examined here through the locus of the habit.

Selecting the Sacred

There is a realm of possibilities in selecting a sacred life-style, from first selecting a contemplative order or an apostolic congregation and then being assigned to perform specific work within that community. For many the first real step in living in chastity, humility and poverty has been and continues to be a dramatic altering of dress. The change into the habit freezes for one moment in time and space the woman's crossing of the threshold from lay to a 'religious'. Thus the habit acts as a kind of portal for the difficult process of memory and forgetfulness which the woman religious must undergo in order to reconfigure her identity to conform with her new spiritual community. In the modern era until the sweeping reforms of Vatican II, the clothing ceremony was the most important moment of transition for postulants, women who had only taken temporary vows while living in the community. In front of a private congregation of family, friends and church officials women were given their first religious garment, their hair was shorn in anticipation of their bodily clausura and new names were bestowed to mark the death of old identities and the beginning of new lives in the Church.

In her landmark anthropological study on two British religious institutes, Suzanne Campbell-Jones offers a rare glimpse into this sacred gathering. During their first year in the convent candidates wore simple clothing approved by their superiors, like white shirts, dark skirts and hosiery and sensible shoes. Since they were still considered a part of the outside world and could rejoin it with impunity, fashionable accessories and cosmetics could be used occasionally. On the day of the ceremony, with the full splendour of a debutante's ball, the women would spend long hours and the families much money for this final enjoyment of luxury and style. In some cases, postulants would wear elaborate and expensive bridal gowns provided by the families. In other, simpler ceremonies a white dress would be provided by the convent for all the women. Their hair was carefully styled the night before and hung loose with a white veil and flowers encircling their heads. The bridal imagery was no accident; this ceremony was their marriage to Christ, complete with a white gown, veil and ring. In fact, the few articles of clothing which a woman brought with her to the convent were customarily called her trousseau. The bridal motif derived mostly from a chapter in the Old Testament, the *Song of Songs*. It is a long, erotic poem of Christ's love for his bride who is at once the Church, the perfect souls in the Church and the most perfect soul of all, the Blessed Virgin Mary. By the end of the middle ages, it was common enough to call a woman religious a Bride of Christ and many woman mystics, including the only two women Doctors of the Church, Theresa of Avila and Catherine of Sienna, referred to themselves as such. Catherine even went so far as to claim that her wedding ring was made from the circumcised foreskin of Christ, although the more reserved male Church officials preferred to describe it as gold encrusted with pearls (Bynum 1991:186). It seems evident that in the clothing ceremony, postulants were committing to a spiritual marriage. Even her virginity was symbolically given to Christ: as each bride approached the altar, the officiating priest would cut a lock of her hair, a symbol of women's erotic power. Carrying their habits, the postulants would file out of the church for the complete transition to take place away from the gaze of the congregation. When the postulants returned all together in a repeat of their first procession, they were shorn and fully dressed in the habit, their bodies forever hidden from the people who once knew them best. It was an emotionally-laden moment of transformation from young girls to sombre women religious (Campbell-Jones 1979:174).[3]

Since the habit was the first signifier of religious commitment, its symbolic potential predominated in the life of a nun. Each article contained particular pietic meaning which demanded meditation twice a day, upon dressing in the morning and undressing at night. Mary Jackle OSB provided me with

---

3. Representations of the clothing ceremony can be seen in two excellent films about pre-Vatican II convent life: *The Nun's Story* (1959) and the Australian television mini-series, *Brides of Christ* (1992).

the following set of Rising Prayers from the Federation of St. Benedict, a community within the oldest monastic order, the Benedictines. It is interesting to note that the part of the prayers which refer to the sister as a 'new man' had not seemed strange to her until she put her habit away for good. This suggests the degree to which the intense relationship the religious had to her habit actually influenced her own sense of herself as a woman. The sister had to first kiss each part of the religious garb and then recite the prayer while donning it. The long tunic which comprised the major piece of the habit represented renouncement of worldliness and bodily insignificance. 'For it were the words, "Clothe me, O Lord, with the new man who is created according to God, in justice and holiness and truth".' The tunic was loosely tied at the waist by a cincture to symbolize purity while the nun recited, 'Gird me, O Lord, with the girdle of purity, and extinguish within my reins the passion of lust, that the virtues of continency and chastity may remain with me.' Then the coif or headpiece which enclosed the hair and face was put on to signify innocence and simplicity. In this particular set of prayers, the nun reminded herself of the father of her order with the words, 'Pour forth into my heart, O Lord, the spirit of our Holy Father, Saint Benedict, and take away from me all levity of mind and vanity of dress.' Pinned onto the coif is the veil of virginity and humility which summoned the prayer, 'Place upon my head, O Lord, the helmet of salvation to repel all the attacks of the devil.' Finally, overtop the tunic was placed the scapular which bore both the colour and insignia of the convent and represented willingness to labour. The nun would conclude the ritual with 'O Lord, Who hast said: "My yoke is sweet and My burden light," grant that I may so carry it, as to obtain Thy grace. Amen.' As evidenced here, each article of clothing represented a particular relationship of the body not only to the spiritual world but also the outside world. Taken together, the habit was intended not merely to conceal the woman within but to provide her with a tangible artefact to meditate on her constant struggle to sublimate her identity into a more perfect union with her community and with Christ. The religious was held in place between the two poles of social and spiritual responsibility in part through the wearing of the habit, in particular the scapular and headdress, respectively. These two articles of the habit therefore deserve a more in-depth look here.

As the most external article of clothing, the scapular is the carrier of community. It hails her in her relationship to her sisters, her labour and her most immediate choices of sacred living. Scapular colour can signify class, era of origins, devotional dedication, communal work and degree of cloister. The original colour of monasticism since the founding of the Benedictines in the sixth century was black. Later, when other theories of monastic life flowered in the high middle ages (eleventh to thirteenth centuries) one of the primary and most visceral changes was the adoption of either white, like the Cistercians or Dominicans, to represent child-like purity and a dis-intellectual faith or the excessively humble home-spun brown of the Franciscans and other orders who stressed poverty above all other vows. These were simple choices, grounded in the limited cultural economies of early textile production, where colour was a luxury. However, they soon took on other meanings for women considering becoming religious who related the spiritual properties of the habit to the sartorial orders of class and feminine status existent in lay dress. Following the renewal of monasticism during the Counter-Reformation, women seeking to form religious communities did not want to separate themselves completely from their social positions. At their inception, these loose collectives, often with only unofficial recognition by the Church, began with simple uniforms based on the dress of a particular social group with which the women felt most affiliated; although, sometimes this symbolic affiliation could offend their own feelings of propriety and rank. Some of the more educated and urban women who joined Vincent de Paul's Filles de la Charité were at first mortified when he insisted they adopt the costume of the peasant women of the Paris Basin (Rapley 1990:190). In general, the teaching congregations wore the dignified black of the matron and widow dress while the hospitallers were dressed in the dingy greys and browns of the poorer peasant class. Thus, it appears that the initial function of the scapular was to represent the prior social status of its wearer. It is only fairly recently, in the eighteenth and nineteenth centuries, that it became more emblematic of spiritual devotions and the particular dedication of a community to its sacred patron. Orders dedicated to Mary like the Immaculate Hearts of Mary wear different shades of blue. Adorers of the Holy Spirit or the Missionary Sisters of the Holy Spirit have a rose pink scapular. Contemplative communities like the Adorers of the Precious Blood and the Sisters of the Incarnate Word and Blessed Sacrament, who centre their prayers on the Passion of Christ and the Eucharist, sometimes wear a scarlet scapular within the convent walls but, on those rare occasions when they leave the convent, they tend to switch to a less eye-catching white or black with a red cincture.

The headdress and veil can have an even more complex system of social and spiritual meanings than the scapular. The veil was the original and single article of clothing worn by women to distinguish themselves as vowed religious before full religious uniforms were conceived that separated women religious from society. Herrad von Landsberg, the creator of the twelfth-century illuminated encyclopedia, *The Garden of Delights*, depicted the nuns of her convent in Hohenburg wearing the regular dress of aristocratic women of her time but with brilliant veils in the royal colours of red and purple.

Her Rhineland contemporary, the visionary Hildegard von Bingen, was often chastised by the bishops for her lavish taste in clothes, especially her expensive headpieces to secure the veil which she personally designed from memories of the visions she had of Heaven, the Church and Christ. The challenge to the church hierarchy which these two women subtly put forward by their headdress cannot be left unstated. The veil was the most obvious outward symbol of feminine piety. Male monastics received the tonsure to open the mind to receive God but women had to cover their heads in humility and deference, as ordered by Paul in the Acts of the Apostles.[4] Both Hildegard and Herrad reconceived the symbolism imposed upon them into expressions of beauty, wonder and inspiration. They established a tradition of carefully constructed headdresses which extended far past the medieval monastery to become an integral aspect of spirituality for every woman religious. Great care and attention was placed into the precise folding, fluting, pleating and draping of the veil. Such intricate and consuming manual labour offered even more time for meditation on the responsibilities imposed by wearing the veil. In addition, to carry such a weighty and imposing headdress required the full attention of the body. Some communities would embroider biblical mottos along the edge of the veils which enrobed their faces, and design heavy, upstanding coifs which would cause the veil to fall in a particular way. The popularly recognized 'flying nun' hats worn predominantly from the seventeenth to the early twentieth century were, ironically, derived from peasant turbans; as they became encrusted with religious symbolism, elaborate starching and folding were required.

The precision of the veil was matched in the exactitude the habit enforced upon the community as a whole. Everything was written into the rules: cleaning, starching, ironing, folding and storing. Of course, the dress patterns of each article had precise measurements which, as much as colour and material, became distinct emblems of community and piety for many nuns. To alter any aspect, even with good reason, was to alter the religious's direct relationship to her community and to God, as some discovered the hard way. Sr Julia Upton RSM tells this story about Mother Euphrasia, her Reverend Mother during the 1960s:

4. I Corinthians 11:5,7–10. 'But every woman praying or prophesying with her head uncovered disgraces her head, for it is the same as if she were shaven . . . A man indeed ought not to cover his head, because he is the image and glory of God. But woman is the glory of man. For man is not from woman, but woman from man. For man was not created for woman, but woman for man. That is why the woman ought to have a sign of authority over her head, because of the angels.'

One of her unilateral decisions was that the sisters would 'cut their cincture'. People always spoke of it as 'the beginning of the end,' but I never understood what it meant until that conversation with Mother Euphrasia. Apparently the sisters used to wear a very long belt – *much* longer than necessary. The leather was expensive and she thought that since the extra length served no purpose, they should simply wear normal sized belts. She was shocked when the sisters were scandalized by her decision. Such a simple thing . . . or so she thought. Mother Euphrasia has gone home to God, but they're *still* talking about the cincture!

The process of transformation from a practical and socially-dependent symbolism to an atemporal, spiritualized meaning elucidates the complex negotiation women would undergo as they became integrated into a larger sacred order of living. It can be concluded that the shape and characteristics of the habit mirror those of spiritual movements and revolutions. Across the *longue durée* of feminine monasticism there have been many philosophies for this simultaneous shrouding and baring of the woman religious's soul. To briefly summarize this, the first organized sisters from the aristocratic class in late classical Rome debased themselves to such degrees that some even refused to bathe and wore slave's clothes. Later, European royalty viewed this sort of behaviour as a frivolous rejection of responsibility. Members of the royal convents dressed like the queens they were, revelling in God's splendour and setting a glorious example to the people who put their souls in their care. That in turn led to new expressions of humility including discalced or shoeless orders. The Counter-Reformation witnessed both poverty and glory of spirit within the narrow spectrum of bourgeois piety, where women either claimed a lady-like status with the matron dress or adopted working-class garb and a more revolutionary stance. In the eighteenth and nineteenth centuries, a popular fascination with Christian visionary motifs might possibly have prompted the number of communities who adopted colourful habits with elaborate insignias. Finally, in the more recent past there has been a stabilization of symbolism as most of the influential orders have established standards which fossilized habits. Put another way, the clothes which previously connected women to their social environment have been removed from any concrete relationship to a particular time and space and have become a kind of otherworldly adornment denoting a sacred body.

The Productive Forces of Religious Life

Even as clothing became deeply entrenched into the sacralizing of the body, religious communities could not lose sight of the purposiveness of their habit.

Like many uniforms, the habit can signal its wearer as a helper to society or a protectress of the oppressed. Always the religious outfit has been designed to address not only the economic and social responsibilities of the sisters to the people of their district but also those same needs for themselves. While ensuring that the habit was congruent with fundamental religious symbolism was certainly a concern for any community, several fundamental decisions in style or fabric were made to best suit both the environment and working conditions of the wearers. For example, missionary sisters, even of congregations who usually wore black or another dark colour, would change to a white scapular in equatorial climates to avoid heat prostration. With the invention of new fabrics in the twentieth century, women religious had labour-saving and cost-efficient alternatives to the traditional wool, linen and cotton, and sometimes even stiffened coifs and veils with plastic linings rather than difficult starching. Some missionaries wore drip-dry habits, able to withstand both extreme climate and politics and still come out wrinkle-free. The Little Sisters of Jesus, founded toward the end of the Great Depression and a decade of labour unrest, chose to wear denim, the ultimate cloth of the modern working class. Sr Margaret Campbell spoke to me about a pre-Vatican II house of the Canonesses of St. Augustine who wore culottes as part of their regular missionary habit. One of their missions was high up in the Philippine mountains, accessible only by mule. Riding sidesaddle with a long, fluttering habit was treacherous, even deadly for one member. In a time when ladies did not wear trousers, the Church hierarchy agreed to a compromise so that the community could best serve their duties.

The problem of wearing wool to make a special indication of poverty has been not only its increased value as a luxury fabric in the twentieth century but also its heaviness in more hygiene-conscious modern society. An entire house filled with women who each wear their same long wool tunic day-in and day-out can become rather odoriferous, particularly in the summer, and it could be even worse if the community was assigned to an urban centre. Occasionally light-weight habits would be worn for the summer. Grace Ingersoll, a former member of the discalced Poor Clares of Chicago from 1961 until 1969, remembers clearly how it felt to change clothes.

> I certainly do remember the twice a year habit washing days. And the joy of putting on the new, fresh, soft habit of the season. Heat? Sure, it was Chicago, after all. But, we were barefoot too, so that helped. And I remember Sister Charles Borromeo . . . telling us in class one day that she had discovered that she could get used to anything if it's daily. I think there's a great deal of truth in that.

Since, traditionally, the habit was not changed more than twice a year, great care needed to be taken to keep it clean and in good repair. For those who did not own a special Sunday habit, a voluminous apron would be worn over top their clothes during work and sometimes they would receive special permission to wear a work habit, an old and threadbare tunic for extra sweaty and dirty work. During postulant years, women were trained in correct walking, sitting and kneeling postures which would cause the least amount of wear on the habit. Stairs posed a particularly awkward problem because skirts needed to be lifted from behind to protect the hems. Owning regular changes of clothes could be considered contrary to the vows of poverty, so pre-Vatican II convents developed specific rules of laundering to protect their clothes and make them last as long as possible. Just as the women were restricted in their hygiene and toiletries, so too were their clothes. Baths were unusually rare luxuries for a religious body and the habit, as an extension of that body, was also barred from any full immersions in water. Instead, it had to be spot-cleaned once a week rather than receive a washing which would have been considered the same as if the woman had soaked in a tub. Some more conservative orders never completely laundered the habit, only under-tunics. The habit was brushed regularly and spot-cleaned; that way, it could last throughout much of a nun's life. Jane Tobin recalls subverting the rule to avoid the dreary task and simply drenched her habit with a dripping-wet sponge so that it received a 'shower' rather than a forbidden bath.

In-house production and care of the habits was a direct continuance of women's traditional occupation as weavers and sewers which dates far back into Christian history and has been a cornerstone of monastic industry. As early as 747, Church Council decrees tried unsuccessfully to limit the time nuns spent on handiwork: 'Time shall be devoted more to reading books and chanting psalms than to weaving and decorating clothes with various colours in unprofitable richness' (Eckenstein 1896:226). In the same year, St. Boniface, the Carolingian reformer, to the Archbishop of Canterbury in Letter XLII of the *English Correspondence*, complained about the lavish dress of the convents: 'These garments, betraying a nakedness of soul, display in themselves signs of arrogance and pride and wantonness and vanity.' Later, male church officials saw the benefit of these labours because they kept a woman's hands always busy and supplied useful accessories for the habit like handkerchiefs and dustjackets for the books of prayer which religious carried with them everywhere. For centuries, needlework and weaving were one of the few means for single women to earn a living. In the thirteenth century, loose networks of single women combined their skills in textile arts with their spiritual desires to form independent collectives knows as

Beguinages. The Beguinages mark the beginning of the modern era in feminine monasticism, built upon strategies of economic independence through shared labour and egalitarian spiritual companionship. Time and again, convents have utilized the skills and talents of their inhabitants, particularly in embroidery and linen stitching, to earn badly needed extra money. This kind of work has generally been considered by its practitioners as much as purchasers as being outside of the world of commerce and industry since it was not real labour but a feminine and domestic pastime. Because it was often tedious but also productive and useful, it was considered an excellent meditative activity for pious women and has become a significant area of study in the field of religious material culture. Investigation into homework and fabric arts has opened doors to questions about the relationship between gender and spirituality, built upon identifiable systems of preparing and constantly working on the body.

Engendering Piety

For women religious, issues of gender identity were above all the most contingent upon the historical and societal understandings of the normative roles of men and women, more so than sacred living or labour practices. In a belief system which to this day continues to uphold on many levels the social inferiority and sexual transgressiveness of women, to appropriate the potency or prestige of the other sex was highly suspect. As Vern Bullough has contended in his seminal essay 'Transvestism in the Middle Ages', questions of gendered piety revolve more around a problematic of social relations of gender than a problem of gendered psychology (Bullough 1982:45). There are many stories of women religious who are revered after death as extra-holy because they dressed as men and kept their real sex hidden from the world. One of the highest compliments an early monastic could receive from her male counterparts was that she was 'masculine in faith', a tradition harkened to in the Benedictine clothing prayers requesting the habit to produce a 'new man' from the piety of a woman. Of course, the same logic did not hold true for men who were shamed and despised if they displeased God by wearing feminine garments even for pious reasons. More blasphemous yet was a woman who brazenly wore men's clothes without denying her true sex. This ideological valuing of one gender over the other is best exemplified by the trial of Jeanne d'Arc in the fourteenth century. Charged, among other crimes, with wearing men's garments, she was accused of mocking God's divine order. Her attire ultimately sealed her fate since, faced with a lack of evidence, her jailors stole her prison clothes and replaced them with men's. The moment she put on men's clothes, she was easily proven to be a heretic and sentenced to death (ibid.:51–2).

Other women religious saw liberation precisely in gloriously feminine garments. One of the most important philosophers of sacred dress was Hildegard von Bingen. In her two books of visions, dress was regarded as an important aspect not only of women's work but also their spiritual relationship to God through the feminine aspect of Sapientia or Wisdom. Wisdom's vestures were the clothes of creation: the revelation of the beauty, synergy, harmony and grace of God. According to Hildegard, since women were the weavers of society, they not only clothed the faithful in garments but, as the givers of life, they provided the first robe of skin to protect the soul, making nakedness itself a form of sacred dress (Newman 1987:74). In the transcriptions of her visions, Hildegard often described in great detail the dress of each apparition, thus creating a personalized order of symbolic representation based upon adornment of the sacred body of Christ and His Church. Here, in Vision Five of the *Scivias* is an example:

> ... and in this brightness appeared a most beautiful image of a maiden, with bare head and black hair, wearing a red tunic, which flowed down about her feet ... And around that maiden I saw standing a great crowd of people, brighter than the sun, all wonderfully adorned with gold and gems. Some of these had their heads veiled in white, adorned with a gold circlet; and above them, as if sculpted on the veils, was the likeness of the glorious and ineffable Trinity as it was represented to me earlier, and on their foreheads the Lamb of God, and on their necks a human figure, and on the right ear cherubim, and on the left ear the other kinds of angels; and from the likeness of the glorious and supernal Trinity golden rays extended to these other images. And among these people there were some who had mitres on their heads and pallia of the episcopal office around their shoulders (Hildegard 1990:201).

This form of communication of the sacred through references to the material culture of women's lives makes Hildegard a unique figure of both feminine piety and propriety. It leads to the question of how different communities negotiated historically and culturally specific gendered discourses and contended with the sublimated sensuality of the habit and the cloistered body contained within.

It is not merely coincidental that convent schools have been the locus of feminine training in the art of reserving the body from suggestive or erotic behaviour. Although there have been times when even convents have had difficulties in meeting their own standards of deportment. In a 1922 letter from Mother Alfons to her community, she railed against the infiltration of flapper-like styles into her spiritual house:

A number of abuses which may not in any way be tolerated have crept into the community. Sisters walk around in the house, sit around and study in their kimonos. In the strictest way, I forbid all Sisters to wear their kimonos anywhere except in the bedrooms. Another serious irregularity is that Sisters use powder, rouge, cosmetics and lipstick. For God's sake! How far will worldly-minded Sisters go![5]

With all due respect to Mother Alfons' outrage, it has not been so easy for sisters to simply ignore the social discourses of femininity, especially once the strict rules of the habit were relaxed. Controlling women and the limits of gender by dress is not unique to religious organizations but with the added threat of eternal punishment and the strict administrative hierarchy bearing down on the convents, dress codes and styles were perpetually sites of conflicts and contestation in determining a distinctive identity and a certain degree of power from the habit. It is in this final arena of power relations and community homogeneity where struggles for identity and piety are ultimately played out.

The Politics of Habits

The habit has always been used by the Church as a device for establishing terms of self-governance and community control. When convents were ruled by members of European royalty, women were loathe to give up the status and rank which sumptuary laws accorded them. Thus, they dressed as lavishly as they could with only the veil to mark them as religious. Later, the poorer Beguines and apostolic congregations could ill afford a specially designed uniform and so wore their regular bourgeois dress with a veil to symbolize their simple vows. In 1547 the Council of Trent, fearing that women religious were acting too independent and enjoying too many benefits of both the social and sacred world, banned lay adaptations of dress and insisted upon a fully cloistering habit. By the twentieth century, women were caught between an over-standardization of the habit and the requirement to have distinguishable form of dress duly representative of their community's origins, labour and pietic practices. It is not surprising, then, that the length of a belt or particular weave of fabric would become over-valued. As new communities flourished, they had to go to the bishop for final approval of a habit and a sort of quality control to ensure that the design was appropriately differentiated enough from all the others in circulation. Some men took this

5. Excerpt from the Circular letters of the Superior General, Archives of the School Sisters of St. Francis, Milwaukee, WI. I am grateful to Dr Margaret Susan Thompson for discovering this letter in her own research and bringing a copy of it to my attention.

job quite seriously, commenting upon the cut, length or fabric of any particular piece, from the scapular to the collar. There is even a story about the late nineteenth-century Bishop of Salford who actually tried on the new headdress of the Franciscan Missionaries of St. Joseph in front of its foundress, Alice Ingham, to demonstrate what he felt was an improved style. Chaplains also frequently made suggestions, which were just as frequently unwelcome in the convent. In 1904, the Vatican demanded that the Sisters of Loretto remove an embroidered inscription and add a white lining to their veils to cut the harshness of the all-black habit. Officials said the imposing starkness of the habit would discourage young women from entering but Mother Praxedes, the Superior of the house, responded rather tartly that they had more than enough candidates and clearly did not appreciate the intrusion into the life of her community. She called for a vote on the matter and wrote, 'I shall not grieve or be the least disappointed if the majority are not in favour of the addition. All I request is to act honestly and before God what you think will promote his honour and glory and the welfare of the Society.'[6]

Sometimes the advice of the male clergy was crucial since they were much more likely to travel around to the different houses and provide useful information about innovations in production and display. Since communication between houses could sometimes be difficult, especially for remote missionaries, and description not always clear, women religious used their talents in needlework and handicraft to create special habit dolls which they would send to their sisters living elsewhere. The dolls were carefully and intricately dressed miniatures in full attire, including accessories and under-clothes, in the exact fabric and colours of the convent. Much care and devotion went into the preparation of the habit dolls, although not without some humour. The Prioress M. Monica Rohrner wrote a fanciful letter in 1889 to her counterpart in Racine:

> Do not be too frightened when you discover that I have smuggled a nun into the package. She is a Dominican from the Convent of Heilig Kreuz, judging at least from her religious habit; and she wants to visit the dear, dear Dominican Sisters in far-away Racine. To the loyal sisters of our dear foundress of their convent, M. Benedicta Bauer, she is bringing a picture as a remembrance, and also a veil as it is now worn in our convent.[7]

6. Typescript from the 'Mother Praxedes Carty' file in the Sisters of Loretto Archives, Nerinx, Ky (postmarked Rome, Italy, 12 January 1904). I am grateful to Margaret Susan Thompson for discovering this letter in her own research and bringing it to my attention.

7. Correspondence from M. Monica Rohrner, OSD, Prioress of Hl. Kruez, Regensburg, to J.A. Birkhaeuser, Chaplain, Racine (postmarked Regensburg, Bavaria, 13 April 1889). I am grateful to Suzanne Noffke for discovering this letter in her own research and bringing it to my attention.

Between the habit dolls, clothing ceremony and daily clothing prayers, the habit dominated the lives of women religious and was a key factor in the means of identification, differentiation and mechanisms of social control. After over fifteen centuries of Christian monasticism, women religious finally seemed on the brink of striking an effective balance between the individual, social and sacred body through a vital attention to the habit. And then the Vatican decided to transform the monastic habit completely.

In 1952, Pope Pius XII first introduced some minor reforms to modernize the habit. '[H]e caused flutterings and stirrings among the Church's feminine orders everywhere' and even prompted the Italian magazine *Il Tempo* to solicit new styles from top fashion designers, to be judged by a panel of nuns (*Life*, 15 December 1952:16). Eleven years later, in the midst of the Second Vatican Council, *The Nun in the Modern World* by Leon Joseph Cardinal Suenens, Archbishop of Malines-Brussels, was released. Rejecting traditional notions that spiritual dress must be timeless and unworldly, Suenens wrote:

> But the habit must be in keeping with the needs of our time. The world today has no patience with mere ornamentation, useless complications, gofferings and other oddities, whether starched or floating in the wind, which belong to another age: anything contrived or lacking in simplicity is rejected, and anything unpractical or unhygienic, anything that gives the impression that the nun is not only apart from the world but also a complete stranger to its evolution (Suenens 1962:130).

The Council left decisions to the individual orders and their houses, encouraging them to consider nothing so sacred that it could not be modified or done away with altogether. Left on their own, convents often turned to charm schools and dress consultants for advice and support. As they were being called to a more active and visible presence in the world, women religious required some up-to-date training in proper lady-like behaviour. During the 1950s and 1960s some of the new skills they were told were necessary to participate in the modern world were getting in and out of cars with the shorter, modified habits; when and how to put on and take off gloves in the summertime; and to stop wearing white after Labour Day – a rather odd lesson, remembers Sr Anne Anderson, for the Sisters of St. Joseph who wore black habits all year round. Experts were called in to teach the complex codes of class, femininity and society into which women religious would more deeply implicate themselves.

In the years since Vatican II one convent has received instruction from the Principal of the Continental Airlines Stewardess School and another invited a representative of Estée Lauder to advise them. Consultants would often meet with each woman individually, discuss her work and responsibilities to her community, experiment with styles and fabrics to best suit her age, colouring and body size and then recommend a dress or skirt-and-shirt combination which would safely traverse the line not only between community affiliation and individuality but also a sacred life in the secular world. Even the mini-skirt was seriously considered, especially among those working in urban slums who wanted to fit in (Campbell-Jones 1979:29). It was not a peaceful time for the convent, as the thought of removing one of the principles of monastic life, bodily clausura, caused great anxiety and confusion. Who outside monasticism can really understand how it must have felt to women who had long ago adjusted to tunnel vision to suddenly have their peripheral sight restored when they switched to the modified veil, or the frightening sense of nakedness and vulnerability when the ear was no longer pressed tightly to the skull and covered under layers of fabric? Carefully trained ways of walking had to be untrained, hands were no longer tucked away out of sight inside voluminous scapulars: the drastic changes to the habit affected every part of the body. This very complicated mediation caused some strife in the convents between nuns unprepared for such dramatic changes and others wanting to test the limits of their newly gained freedom. Sr Mary Jackle illuminates the conflict:

> We were in the black-skirt-made-from-an-old-habit and white blouse phase. At a chapter meeting called to accept candidates for final vows a sister rose to object to an acceptance of a novice because she wore lipstick and had (gasp) red shoes. This touched off an argument between us. When she could stand it no longer, one of the oldest sisters in the community stood to speak. Although she had been in authority positions most of her life, she rarely spoke at Chapter, so everyone was pretty interested in what she had to say. 'In all the time I've read the gospels,' she began, 'I never noticed that Jesus chose His disciples according to what they wore or how they looked. I think we should follow His example. Secondly, I hope we don't vote against red shoes because I myself might want a pair someday.' She sat down and a hushed group voted unanimously to accept the young sister. This wonderful elder lived to be 100 years old and never did buy red shoes. But we all knew that she *might*.

Conclusion

It is both the potency and potentiality of this word, 'might', which provides the key to understanding the complex network of negotiations women religious undertake in their dress. Although all the women who contributed stories to this article have ceased wearing the habit – some even returning to the laity – it is clear that the habit still exerts some force upon their sense of identity and piety. As they remember with love and respect their work, their debates and their instruction on sacred dress, they continue the living link with past sisters, extending their legacy past the material confines of the habit. The habit is historically contingent upon tradition and convention; it is responsive to work and climate; and it is culturally sensitive to symbolic references of piety, femininity and social status. Thus, as matters changed in the relations of the religious to the outside world, to her sisters and to her Church, it called direct attention back to the corporeal body and how the habit must mediate those dynamic relations. Whereby the structures of monasticism are crucial in the formation of a religious woman into a woman religious, so too are the fluid processes whereby individual members are 'monasticized' through both daily and ceremonial activities which accentuate the habit (Gilchrist 1994:18). Examples of external pressures by Church officials and even internal struggles within communities over seemingly insignificant factors like veil trimming or belt length become urgent when it is realized that the totality of meaning which goes into bodily clausura relied upon each woman's dedication to minute and intricate practices of dress. The woman religious is a living embodiment of that totality, a concrete and symbolic body who navigates across the social landscape, forming and reforming her sacred self within the practices and perceptions of her community. As a social group, women religious determine their access to the world and represent those choices to that world most viscerally and fundamentally by their habit. As more women are choosing to put aside the habit and wear regular lay clothing and as any gathering of religious from the same community can include attire ranging from a full traditional habit to the modified jumper habits to simple dresses or even pants, the question of unity without uniformity has only begun to be addressed. Today, only a pin or necklace may identify a woman as a religious. Or perhaps a combination of styles in lay dress which defies contemporary fashion codes of colour, fabric and cut will alert the observer to realize that this woman is under religious vows. What is for certain now is that the habit as both social reality and sacred ideal will continue to work upon the body of the woman religious as she continues to define and identify herself through richly complex signification systems of service and faith.

Acknowledgements

I am grateful to the members of the Sister-L listserve (sister-l@listserv.syr.edu), an electronic mailing list dedicated to discussion of the history and contemporary concerns of women religious, for their unique insights into the habit. I would especially like to thank the listowners, Ritamary Bradley and Margaret Susan Thompson as well as the women who allowed me to use their stories and who provided archival material for this article.

Bibliography

Anonymous (1952), 'Speaking of Pictures: Pope's pronouncement on modernizing nun habits leads designers to some surprising suggestions,' *Life Magazine*, 33(24):16–17.

Boniface (1911), *The English Correspondence of St. Boniface*, Edward Kylie (ed. and trans). London: Chatto & Windus, Publishers.

Bourdieu, P. (1984), *Distinction: A Social Critique of the Judgement of Taste*, trans. by Richard Nice. Cambridge, MA: Harvard University Press.

Bullough, V. (1982), 'Transvestism in the Middle Ages.' In V. Bullough & J. Brundage (eds), *Sexual Practices and the Medieval Church*. Buffalo, NY: Prometheus Books.

Bynum, C. (1991), *Fragmentation and Redemption: Essays on Gender and the Human Body in Medieval Religion*. New York: Zone Books.

Campbell-Jones, S. (1979), *In Habit*. New York: Faber & Faber.

Chmielewski, Wendy E., Louis J. Kert and Marlyn Klee-Hartzell (eds) (1993), *Women in Spiritual and Communitarian Societies in the United States*. New York: Syracuse University Press.

Eckenstein, L. (1896), *Woman Under Monasticism*. Cambridge, UK: Cambridge University Press.

Gilchrist, R. (1994), *Gender and Material Culture: The Archeology of Religious Women*. New York: Routledge.

Gordon, B. (1993), 'Shaker Fancy Goods: Women's Work and Presentation of Self in the Community Context in the Victorian Era.' In Wendy E. Chmielewski et al. (eds), *Women in Spiritual and Communitarian Societies in the United States*. New York: Syracuse University Press.

Hildegard von Bingen (1990), *Scivias*, Mother Columba Hart and Jane Bishop (trans). New York: Paulist Press.

McDannell, C. (1991), 'Interpreting Things: Material Culture Studies and American Religion,' *Religion*, 21: 371–87.

Newman, B. (1987), *Sister of Wisdom: St. Hildegard's Theology of the Feminine*. Berkeley: University of California Press.

Rapley, E. (1990), *The Dévotes: Women and Church in Seventeenth Century France*. Montréal: McGill-Queens University Press.

Suenens, L.J. (1962), *The Nun in the World: New Dimensions in the Modern Apostolate*. Westminster, MD: The Newman Press.

Wilson, E. (1990), 'All the Rage.' In Jane Gaines and Charlotte Herzog (eds), *Fabrications: Costume and the Female Body*. New York: Routledge.

8

À la Mode: Fashioning Gay Community in Montreal

Ross Higgins

Once upon a time in North America, any man with an earring was sure to be queer. But how times have changed! Today a man in jewellery is just as likely to be a queerbasher as someone with whom to share your passion for opera. Once, *not* wearing earrings, tight white slacks, perfume, or a lush, colourful sweater was essential to being a 'real man'. Any evidence of attention to style threatened a man's reputation just as much as standing the wrong way, having a mincing walk, or sitting with your legs crossed like a girl. A 'real man' in those days could not be seen to have style; style was for queers like Liberace, bedecked with furs and rings. And queers not only dressed in style, so the popular conception went; they promoted and profited from it, imposing their vision of fashion on women, as hairdressers and dress designers, while a lucky few got to do costumes or sets for tinseltown Hollywood or the follies of Broadway.[1] You couldn't get any further from the 'no-style' required for authentic masculinity.

Of course in anthropological terms, for a 'real man' to say he was dressing without style was as meaningless as claiming to speak without grammar, make music without notes, or walk without taking steps. Human activities like these rest on an ineluctable substrate of form – a walk in the park is formed of steps and turns and periods of sitting down, as surely as an opera is composed of scenes, or an outfit of clothes and accessories. You can't

---

1. For a thoroughly tautological explanation of the attraction of gay men for show business design and vice versa, it would be hard to surpass Mast (1987:37): 'Perhaps there is something in two cultural clichés that make musicals and gay people especially suited to one another: musicals represent an extravagant and excessive frippery and gay people possess some special sensibility that finds an outlet in extravagance, excess, and frippery.' Feeble as this explanation is, Mast does offer one of the few accounts of the role of minorities in the history of American entertainment to refer to gays as well as to Jews and Blacks.

dress unconsciously, though you can dress as you are told. And unlike many other cultural activities involving the elaboration and manipulation of forms, dress is one area where almost anyone can express themselves. Moulding pottery or building missile systems is much harder work than choosing a necktie.

Sets of forms can always serve as contrasting members of a meaning structure or schema, a systematic organization of shared knowledge which enables the exchange of social meanings. The adamant refusal of style by 'real' men thus appears as simply an ideological ploy, a rampart of the sex-gender system that consecrates male privilege (Brydon, this volume; Rubin 1975). Men assert superior social rank by making themselves the 'unmarked' category, to use a linguistic term. Gay men are marked in stereotypic portrayals which evince the opinion that they transgress the gender line by failing to acknowledge the ban on taking an overt interest in how a man should dress and groom himself. The rules of maleness which boy children learn to qualify for entry into North American maledom are constantly promulgated in discrete discursive interventions in the myriad of social contacts with peers and authorities. A challenge to scholarly understanding, then, is the remarkable feat of how gay men, subject to sanctions that could go well beyond the discursive (loss of job or residence, public disgrace, arrest, violence or murder), fashioned a new collective self-image and an effective organizational basis for a self-affirming collective life. In this paper I will argue that fashion provides important clues to solving this puzzle.

New Men in the 1980s

The relation of gay men to fashion is even more interesting when the changes in all men's relation to fashion in the 1980s are considered. Up to the early years of that decade, male conformity to the dictates of the 'no-style' style was still absolutely obligatory. As evidence of this, Mort (1988:212) cites the early 1980s failure of a new fashion magazine aimed at late teen male readers, with the explanation that, 'speaking to young men as men is a risky business, because it targets men in gendered terms rather than the norm which defines everything else. Masculinity's best kept secret is broken open.' Young men resisted the idea of male fashion because that would mean losing their status as the 'unmarked' category, the standard from which women deviate; it would undermine their 'no-style' style and violate the male claim to just being 'natural', while women fuss and fret over their appearance.

But within a few years this failed magazine was followed by others that did not fail, marking the beginning of a new phase in male fashion. Not just in Great Britain but internationally, as men reacted to major social changes resulting from the second wave of feminism, most notably in the workplace, the 'new man' became a media icon (Spencer 1993). This change occurred in the 1980s and has brought about a new regime in men's clothes and grooming that signals a new male style-consciousness and a radically new willingness on the part of men [2] to admit to wanting to be seen as sexual creatures. This change was unmistakably demonstrated by the appearance, looming over downtown streets and expressways in cities throughout North America, of immense billboards for Calvin Klein underwear and other fashion products, showing men with less on than had been seen in advertising before. This shift in the visual attributes of masculinity, the representation of the male as sex object, has been documented by Mort and others.[3] But there is a surprising dearth of studies of gay men's multiple relationships with fashion beyond a few magazine articles and books on 'how to look good' for the gay market and commentary on the change to masculine fashion in the early 1970s.[4] This paper is an attempt to map out the issues that are raised by the subject.

2. This change was especially important in Anglo-Saxon men, where the ban on effeminacy was particularly intense. A comparative study of gay style and menswear across cultures would be a useful asset to the growing literature on fashion.

3. See Craik's (1994) chapter 'Fashioning Masculinity'. Spencer (1993) points out that in Britain at least, the proportion of men who follow fashion is tiny. Pumphrey (1989) analyses the problems of representing masculinity in movie Westerns, noting that the disappearance of the genre coincided with the shift in male fashionability. Also concurrent with the change, was a shift to a new form of industrial organization in fashion, marked by the rise of the new star designers who were responsible for the billboards (Coleridge 1988).

4. Loovis's (1974) guide to how to look good for cruising is a classic in its genre, affording insight not only into the clothes but also the body culture of the period. Laud Humphreys' (1972) 'New Styles of Homosexual Manliness' analyses the relation of the 1970s gay 'virilization' in relation to both the hippie movement and the gay bar market; Martin Humphries (1985) discusses the advent of the clone and denim or leather as two styles of 'surface masculininty'. David Fernbach (1981:101) coins the term 'butch shift' for the newly masculine look of the 1970s. Blachford (1981) examines how this shift in some ways reproduces heterosexual cultural values, particularly male dominance, while also expressing gay men's resistance to them. Henley's (1982) *Butch Manual: The Current Drag and How to Do It*, ostensibly a how-to guide, is actually a vigorous send-up of the new manly styles. The book's sub-title indicates gay awareness (military drag; biker drag, and so on) that *all* dress is costume. Rubinstein's (1995:215–17) dates are inadequate, but her book is useful for illustrating the 'Old Clone' of the 1970s and the 'New Clone' of the 1980s in plates from a magazine article by Signorile (*Outweek*, 28 November 1990).

Gays in Fashion as Workers and Shoppers

I want to look at two points of intersection between fashion and the lives of gay men in the pre-earring period, before the changes of the 1980s. The first aspect which I will look at is the presence of gay men in the fashion industry itself, contrasting information from life histories of gay men in Montreal with the widely held conception that this is an occupational ghetto full of gays. Secondly I will examine fashion consumption, how the signifying properties of style were used by gays in ways more subtle and effective than the no-style ideologists had imagined. I suggest that these symbolic elements should be looked at using an approach that casts fashion as an ongoing social process, not only the physical product of textiles and stitches, but as a product of discourse as well, since clothes emerge from a set of discourse practices among manufacturers and designers, distributors, advertisers, commentators, retailers and consumers.

In pursuing this investigation into one particular set of discursive practices and meaning structures which I believe were integral to the emergence of a collective gay identity in the middle of the twentieth century, sketching a fragment from the broad canvas of themes and viewpoints that represents gay men's multiple relationship to fashion, I hope to contribute to a better understanding not only of gay life but of the social processes underlying the formation of collective identities in general. It is not news that clothing symbolizes group membership, but so far there has not been enough attention paid to *how* let alone *why* that is so. What particular practices effect the link? How do certain attributes of the body and its adornment come to signify appropriate or inappropriate gender identification, and thereby cast doubt on the wearer's sexual orientation? We need to look at discursive as well as visual data to get a deeper understanding of communities in mass society. The multiple relations of the gay and fashion worlds, past and present, offer a potentially rich source of insight for an exploration of these issues, and I will conclude with some suggestions of research directions for the future.

The Discourse Community Model

The second point of intersection between gay men and fashion is consumption and the symbolic properties of style. For many in the gay world, fashion is an object of attention, a domain around which people develop more and more knowledge, using what cognitive anthropologists[5] see as a series of interconnected knowledge structures or schemata. Shopping involves comparing notes, reacting to others' purchases, developing a definition of style in a peer group and scorning last year's look. In examining gays as consumers of fashion, I use Swales' (1990) 'discourse community' model in order to study its relation to the development of public gay communities in the mid and late-twentieth century. Unlike the polysemic word 'community' used alone, the term 'discourse community' has a precise definition, and thus its applicability in a specific instance is subject to verification, and the concept can be extended and deepened in a confrontation with empirical data. One concrete manifestation of a discourse community is its relation to a set of speech genres or other conventional arrangements of discourse. A discourse community uses its genre for the expression of knowledge and attitudes particular to its social viewpoint. For example, as Swales found in his examination of the formal set of genres that academic disciplines maintain, such as the scientific research paper, these formal schemata are made up of sets of conventionalized rules governing the structure of a text, and the parts are characterized by syntactic and pragmatic regularities. These sets of habits 'belong' to discourse communities (institutionally manifest as academic institutions, professional associations and the like),[6] which create genres, maintain them and adapt them over time, and use them to enforce the standards and norms of the collectivity on members and would-be members.

In this examination of fashion and gay life, I have broadened the applicability of the term 'discourse community' beyond that advanced in

5. D'Andrade (1995) and Keller (1992) offer introductory discussions of the theory of schemata or knowledge structures in anthropology. Fashion schemata encompass knowledge of many types: who the designers are, where they work, and so on; retail outlets; fabrics and fabric care; knowledge of colour, and much else. They are carried to the mass market by the media, there to be shaped and channelled in local social networks or 'circles of opinon', as discussed below.

6. As Swales puts it: 'Genres themselves are classes of communicative events which typically possess features of stability, name recognition and so on. Genre-type communicative events (and perhaps others) consist of texts themselves (spoken, written, or a combination) plus encoding and decoding procedures as moderated by genre-related aspects of text-role and text-environment' (1990:26). Genres combine formal properties with communicative purposes. Equally important is the relation of genres to knowledge about the world and about previous texts, on which skill in their acquisition and use depends (1990:9–10). Such skill is a measure of an individual's membership in the discourse community. Cohen and Dyer (1980:172–3) recognize the importance of collective knowledge of the gay community in their discussion of cultural production.

Swales' formulation, giving more consideration to oral genres, whose conventions and situational usage may not correspond as neatly to the model as more formal written texts. I argue that genres of all types are subject to such social processing, whether by formally constituted groups or by informal groupings. I find this model a particularly useful tool for the study of gay collective life since the discourse community concept inherently focuses attention on the dynamics of discourse in society and thus on individual and collective agency. Unlike many terms for social groupings which are simply passive rubrics for categorization, 'discourse community' incorporates social change as an integral aspect; it is the result of actions and decisions taken by individuals or groups. Sanctions are applied or benefits accorded based on knowledge of discursive skills and their appropriate deployment on social occasions and on the accumulation of knowledge judged interesting or useful by the group. In the use made of the discourse community model here and in other work, I have looked especially at the schematic under-pinnings of shared discourse, arguing that in a similar way to information on gay bars, fashion constituted a conversational focus whose elaboration was constitutive of a sense of gay collective identity. The model incorporates individual agency and the possibility of resistance in word as well as in dress.

Gay Men in the Fashion World

Popular discourse often assumes that men involved in fashion work and related fields of design are gay. A male model, as Pumphrey (1989) points out, is inevitably thought to be gay. Today when glimpses of the fashion world have become a staple of cable television, no one will deny the promin-ence of recognizably gay designers, as a casual scrutiny of the new fashion television reporting (e.g. *Fashion File* on the CBC Newsworld channel) shows. Research into the history of fashion photography has also reinforced the view that there was a significant gay presence in the highest spheres of fashion. In the 1930s and 40s, as Waugh (1996:106) argues, there was a 'highly interconnected trans-Atlantic web of gay intelligentsia and denizens of high Bohemia' operating to define the image of glamour at the top level of the London-New York worlds of show business, fashion and design. Its members included Noel Coward, Cecil Beaton, George Hoyningen Huene, Jean Cocteau and Horst. Gay men are apparently well represented in the rarefied circles of world fashion leaders and their helpers and hangers on.

One journalistic book on the American fashion world in the 1960s, Bender's *The Beautiful People* (1967), discusses the question more openly than most writing on fashion history:

There are no statistics to prove that Seventh Avenue has more homosexuals than Wall Street. But clearly, the arts – fine, performing and commercial – are more hospitable to those with unconventional sexual habits than investment banking and heavy industry at the moment. [. . .] The homosexual doesn't have to camouflage himself on Seventh Avenue. He can flaunt (Bender 1967:36–7).

Bender's text is full of querulous and disparaging references to the 'ubiquitous bachelors' of fashion. One of those mentioned is Rudi Gernreich, a California couturier who in 1964 introduced the topless swimsuit and achieved sudden notoriety. Though Bender devotes several pages to this designer, referring in passing to his 'bachelor abode in the Hollywood Hills' (pp. 175–7), she nowhere notes that Gernreich had been among the founders of the first homophile organization in the United States, the Mattachine Society, launched by Harry Hay and friends at the beginning of the 1950s (D'Emilio 1983).

Gernreich is one of several 'bachelors' whose contributions to fashion in Europe and America are well known, but in this chapter, I would like to go beyond 'big name' research and look at ordinary gays working in the industry as part of a more extensive project to map out the 'political economy' of gay life. Only within this broader context of how gay men have found secure employment, how their interconnections have served as one sort of 'back channel' in some activity sectors can we fruitfully examine the often heard claim, repeated by Mast (1987) as well as by Bender, that theatre, fashion, and other artistic domains are more tolerant of gays than other occupational groups. In this study I want to present data from my study of the formation of a self-identified and increasingly vocal gay community in Montreal between 1945 and 1970 which indicate at least a few older gay men's work experiences in the fashion industry.[7]

Montreal Gay Men in the Fashion Trades

In thirty life history interviews conducted with men who participated in Montreal's gay world before 1970, my objective was not to document the relationship between gay men and fashion but to trace the processes of collective identity which led to the emergence of a sense of community among gay men in postwar Montreal. Thus I did not ask for detailed information on clothes or other style-related topics, and the information that I received

---

7. Textile and garment manufacturing were among the most important sectors in the process of industrialization in Quebec; in Montreal they accounted for 55,000 jobs in 1951, for example (Lacoste 1958:216), far more than any other Canadian city.

came because the narrators in my interviews decided to mention them. In addition, there is documentary evidence suggesting that the Montreal fashion scene of the 1920s indeed followed the same pattern as the major fashion centres, since it indicates that at least two of the prominent male couturiers were homosexuals. However this visible role for gays in fashion was not confirmed by the two men interviewed who worked in other, less exalted, segments of the industry. I will examine these sources for what they can tell us about the widely assumed prominence of gay men in the fashion world.

Documentary sources afford only a few tiny glimpses into the life of a prominent designer named Lucien Lacouture, who worked in Montreal in the 1920s and 1930s. The earliest information on this man comes from the autobiography of a well-known San Francisco lesbian writer, Elsa Gidlow, who grew up in Montreal at the beginning of the twentieth century and later lived in San Francisco. Gidlow relates how she met a circle of gay men of literary and artistic tastes at the end of the First World War. One of these was Lucien Lacouture, who told her how he had lost his vocation for the priesthood after being raped by his confessor at school, and decided to become a couturier (Gidlow 1986:114–16). Lacouture later visited Gidlow when she lived in New York on his regular fabric buying trips until her departure for the West Coast around 1930, when they seem to have lost touch.

The second story about Lucien Lacouture emphasizes his prominence in the small Montreal fashion scene of those years. An anecdote told by labour organizer Léa Roback (Lacelle 1988:135–7), who met Lacouture in the early 1930s, provides a unique insight into public discourse on homosexuality. In 1934, Roback was working for the Young Women's Hebrew Association run by Mrs. Bronfman, wife of the owner of Seagram's Distilleries and a customer of Lacouture's couture dress shop, which shows that his customers included women from Montreal's most affluent social circles. But when Mrs. Bronfman heard from Lacouture that they were friends, she insisted that Roback should stop seeing Lacouture at once since he was 'not like a man'. She reacted by contacting two working-class women that she knew on the association's board, who, says Roback, succeeded in making the point that people should be hired on the basis of their abilities and not who their friends were. A few years later Lacouture's career was cut short when he died suddenly in the mid-1930s at the apex of his fame (Guernsey 1982:100–1). His friend milliner Émile Phaneuf is also mentioned by the sources, but all we learn about this second gay designer of the 1920s and 1930s is that he was small, blond and made hats for the same wealthy clientele as Lacouture. Some of Phaneuf's work is preserved in the fashion collection of the McCord

Museum. Given their reputation, it is likely that further research could turn up more information on both of these rather enigmatic figures.[8]

Fortunately, two vivid life history accounts from gay men working in the Montreal fashion world are available, though they relate to a later period and come from less prominent participants. The first narrator, whom I call Walter, was interviewed in 1990 with Percy, his lover for nearly sixty years. Walter related that he had always been obsessed with being well dressed and well groomed, to which Percy intoned, *sotto voce*, 'He still is!' Walter continued, 'I was always quoted as being the best-dressed guy in the school, and if I got dirt on me, I'd scream.' He loved it when his school cadets got to parade for the Prince of Wales' visit to Toronto, because he thought the uniforms, red jackets with shiny buttons, were superb. Later, he quit his first job in a department store when they tried to put him in charge of a donut-making machine that got dough all over his clothes. Walter attended large drag parties hosted by a transvestite heterosexual couple in Toronto in the early 1930s, but soon after he met Percy and followed him to Montreal when he was transferred there by his employer. In Montreal Walter established a workshop in their apartment and supported himself by offering custom leather work for sale through a department store and on the ships of the Cunard Line. The two men always had a relatively open relationship, so one night when Percy picked up a man who must have been one of Lacouture's competitors in the couture business in the notorious cruising park on Mount-Royal, he brought him home and introduced him to Walter. This led to a lucrative new line of business for Walter:

> I did a lot of work for him. His gowns used to sell for $1000, and at that time, stores were not making handbags to match shoes. So customers would bring in a pair of shoes to match up the whole outfit and say, 'If I could just get a handbag to match my shoes . . .' He'd say, 'Well, I think we can arrange that.' . . . I used to say, 'Sure. I'll take the shoes to match the colour. I'll go to the factory and get some leather.' So I'd buy a skin of leather – not very big, because they were calf skins – and make the handbags for him. I used to make hand bags out of fur – the fur would cost about $200 just for the material, and he'd sell the stuff for $500–$600.

For several years Walter and Percy saw the couturier and his wife socially, and were sometimes invited for weekends at their country house. When the war came in 1939 however, the connection was broken. After serving in the

---

8. The McCord Museum fashion collection contains no work by Lacouture but they do have several hats by Phaneuf, as curator Jacqueline Beaudoin-Ross kindly brought to my attention. She also provided me with general information on the history of the Montreal fashion scene.

army for the duration, Walter took three design courses in New York and tried to set up as a couturier himself with three or four women sewing for him at home. Though he had financial support from his father, he found the business too difficult, so in the late 1940s he went to work as a dress designer in a factory and followed this profession for the rest of his working life.

Walter had little use for my assumption that this meant he worked in a gay profession. When asked about gays in the fashion industry, he replied:

> I never had anybody – never had any association with gays at work, as far as I know. We didn't have anybody – they were all married men. Never ever tried to encourage it, because I knew it'd be rather taboo as far as the factory was concerned. They suspected I was; I'm sure they did. Because I didn't bother with any of the gals or anything. I just minded my own business. Some of the other boys were always making plays for the girls. Even the bosses were screwing them whenever they got a chance to.

As far as the supposed predominance of gay men in fashion careers, he said:

> Well, that's on the creative end of it, but not on the actual production end. That's just a job for them. They either cut the dresses, or couldn't care less.

Walter would spend three decades working in this environment. The job had the not inconsiderable advantage of requiring frequent trips to New York City, often accompanied by Percy, to keep up with the latest dress styles for work, while incidentally seeing a show or two, checking out the latest gay bars, and keeping up with a far-flung gay social network.

Walter's rejection of the idea that gays abound in the fashion industry was echoed by a second narrator, Ralph, who moved to Montreal to study fashion design in about 1960. Like Walter, Ralph's fascination with clothes went back to his childhood. Asked how he got interested in fashion, Ralph replied:

> I was always interested. I had a fascination with material, with fabric. I remember – mother didn't sew – she bought fabric and there was a dressmaker in our town. I would go to the general store and pick up bolts of fabric for her. A week later you'd see it again and my sister was wearing it as a dress or I was wearing a shirt. Even today I think it's amazing – from thread comes fabric, from fabric comes clothes, and clothes tell a story. It tells a lot about you, the kind of clothes you wear. Growing up interested in dressing dolls and making dolls' clothes – I was close to my sister so I played with toys and dolls. It was okay when father was away. Mother would say 'Now your father is coming, so get it all away.' So I knew it wasn't okay.

Ralph had to fight to get into the career he knew he wanted:

> Later at school I was interested in art work. It became an obsession, and this was offensive to my father. So long as he was away I was allowed to paint, but I knew what I was doing was wrong. In 9th grade we started to have lay teachers. There was a French teacher from Belgium. He was very taken up with my art work, my creative side. I didn't realize he was gay until years later I met him in a gay bar in Toronto. Lucky he didn't come on to me, but he wasn't like that. He was really interested. He was aware my parents were not aware of my talent. They were ashamed of it. He got me to have him invited to dinner and brought a file of my drawings. Because he believed in it, my parents said maybe I should take an art course in grade 9, 10 – grade 11.

When it came time to choose where he would go after high school, Ralph resorted to devious tactics:

> I wanted to go to Fashion Arts Academy. My father wouldn't allow that, but he would allow the Commercial Art School. So I came to Montreal with no idea of doing that, looked for schools and found the Fashion Arts Academy. I told my father it was a commercial art school and studied fashion art.

Based on his experience there and afterward, Ralph wholeheartedly agreed that the stereotype of gays in fashion was misleading; instead he notes the gender prejudice at work:

> At the Fashion Arts Academy there were 22 students and 21 were girls. This was 1959–1960. When Dior died there was a sudden fad for male designers. At the Academy there was a small number of serious students. I had five [job] offers; none of the girls did. When one of owners of the school got sick, I taught evening courses. That was the first time father accepted it.

Looking at a later period than Walter, Ralph repeated that it was only at the top of the fashion industry that gays were known. He spoke of the arrival of the more or less open gays among the new crop of designers of the late 1960s:[9]

> Some male designers were probably gay but there were not a lot of them. This was just the beginnings of male designers in Quebec fashion culture. Afterwards it became very gay . . . But when I went to work, I started with a small company and stayed for 27 years. There was my boss and 7 girls. I never met gays. The boss was anti-gay. He was like my father. I had an operator and we used to go to New

---

9. On this period and especially the success of Michel Robichaud, see Beauregard, Duchesneau and Nadeau (1988) and Charest (1988).

York, buy samples and take them apart to trace them, which didn't work too well. When I started, I worked as cutter, pattern-maker and designer. The boss was almost ashamed to introduce me to customers. He was not comfortable to have a gay man as designer. Yet business tripled – in 27 years we never had a bad season, never lost money. But there was not a lot of gay contact until I leaped into the gay pool.

For Ralph, the 'gay pool' meant his new hangout, a bar called the Café Apollo, described below, where he met a circle of lifelong friends, some of whom would later work for Ralph when he set up his own clothing manufacturing business, selling clothes to the increasingly visible gay market in the 1980s and 1990s.

What then is the 'political economy' of the gay presence in fashion? Based only on these preliminary interview materials, we can see that the idea that the fashion industry is a gay occupational ghetto must be treated with caution, since it was contradicted by both Walter and Ralph, although their own work histories do indicate at least some gay presence at lower levels in the business. In the small-scale (but long the hub of the business in Canada) Montreal garment industry, these two observers suggested, there were only a few people at the top of this very stratified business who could function openly as gay men. Like management in any field, the owners and supervisors of firms in the mass fashion business shared the values of their homophobic social environment, but they were also willing to have that outweighed by their profit sense. They may have been aware that many designers were gay, but tolerated them if they were good money makers.

To see if in fact the pattern of gay men working in fashion was as restricted to the elite level as the two narrators suggest, we need to know much more. Documentary and interview data can help build a model of what looks like a key area for understanding the political economy of gay life. For research on men who worked in fashion, particularly at the top, only contact with key informants can resolve the question of how large a role gays played in the various stages of the history of clothing design and production and at various points from the metropolitan centres of international fashion to a smaller centre like Montreal.[10] In the next section, I will turn to the consumption side of fashion. Here ethnographic research with a much wider

10. Designers, workshop assistants, journalists, and many other categories of informant could be interviewed. Finding them will take perseverance and luck. In the light of the central role of publicity in the industry, it is crucial to find out who the local photographers of fashion were, and what their work can tell us, if indeed it is accessible. Similar research could be done in other design fields such as theatre and film design, interior decorating (e.g. club interiors), and architecture.

range of narrators can help answer the question of how gay men use and have used style to communicate with both outsiders and with each other, not only their sexual orientation but a complex range of social meanings that clothes can convey. 'Clothes tell a story,' as Ralph said, but we need to write it down to make sense of it sometimes.

Gay Men à la Mode

In the 1950s, one of the expressions gay francophones used to covertly signal that someone was gay was, 'Il est à la mode.' This stereotypic perception corresponds to such English expressions as that someone is 'musical' or 'light in his loafers'. All of these relate to the purported gay penchant for following styles, whether in music, footwear or art, and it was one of the signs that could lead to labelling of a man as a 'faggot' in the working-class friendship groups studied by Dunk (1991:96). Cohen and Dyer (1980:176) stresses the close association in his mind between being queer and being cultured as he came out in England in the late 1960s. In considering gay men as consumers of fashion, I want to highlight two sub-topics. I begin with the way style in clothing is used to signal a gay identity to society at large, and then look at how style functions internally in the gay world as a set of codes carrying meanings between gay men, within gay culture.

Gay men use style to proclaim who they are, and have been doing so since long before the in-your-face styles adopted by youth in the 1990s. But in the past, the discursive environment presented by society contained no gay voices, or only very weak ones, to satirize or otherwise counteract the savage verbal attacks perpetuating prevalent homophobic stereotypes in interpersonal discourse or in the media. One of the techniques used in these attacks was a heavy-handed emphasis on the ridiculousness of gay men's interest in fashion. One such attack, though a relatively mild one, was a skit in the British hit revue *Beyond the Fringe*, which opened in London in 1961, and on Broadway one year later. 'Bollard' satirizes the contrast between the pre-shoot conversation of actors making a commercial and the commercial itself, which is for 'a man's cigarette,' for which they have to shift their voices down an octave. In addition to voice and intonation, one of the markers of their gayness is an obsessive focus on hair and clothing (one wanted a vest in mauve, but had to settle for Lincoln green).[11]

11. Beyond the Fringe Original Broadway cast recording, Capitol SW 1792, n.d. [1962], comedy revue starring Alan Bennett, Peter Cook, Jonathan Miller, and Dudley Moore. Much attention has focused in recent years, or even decades, on 'camp' style in the gay world. Recent

We can read traces of this 'gay aestheticism' even in the pages of Quebec's thriving weekly scandal press in the 1950s. This very particular local documentary source, in which gossip and jokes about homosexuals were far more common than in mainstream publications of the period (Higgins and Chamberland 1992), provides another indication of the close relationship between gays and fashion, style and 'high culture' generally. In the inevitable lonely hearts ads at the back of these scruffy little newspapers, the gay advertisers are easy enough to spot since quite a few specify that they want to meet correspondents of the same sex, while others list their interests as art, music, literature and physical culture. A phrase that frequently recurs in self-descriptions offered by those who place such ads is *'aimant tout ce qui est beau'* (loving all that is beautiful), a sort of mini-manifesto of gay identity in the making.

A particularly flagrant example of mainstream media stereotyping is the use of fashion to code gayness in a news report related to a 1956 gay murder investigation (Higgins 1995). In that year, when the heat was on the police due to a stalled investigation into the death of a gay man, they decided to look busy by arresting a few queers. Thus in January 1956, Montreal newspapers reported the arrest of 34 men for 'insulting or obscene language'.[12] One paper, the *Herald* went into more detail than the others, noting: 'Morality cops stressed the suspects were not leather jacketed youngsters, but older men dressed in neat if somewhat chi-chi clothes.'[13]

In fact, the objective of most gay men in 1956 was to stay as far away from chi-chi street clothes as possible, precisely because they wanted to avoid conforming to the popular stereotype in order to keep their homosexuality a secret. Most went along with the cautious advice of a 1948 book (preface to the Second Edition Canada, July 1948) called *The Invert* by 'Anomaly':

---

collections by Meyer (1994) and Bergman (1993) highlight the camp 'sensibility' made into an object of intellectual consideration after Sontag's 'Notes on Camp' in 1964. Camp speech styles are much commoner than dressing in drag however, and the topic of camp is more closely tied to the connections between gay style-sense and show business than to the way most gay men dress.

12. Using an obscure section of the Canadian criminal code. The cases were later dropped.

13. '34 to Face Court For Obscene Talk,' (*Herald*, 23 January 1956:15). Several days previous to these arrests, the papers reported that the Quebec censors had banned the Marlon Brando film *The Wild One* which made leather jackets all the rage among rebellious young North Americans. This development, as Craik (1994:194) points out, was the start of a new trend that would eventually make jeans and leather expressions of youthful rebellion, but the impact would not be fully felt until a decade later.

Don't be too meticulous in the matter of your own clothes, or effect extremes in colour or cut; don't wear conspicuous rings, watches, cuff-links, or other jewellery; don't allow your voice or intonation to display feminine inflection – cultivate a masculine tone and method of expression; don't stand with your hand on your hip or walk mincingly; don't become identified with the groups of inverts which form in every city; don't let it be noticed that you are bored by female society (pp. 135–6).

The author claims that his list of 'Don'ts' is intended only to help homosexuals protect themselves, not because the conspicuous peculiarities are in themselves undesirable.

One man told a story of such avoidance. Before he moved to Montreal, Donald, a life-history narrator who grew up (and came out) in Trinidad in the late 1940s, was leery of becoming too close to someone he knew in the small social world of the island elite:

Edmund was flamboyant, but not in a faggoty way. He was just a bit too different for Trinidad. He was like, I would say, a Noel Coward – that type. He dressed just too well. And he was so fabulous-looking . . . You see, he worked for the oil fields . . . And he would go to New York and New Orleans and come back with all these stories and clothes. He was quite a clothes horse.

For Donald, contacts with the expatriate Americans and others were safer socially.

But clearly some Montreal men gloried in the flamboyant faggoty style in the 1950s without necessarily doing full drag.[14] One of the men I interviewed remembered his father coming home and telling the family that at a local tavern in the nearly suburban east-end working-class district where they lived, there was a row of tables at the back that was occupied by *les tapettes*, or queers, men in pastel pants whose hands were covered with rings. 'Overt' gays are linked symbolically with the eastern part of the city. In the sociolinguistic cultural divide that characterized Montreal before the rise of Québécois national pride in the French language, at a time when 'English' and 'West' coded 'high-class' and 'French' and 'East' meant 'lowlife' (depending on who was talking, and to whom), the divide between flamboyance and caution crosscut the difference between English- and French-speaking

14. Semantically 'full drag' fits into a hierarchy with professional female impersonators at the top and variably feeble attempts to imitate female attire, ranging from a fair attempt, like the fabulously-dressed 'women' Walter saw at his drag parties, to the length of fabric employed by one man at a party in the Canadian West described in a letter cited by Leznoff (1954:117–18), or the inexpensive 'hat parties' described by another narrator. These terms map a knowledge set of the gay discourse community, as discussed below.

gays. This adds another dimension to their more usually noted link to the class distinction.[15] 'Lowlife' characters abound in the dramatic and fictional work of Michel Tremblay, where they serve as symbols of francophone oppression and self-oppression. When, in *La duchesse et le roturier* (1982), Édouard, the Duchesse de Langeais, gets his sister a ticket to see Tino Rossi, and then gets the adjacent seat where he himself will sit in full drag (she doesn't recognize him), one of the descriptions of the crowd is that it is full of men just like those who went to the east end tavern.

Wearing a dress was only for special occasions unless you were an entertainer, but it was enough to signal who you were merely by wearing a style or colour of pants. In those days, any kind of jewellery beyond a tie clip and a pinkie ring was taken as a marker of gay identity by the outside world. Only a small proportion of gay men, the 'screaming queens', adopted really extreme visible signs in order to defiantly proclaim their difference for anyone to see. Quentin Crisp (1968) has given eloquent expression to the point of view of a man who deliberately chose to use style to confront society in a form of street theatre, which took enormous courage in the pre-liberation days.

Most men, however, wanted to do just the opposite. In his study of Montreal homosexuals, Leznoff (1954)[16] included a section on the 'Role of Dress' in a chapter on 'Contact Techniques'. He divides gay men of the early 1950s into the 'Overts', those whom Donald referred to as flamboyant, and the 'Coverts', whose professional status motivates their greater concern with secrecy. Thus class difference is a premise of Leznoff's study. He explains his informants' attitudes to clothes in relation to the question of secrecy and thus to social class:

> In some cases identifying dress consists of a pair of tight fitting slacks designed to reveal the outline of the body, a sports shirt open at the neck and a pair of sandals. To homosexuals, this clothing arouses suspicions of homosexuality (1954:164).

15. A comment in Pollak's (1988:46) study of homosexual society in France indicates that drag has the same lower-class association there.

16. Leznoff's (1954) sociology master's thesis is the earliest known full-scale gay ethnography of a North American city. Other than a massive study of German homosexuals published by Magnus Hirschfeld in 1914, this is the most detailed gay sociological research into the social aspects of homosexuality. Leznoff, for reasons of protecting the confidentiality of his sources, concealed the name of the city itself, as well as those of the men and the bars they drank in, so he was unable to include a discussion of Montreal's specific French/English cultural divide, the one major drawback to his extraordinary accomplishment.

As a result of their suspicions, the way the men dress is dependent on their class position in more ways than the quality of the fabric alone:

> Since they generally consider that heterosexuals are as suspicious of certain types of dress as they are, those who attempt to conceal their homosexuality are careful to avoid fashions defined as 'gay'. For those who make no attempt to conceal as is the case of Overts, dress may be used to aid in making sexual contacts (1954:165–6) (Fig. 8.1).

Though there is little indication that heterosexuals generally perceive the signs that gays consider so revealing, Leznoff adds, the Covert homosexual, 'consciously avoids those fashions, colours, or combinations which homo-sexual society defines as being 'gay'. Thus Coverts use dress as a means of concealing' (1954:165). On the other hand, one of the Overts boasts, 'It's amazing what a pair of slacks can do for you. I find that the most successful way to cruise. You really get the looks that way' (1954:165) (Fig. 8.2).

Leznoff's dichotomy of class and flamboyance types is useful in that it highlights the class distinction, but it fails to provide an adequate model of the many subtle gradations of costume that are available for the coding of interpersonal meanings. Other sources and common sense deduction from the clearly established predisposition in many gay circles, including those with comfortable incomes, to explore style and buy beautiful objects, suggest that Leznoff didn't cast a critical enough eye on what the Coverts were wearing and compare it to heterosexual fashion of the day. One respectable homophile leader is reported by Brake (1976, cit. Blachford 1981:189) as exclaiming after being refused admission to a London pub that had banned gays, 'They said I was effeminately dressed. I was furious. I may be queer but at least I'm a man.' Perhaps the Coverts didn't go for those trashy tight white slacks (or maybe only when safely on vacation in Provincetown or Capri), but they were almost certainly better dressed than their straight peers and this difference might be visible to some non-gays as well.

Looked at from the internal point of view, what gay men were really striving for in the way they dressed was, as Richard Dyer (1994) points out in his reflections on gay style, to appear in such a way that heterosexuals wouldn't notice, while unambiguously signalling their gayness to their gay peers. Few others could read the appropriate codes or had the interest to try. The history of such codes and their use within the gay world to facilitate the exchange of meanings among initiated gay insiders has not been fully told. The most complete account of such a system is given by Chauncey (1994:42–54), who stresses the ethnic and generational variations in the codes in use in New York City in the early decades of the twentieth

Figure 8.1. Patrick wearing a see-through shirt of which he was very proud. Credit: collection John Banks.

Figure 8.2. Patrick wearing white slacks. Credit: collection John Banks.

century.[17] Among the common identifying signs, he notes red neckties, a certain style of loafer, and green suits. The latter helps make sense of a folklore belief concerning this colour that Judy Grahn (1990:76–7) says suddenly surfaced in her grade ten class when her peers thought that if you wore green on Thursdays, you were queer.[18]

In the climate of secrecy in which most gay men led their lives however, specific signs like shirt colour or shoe style could be dangerous, since they could easily be learned by outsiders. Chauncey (1994:52) reports one man who said he was sneered at by newsboys who recognized the significance of his red tie, but he notes that such recognition was in the context of a gay cruising area. Elsewhere it would merely have been seen as an eccentric colour choice. Probably gay men have more commonly relied on minor variations on standard fashions than on odd garments or outlandish colours. Small details like the 'excessively bright feathers in their hat band' or 'tightly cuffed trousers' quoted by Chauncey, were, as he points out, less risky than a green suit. D'Arcangelo (1968) provides indirect evidence from England for what this entailed in more recent years:

> An English friend told me that in London there is a definite though very subtle sign language of clothing that communicates one's sexual preferences down to fairly minute details. I don't mean the difference between tennis-court drag and leather motorcycle fetishism, but, for instance, the color of a raincoat, or the way it buttons, whether or not it's buttoned, belted or double-breasted. That sort of thing.

Such elaborate codings may not have been known beyond special gay groups, but everyone recognized attention to style as a maker of gay identity. Taking just a little too much care in choosing a sweater, or being just a little too well-groomed were the minor transgressions of the masculine no-style style that enabled mutual recognition.

Since clothing is an easily changed aspect of self presentation, subject to infinite variation in cut, colour and trimmings, it is likely in fact that a much finer textured analysis would reveal a situationally varying subtle shading

17. Following clues assembled by Ellis (1936), Burnham (1973), Bullough (1976) and Katz (1976), Chauncey documents the practices of New York's pansy craze of the 1920s, when many men used markers of femininity as plucked eyebrows, though I know of no evidence of repercussions of this craze to Montreal. Chauncey emphasizes the change over time that affects the signs used for meanings and highlights class, ethnicity, and gender as axes of difference in signifiers and significations uttered, but does not present a detailed theoretical model of the sign system.

18. Karlen (1971:249–50) reviews the gay significance of this colour and speculates that it can be traced back to a Roman political faction!

of the messages and meanings intended (or otherwise) that arise in gay cultural settings. For the historical development of these coding systems, research can be done using visual materials, as well as contemporary written accounts. No static document can replace a first person account, however, in showing not only what codes there were but what it was like to live with and use them. While often the needs of mutual recognition occupy a preponderant place in discussions of gay styles, it should be remembered that recognition is just the beginning of the story clothes tell. Finding narrators who can explicate the shifting nuances through the years is an urgent priority.

One major constraint on the expression of gayness in dress was the fact that middle-class men like those who drank in the posher downtown gay bars of Montreal in the 1950s had to dress according to the limited fashions allowed for all men. Many of the narrators stressed that a suit and tie were *de rigueur* in the bars of the period, most of which were mixed spaces. This was especially so in the hotel bars, where gay men congregated at the bar itself while straights drank at the tables, supposedly oblivious to the gay scene. Len, a narrator who began to frequent gay bars in the early 1950s, explained how he dressed at the time. Of one bar, the Piccadilly Club, situated in a major downtown hotel, he said:

> I don't know if they would let you in without a shirt and tie, but in those days we all dressed up a lot more. I started work when I was 18. I wore a shirt and tie to the office every day and if you were going out anywhere very respectable in the evening, you wore a shirt and tie. Shirt and tie, sometimes with a sweater, but still wearing a shirt and tie. It made it a lot easier in some ways if all your clothes were dress-up clothes.

Correct clothing was not the only prerequisite for acceptance at the Piccadilly, however. Walter and Percy became regulars there soon after they arrived in the city in the early 1930s, and said that they had seen 'obvious' gays refused service (which they recounted with approval, taking the bartender's side). Such people would have to drink at places lower down on the social scale. The characteristic divide of the 1950s was sharpest between the jacket and tie set downtown and the work clothes and casuals of the 'Main' (Boulevard Saint-Laurent), ten blocks further east and scene of many of Michel Tremblay's dramas,[19] but each sector of these two poles of gay life at the time had its internal gradient as well. Donald said that when he got his

---

19. And twenty years later a tabloid headlined 'Les homosexuels: l'est pour les durs, l'ouest pour les raffinés,' *Photo-Journal*, 6 au 12 septembre 1971, p. 6. Roughly: 'The East is for Toughs, the West for the Refined.'

initiation into the Montreal bar scene from two queens who worked at the same department store, they told him they were only able to visit the tavern in the same hotel as the Piccadilly Club because they were with someone as respectably masculine as him. Otherwise they had to go to the Tropical Room or the Hawaiian Lounge, which were much less choosy about their customers than the hotel bars.

But by the early 1960s, there was evidence of changes in this hierarchical bar system and its fashion component. One narrator, Patrick, believed that around 1960[20] a historic change had occurred:

> . . . when gay visibility suddenly came into being. You suddenly recognized people as being gay, mostly because of what we wore, and because the cover-up of going out with girls seemed to have ceased.

They were still not out in tight white trousers, but men whom Leznoff would have called 'Coverts' felt emboldened to go to restaurants or the theatre three couples together, without the women they had formerly needed for cover. Their identity as gay was rendered even more visible by the attention to detail evident in what they wore. Such perceptions of social change, however, are notoriously unreliable, even in popular discourse. To bolster his assertion, Patrick recalled that about then he had read something in the newspaper that made him aware for the first time that not only could individuals be recognized as gay, but a crowd attending a public event could be visibly gay as well.

> I remember things like Tallulah Bankhead and Tab Hunter doing Tennessee Williams' *The Milk Train Doesn't Stop Here Any More* in New York and Ed Sullivan in his column writing: 'We haven't seen so many lavender lads out together since the last time the Ballets Russes de Monte-Carlo played New York.' And I think it was one of the first times I read in print a direct reference to the fact that a play was getting an enormous gay audience.

As an adolescent from a comfortable but confining suburb, Patrick (a native speaker of both languages thanks to mixed parentage) and his best friend had escaped early into the gay life downtown, meeting older men at the

---

20. Rubinstein's (1995:215) treatment of the history of gay visibility is quite inadequate. Basing her comments entirely on one magazine article by Michelangelo Signorile, she situates the beginning of gay visibility in the early 1980s when a new generation of 'free-spirited rebels' rejected the 'clone' look of the 1970s, which had itself replaced the preceding 'invisible' style. Rubinstein's simplistic typology fails to do justice to the complexities of gay fashion, and ignores many other earlier and contemporary styles.

train station and getting to know the tourist room circuit, as well as forming lifelong friendships among their new peer group. After becoming more established in the early 60s gay world, Patrick was not shy to experiment with dress.

> But such things! I remember going out in white trousers and having people on Sherbrooke Street spin around and gape, like . . . You couldn't be stared at like that today [1990] if you were out in flaming pink! Men wore white trousers in the country or by the sea shore but not in Montreal, in the city.

Patrick admitted that in addition to what they wore some of their behaviour was intended simply to shock. Holding hands or giving each other pet kisses on the street expressed a new impatience of young gays with the social denial of their existence.

Even without such intentions, some specific forms of attire were forbidden and could get you into trouble with the police, as Patrick and his Danish lover Nicki learned to their astonishment in about 1961:

> And Nicki getting arrested for wearing short shorts! They put him in the car and brought him home. He had to change trousers. And he was wearing just short shorts that he had brought from Europe. The police told him 'No. Get in the car.' And they drove him right up to the door. . . . And he was European. He was wearing short shorts and socks and shoes and a shirt. Wasn't at all like a display of his body!

Montreal's zealous concern with vestimentary conformity may have been uncommon among large cities,[21] but this story highlights two key elements in the meaning structures coded by gay fashion schemata: their international scope and their intergenerational variation.

In the postwar period, travel to Europe led to direct social ties, reciprocal visits and other types of connections to an extent that generations living before cheap air travel had not known. In addition to travel, international migration was also a factor in the diffusion of gay fashion networks, and perhaps a more important one, since migration tends to create long-term connections between friends left behind and new friends abroad, who can all get to meet as travel allows. Donald's account of gay life in Trinidad and Stefan's story of his move to Montreal from Berlin soon after the Second World War, illustrate the types of connections through which the international gay fashion discourse community maintained its links, as friends meet friends

---

21. These regulations were primarily intended to control feminine modesty, as Thivierge (1991) discusses.

over the decades. Secondly, Patrick's tale also reveals a way that fashion expressed intergenerational meanings. Dressing differently than your elders is a well established habit in commodity capitalist industrial societies.[22] Each wave of young gays, on arrival in the midst of the flow of gay fashion and its ongoing discourse, deliberately breaks away from the past. Mort cites the rejection of the clone look of the 1970s by young gays in Britain in the 1980s (1988:204–5). Between the generation of the fifties and that of the sixties, the fashion shift signalled more than new clothes. It marked a sudden spurt of daring to be seen.

As the 1960s advanced, a new generation began to frequent the clubs, with a generational attitude that had a lot less patience with discretion. Moreover, a new bar economy came into being with the arrival of gay-staffed, managed and eventually gay-owned bars. In all of them, while the snooty dress codes of the past disappeared, the ban on obviousness was largely held in place and the class distinction underlying the contrast between 'overts' and 'coverts' prevailed almost everywhere. Drag was rare outside the cabarets of the 'Main,' the old Red Light district where the clubs that figured in Tremblay's early work were located. In the downtown centre of gay life in the 1960s and 1970s, drag was only allowed at one club, PJs, which thus had a reputation as a lowlife hangout.

With the opening of more and more new spaces for drinking and socializing towards the end of the 1960s, fashion as a factor in public gay culture came into its own, as gay conversation came into its own in these relatively safe public spaces. Now people could get together and talk about what to wear without needing to already know someone to get invited to a private party or dinner. Conversation flowed faster than beer, in an atmosphere free from the supervision of the surly straight waiters of the past (who gave no evidence of great style sense). Much talk revolved around getting and giving advice or shopping tips, or commenting on what other people were wearing. Moreover, the bars provided gays with a place to try out new looks in safety, within the limits of the taboo on being too 'obvious' for the establishment.

When Ralph came out in 1969, and fell in with the crowd at the Café Apollo, he said, the bar had a 'family' atmosphere. The customers were a mix of:

22. Donald voiced another style choice to explain his increasing social distance from Walter and Percy, who had been his first mentors in the Montreal scene. When he and his new lover finally got to furnish their own apartment, they went more for Swedish modern than the old 'fuddy-duddy' stuffed furniture they saw at the homes of the older gays.

insurance agents, seamstresses, window decorators, waiters from other bars, professional dancers who sometimes gave social dancing lessons, cha-cha and so on, to the other customers, taxi drivers, artists . . . People brought cakes and popcorn to share. They were mostly French but spoke English.

As an anglophone, Ralph had to expand his factory French to a broader range of topics to keep up with conversation at the club. In terms of clothing, Ralph went on:

Then life became complex. I had two sets of clothing, one for work and trips home, another for the bar. I couldn't get over people wearing tank tops in the bars in mid-winter.

In the climate of Montreal, a tank top in January would be considered pure madness by most people. It is almost too symbolic: the real gay body hidden under the layers of heavy winter clothes and the layers of secrecy covering the real self. The dual sets of clothing for different publics added a metaphoric restatement of the gulf between the gay world and straight society. Ralph's comments also show the strength of style rules in the community. As in other clubs, 'obviousness' was socially devalued at the Apollo, as Ralph also stressed that it was 'important not to be effeminate'; there were effeminate types at the tables but the butches stood by the bar, a spatial separation underlining their difference.

The design of clubs in general was changing with the arrival of the discothèque at the end of the 1960s and the Apollo kept up with new trends in bar interiors. Ralph remembered the impact on fashion of the introduction of black lights:

You dressed for it. God forbid you'd wear a black sweater. There'd be no lint on it when you left home, but when you walked into the club it looked like polka dots. And people started rubbing the crotches of their pants so the white showed. You had to know how to dress. Certain prints stood out. And we discovered the effect of Murine under black light: it gave you lime green eyes.

Ralph's 'we' in this context is direct testimony to the group process that underlay the fashioning of style in this very specific socio-cultural microcosm. His testimony is a direct reference to the way collective ideas about fashion develop in the course of ordinary social encounters.

The new discourse community model can be connected to a much older concept of 'circles of opinion' advanced by Mills (1963:591). In these circles, there was an 'opinion leader' who channelled the reactions of their group to media-carried messages, doubtless including opinions on what people wore or should wear (pp. 593–4). In gay social groups, which functioned with increasing openness in the new gay spaces across North America, it would be easy to discern such circles and their opinion leaders helping to shape gay fashion. An important feature of the opinion circle is, Mills explains, that it can act as a site of resistance to the dominance of media influence on the 'primary public' of the circle. For gay men merely having a style that was not 'no-style' was resistance, a political response to ostracism and cultural invisibility.

Resistance also found expression in parodies of mainstream messages. When black light came to the Apollo, not only did Ralph's 'gang' follow the general switch to jeans that swept all of their generation, they took to brushing and soaking these icons of rough masculinity to heighten the message of sexual availability and sexual freedom. They took ghoulish delight in using eye drops under black light to give their eyes a greenish tinge. This insider game could have awkward consequences, as Ralph recalled:

> We had a lot of fun around black light, but it could make you look awfully silly. I remember one time I cruised someone all night until the waiter André came up to me and said 'Jesus, Ralph, what's on your face? The Murine had run down my cheeks in lurid green streaks. And I had spent hours talking to the guy and wondering why he didn't respond.

Ralph's description provides a good example of the expressive use of fashion and style among gays as a focus of collective attention, similar to the British youth style subcultures described by Hebdige (1979); groups like the Teds, Rockers, Skins, and so on, developed clothing styles to express their identity, in some cases mining upper-class fashions of the past in their self-affirming *bricolage*. Collective selfhood is made manifest in the clothes, but the clothes depend on the shared discourse that surrounds them and on the discourse's underlying schematic structures to achieve their symbolic function of group identity.

Much more than the old flaming queen fashions of the past, for which the primary audience was outsiders, now fashion play, fashion work and fashion talk came to be recognized as an expression of gay community. The late 1960s androgynous gay hippie look was followed by the new masculine 'clone look' of the early 1970s, which in turn gave way to the radical clone of the 1980s. Dyer recalls the sixties rise of colourful Carnaby Street boutique styles: 'My most delirious memory of indubitably queer gear passing if not unnoticed then at any rate unmolested is strolling out of a Carnaby Street boutique and through London in a newly acquired pair of white lace trousers' (Dyer 1994:184). He describes this period as the last fling of a gay male style which involved 'incorporating the feminine into male clothing' before the move to the new phase of 'quoting male styles'. The move to the masculine clone was not without its critics. Fernbach (1981:101) expresses the dim view many in the 1970s radical gay movement took of the rise of the 'clone' look. Though he suggests that this is the result of general changes in masculinity, he says:

> Yet this is not sufficient to explain the pronounced 'butch shift' that has taken place in the gay subculture in the last few years, the emergence of the clone look, the denim and leather cult, even the rise of sadomasochism. . . . It is indeed sad, and more than a little ridiculous, that large numbers of gay men feel the need to adopt the external signs of masculine toughness, to dress as cowboys, policemen, soldiers, even Nazis (1981:101).

He sees but does not appreciate the importance of the recognition among gay men that the change was one of image only, and thus neglects to see it as a symbolic expression of community.

> Yet the 'butch shift' does not signify, except for perhaps a tiny minority of gay men, any serious attempt to repress their effeminacy and rejoin the male club on the most traditional terms. The fact that in San Francisco, for example, where this tendency is most extreme, you can tell a gay man from a straight man by the gay man's more 'masculine' appearance, should precisely be taken for the surface appearance that it is . . . The 'butch shift', then, is simply a ploy designed to heighten sexual tension among gay men by presenting an image of masculinity designed to fit the fantasy of a 'man' (Fernbach 1981:101).

Here we are to understand that sexual ploys are unworthy of us, in keeping with the opposition to sexual objectification that was current in the androgynous period.[23] This view was not shared by the majority who were certainly interested in 'heightening sexual tension' by any means at their disposal.

At each stage then, successive younger generations have contributed their fashion schemata and discourse to an already considerable array of other discursive foci in an emerging conversation that binds together the gay community. Paradoxically, while Innis (1951:75; 89) has pointed out that in our space-oriented society, fashion reflects the dominant conception of time as a series of brief flashes, as a discourse topic, fashion (at least in the gay community) can be seen also as the focal point for a process of ongoing

---

23. Montreal's lesbian and gay bookstore, founded in 1973, was (and still is) called Androgyny/L'Androgyne.

community self-awareness, a collective identity anchored in the other sort of time, that of duration, of permanence. The clothes change but the conversation continues.

Conclusion

In this paper I have argued that the stereotypic assumption that fashion is in some sense a 'gay domain' or employment ghetto needs to be handled with caution. We have also seen that fashion is a gay consumer interest and therefore a topic of discussion grounded in shared knowledge and value orientations, which was as important as a topical focus around which a distinctly gay social voice formed as the developing network of gay bars, where many conversations about style and clothes shopping no doubt took place. In both cases there was a conjunction of economics with the emergence of a shared symbolic universe, the dual development which marked the collective construction of the public gay community in mid-twentieth century Western urban societies.

Clearly the material presented here is just the beginning of long-term research both on the work of gay men in various segments of the fashion industry and on the symbolic uses to which fashion is put among gays to express their identity. As a salient aspect of gay relations with society, fashion should be a key area for research rather than being regarded as a frivolous domain with little to offer scholars. Fortunately such attitudes are retreating and we can begin to envisage a general view of the political economy of gay life, and perhaps move on to examine some of the other interesting questions which are arising from the emerging synthesis of recent work in gay ethnography. Does, for example, the presence or absence in a city of a garment industry (or other buyers of design skills) have an impact on the configuration of the local gay community?

Studying the international diffusion of gay fashion could be a key indicator in understanding its concomitant: the international spread of the idea of a gay identity to countries like Mexico or India, where it has made itself a place alongside the established sex/gender systems of these cultures, as has been increasingly apparent since 1980. Another crucial aspect of the consumption side of fashion and the role it plays in the pragmatics of group identity in mass society is the set of meanings attached by the generations to fashion. With the appearance of the 'new men,' a new set of questions have opened concerning the symbolic analysis of fashion and issues of the gender politics which underlie fashion choices. As I suggested at the outset, men have long wielded their disinterest in fashion as a weapon over women, who are stereotyped as fashion-obsessed, while men don't (mustn't) care how they look. Communications research since the rise of feminist theory has, as Pumphrey (1989) recalls, highlighted the gendered nature of the gaze, of who looks at whom, coding the opposition of female object and male subject, male as the unmarked category, the watcher, female as different, marked, the prey. Much of Pumphrey's analysis suggests essential areas to explore at the intersection of mass media, personal self-image, masculinity and sexual orientation.

Although I have considered gay men working in the industry separately from my discussion of fashion as content for shared discourse and schemata construction among gay men, what links can be found between the two aspects of gay men's relations to fashion? Ralph's story of black light at the Apollo suggests a connection between the two. It was not only of interest because it showed the peer group which he joined as a collective fashion 'circle of opinion' alone. Ralph worked in fashion and was clearly influenced in his professional life by the fashion discourse of the Apollo and its successor bars of the 1970s and 1980s, as well as by the flourishing gay press and clothing stores in the gay shopping districts found in most major cities today. Later, as a clothing manufacturer himself, this context influenced Ralph to reorient his business to supply the new fashion niche. The perception of the new gay market was an element in the worldwide changes effected as a new generation of internationally famous designers reshaped the industrial and commercial organization of the fashion business. While the larger scale of this change lies beyond the scope of this paper, I want to emphasize the continuity between gay fashion discourse and the discursive environment in which any industry shapes itself and evolves.

This discussion could be expanded to include two other aspects of gay men's relationship to fashion. In light of both the role of gays in the fashion industry, and the accepted perception that gay men act as style-conscious, to what extent do gays influence men's fashions overall? Dyer (1994) suggests that since concern with appearance in a man has itself been considered a sign of homosexuality, heterosexual men have generally left decisions about what to wear, how to decorate the house, and so forth, to mothers, sisters and wives. Since women shopping for their men have not been able to try fashions out, nor to pioneer new styles, gay men have had an influence beyond their numbers in setting trends which, despite resistance, have ended up changing fashions for all men. With a closer study of the discursive processes and their economic concomitants in the industry, we have some hope of shedding light on this question.

A final aspect of the connection between gay men and the fashion world that could be explored is the link with show business. Comments made by one of Montreal's best known gay entertainers, Armand Monroe, who was the host at the Tropical Room and later at PJs bar in downtown Montreal over the course of three decades, highlighted the advantage for a performer to be well connected with the world of designers, since he said on different occasions he was 'dressed' by one or another of the local gay designers. A photograph of the all-gay staff of PJs in about 1969 shows a group of young men in rainbow coloured lamé kaftans, no doubt the work of one of his well-placed friends. Here is another web of social connections within which the gay world intersects with the fashion world which needs to be examined.

Today there is still a gay style, a certain way of wearing tight pants, that not only gets the looks, but broadcasts one's commitment to the universe of gay fashion. We need to know more about how fashion decisions are effected and enforced and updated in social groups like the gay world, and I want to close with an urging to ethnography. Explorations of the fashion connection lead to investigations of many aspects of the social organization based on sexual organization and contribute to the emerging gay political economy. All the fine-tuned semiotic statements based on a limited set of cultural productions cannot afford the authority of actually finding out what people in the population say and do in a particular area of life. Studying how schemata are shared in circles of gay opinion, of fashion opinion or in politics gives us a new and, I argue, effective tool for gaining deeper insight into central social practices of meaning which affect the evolution of social wholes or communities of all kinds.

Bibliography

Anomaly (1948), *The Invert and His Social Adjustment* (Sec. ed.). London: Baillière, Tyndall, and Cox.

Beauregard, Yves, Alain Duchesneau and Jocelyne Nadeau (1988), 'Vingt-cinq années de carrière: Entrevue avec le couturier Michel Robichaud,' *Cap-aux-Diamants*, 4(2):63–8.

Bender, Marylin (1967), *The Beautiful People*. New York: Coward-McCann, Inc.

Bergman, David (1993), *Camp Grounds: Style and Homosexuality*. Amherst: University of Massachusetts Press.

Beyond the Fringe (n.d. [1962]), Original Broadway Cast. 'Full Dimensional Stereo' recording. Comedy revue with Alan Bennett, Peter Cook, Jonathan Miller, and Dudley Moore, Edinburgh 1960, London 1961, New York 1962.

Blachford, Gregg (1981), 'Male Dominance and the Gay World.' In Kenneth Plummer (ed.), *The Making of the Modern Homosexual*. London: Hutchinson.

Bullough, Vern L. (1976), *Sexual Variance in Society and History*. Chicago: University of Chicago Press.

Burnham, John (1973), 'Early References to Homosexual Communities in American Medical Writings,' *Medical Aspects of Human Sexuality,* 7:34–5; 40–9.

Charest, Nicole (1988), *Michel Robichaud: Monsieur Mode.* Montreal: Éditions de l'homme.

Chauncey, George (1994), *Gay New York: Gender, Urban Culture and the Making of the Gay Male World 1890–1940.* New York: Basic Books.

Cohen, Derek and Richard Dyer (1980), 'The Politics of Gay Culture,' in Gay Left Collective, *Homosexuality: Power and Politics.* London: Allison & Busby.

Coleridge, Nicholas (1988), *The Fashion Conspiracy: The Dazzling Inside Story of the Glamorous World of International High Fashion.* New York: Harper & Row.

Craik, Jennifer (1994), *The Face of Fashion: Cultural Studies in Fashion.* London: Routledge.

Crisp, Quentin (1968), *The Naked Civil Servant.* London: Jonathan Cape Ltd.

D'Andrade, Roy (1995), *The Development of Cognitive Anthropology.* Cambridge: Cambridge University Press.

—— and Claudia Strauss (eds) (1992), *Human Motives and Cultural Models.* Cambridge: Cambridge University Press.

D'Arcangelo, Angelo (1968 [1969]), *The Homosexual Handbook.* New York: Ophelia Press.

D'Emilio, John (1983), *Sexual Politics, Sexual Communities: The Making of a Homosexual Minority in the United States, 1940–1970.* Chicago: University of Chicago Press.

Dunk, Thomas (1991), *It's a Working Man's Town: Male Working-class Culture in Northwestern Ontario.* Montreal: McGill-Queen's University Press.

Dyer, Richard, (1994), 'Fashioning Change: Gay Men's Style.' In Emma Healey and Angela Mason, (eds) *Stonewall 25: The Making of the Lesbian and Gay Community in Britain.* London: Virago Press.

Ellis, Havelock (1936), 'Sexual Inversion.' In Havelock Ellis, *Studies in the Psychology of Sex,* vol. 2 part 2. New York: Random House.

Fernbach, David. (1981), *The Spiral Path: A Gay Contribution to Human Survival.* London and Boston: Gay Men's Press and Alyson Publications.

Gidlow, Elsa (1986), *Elsa, I Come with My Songs: The Autobiography of Elsa Gidlow.* San Francisco: Booklegger Press.

Grahn, Judy (1990 (1984)), *Another Mother Tongue: Gay Words, Gay Worlds* (rev. ed.). Boston: Beacon Press.

Guernsey, Betty (1982), *Gaby: The Life and Times of Gaby Bernier, Couturière Extraordinaire.* Toronto: Marincourt Press Ltd..

Hebdige, Dick (1979), *Subculture: The Meaning of Style.* London: Methuen.

Henley, Clark (1982), *The Butch Manual: The Current Drag and How to Do It.* New York: New American Library.

Higgins, Ross (1995), 'Murder Will Out: Gay Identity and Media Discourse in Montreal.' In William L.Leap (ed.), *Beyond the Lavender Lexicon: Authenticity, Imagination, and Appropriation in Lesbian and Gay Languages.* New York: Gordon and Breach.

—— and Line Chamberland (1992), 'Mixed Messages: Gays and Lesbians in Montreal Yellow Papers in the 1950s.' In Ian McKay (ed.), *The Challenge of Modernity: A Reader on Post- Confederation Canada*. Toronto: McGraw-Hill Ryerson.

Humphreys, Laud (1972), 'New Styles in Homosexual Manliness.' In Joseph A. McCaffrey (ed.), *The Homosexual Dialectic*. Englewood Cliffs, N.J.: Prentice-Hall.

Humphries, Martin (1985), 'Gay Machismo.' In Andy Metcalf and Martin Humphries (eds), *The Sexuality of Men*. London: Pluto Press.

Innis, Harold (1951), *The Bias of Communication*. Toronto: University of Toronto Press.

Karlen, Arno (1971), *Sexuality and Homosexuality: A New View*. New York: W.W. Norton & Co. Inc.

Katz, Jonathan (1976), *Gay American History: Lesbians and Gay Men in the U.S.A.* New York: Crowell.

Keller, Janet Dixon (1992), 'Schemas for Schemata.' In Theodore Schwartz, Geoffrey M. White and Catherine A. Lutz (eds), *New Directions in Psychological Anthropology*. Cambridge: Cambridge University Press.

Lacelle, Nicole (1988), *Madeleine Parent, Léa Roback: Entretiens avec Nicole Lacelle*. Montréal: Les Éditions du remue-ménage.

Lacoste, Norbert (1958), *Les caractéristiques sociales de la population du Grand Montréal*. Montréal: Université de Montréal, Faculté des Sciences sociales, économiques et politiques.

Leznoff, Maurice (1954), 'The Homosexual in Urban Society.' M.A. thesis: McGill University, Montreal, Department of Sociology.

Loovis, David (1974), *Gay Spirit: A Guide to Becoming a Sensuous Homosexual*. New York: Grove Press.

Mast, Gerald (1987), *Can't Help Singin': The American Musical on Stage and Screen*. Woodstock, N.Y.: The Overlook Press.

Meyer, Moe (1994), *The Politics and Poetics of Camp*. London: Routledge.

Mills, C. Wright (1950 (1963)), 'Mass Media and Public Opinion.' In Mills (Horowitz, ed.), *Power, Politics and People*, Oxford: Oxford University Press.

Mort, Frank (1988), 'Boy's Own? Masculinity, Style and Popular Culture.' In Rowena Chapman and Jonathan Rutherford (eds), *Male Order: Unwrapping Masculinity*. London: Lawrence and Wishart.

Pollak, Michael (1988), *Les homosexuels et le SIDA: sociologie d'une épidémie*. Paris: A.M. Métailié.

Pumphrey, M. (1989), 'Why do cowboys wear hats in the bath: Style politics for the older man,' *Critical Quarterly*, 31(3):78–100.

Rubin, Gayle (1975), 'The Traffic in Women: Notes on the "Political Economy" of Sex.' In Reyna Reiter (ed.), *Toward an Anthropology of Women*. New York: Monthly Review Press.

Rubinstein, Ruth P. (1995), *Dress Codes: Meanings and Messages in American Culture*. Boulder, Colorado: Westview Press.

Sontag, Susan (1966), 'Notes on "Camp".' In Susan Sontag, *Against Interpretation and other Essays*. New York: Farrar, Strauss and Giroux.

Spencer, Neil (1993), 'Menswear in the 1980s: Revolt into Conformity.' In Juliet Ash and Elizabeth Wilson (eds), *Chic Thrills: A Fashion Reader*. Berkeley: University of California Press.

Swales, John M. (1990), *Genre Analysis: English in Academic and Research Settings*. Cambridge: Cambridge University Press.

Thivierge, Nicole (1991), Modes et modestie féminine.' *Cultures du Canada français*, 8:18–29.

Tremblay, Michel (1982), *La duchesse et le roturier* (roman), Montreal: Leméac.

Waugh, Thomas (1996), *Hard To Imagine: Gay Male Eroticism in Photography and Film From Their Beginnings to Stonewall*. New York: Columbia University Press.

Willis, Paul (1990), *Common Culture: Symbolic Work at Play in the Everyday Cultures of the Young*. Milton Keynes: Open University Press.

9

A Tale of Three Louis: Ambiguity, Masculinity and the Bowtie

Rob Shields

Waiter, Bouncer, Musician, Architect, Magician, Academic . . . Who wears bowties? There is a masculine mythology surrounding the bowtie itself and men who wear it. The bowtie is an accessory or ornament with unrivalled connotations, both positive and negative. It is heavily overcoded with signifiers of both arrogance and enslavement; of both masculinity and femininity; of both nobility and servitude. Even in its cultures of origin, it has been the exception for men to wear a bowtie. It has always been remarkable, extraordinary and provocative. The bowtie is outside the everyday dress codes, what Victor Turner would have called a 'liminal zone' at the neck (Turner 1979). Just wearing a bowtie is to be dressed in a mantle of contradictory signification; it is to locate oneself at an unstable nexus of a contradictory flow of sense and sensuality. No other accessory in the male wardrobe is as ambiguous, as concealing of intention. No other item is as threatening. Surprisingly, however, there is almost nothing in print on this clothing ornament. Where does the bowtie stand in the pantheon of symbols of masculinity or the lack thereof?

This chapter is a 'tale of three Louis' which examines the history of the bowtie and its meanings in relation to male gender and to the male body, stretching back from Louis Farrakhan, through the architect, Louis Kahn, to Louis XIV. These three exemplars, taken *sub speciae aeternitatis*, with a supporting cast of aristocrats and waiters, professionals and hand-puppets, sorcerers and their apprentices, provide the contrasting elements of an interpretation of the ambiguity of the bowtie, rather than a documented history of a form of dress or a specific article of clothing. Thus, we are less concerned with cloth and historical correctness than with the imaginary 'range' of the bowtie; that is, its ability to serve as an indicator of diametrically opposed meanings, wearer-characteristics, and their personae. A Bachelardian phenomenology of clothing is called for (cf. 1961). How does the bowtie do this? Could its relation to the body of its wearer provide part of the answer?

Louis XIV and the Butterfly Knot

The origin of the bowtie is reputed to go back to the style of a cravat adopted by Louis XIV of France after the uniform of his Croatian mercenaries, called *cravates*. For the soldiers, the bowtie was a lucky charm against decapitation. Louis XIV adopted their white kerchief with added lace and secured it with a small bow at the front (Spooner 1995:48). Over time, this kerchief narrowed and the lace was removed to become the *'noeud papillon'*, the familiar bowtie, worn in front of the collar. The cravat itself became a separate item worn under the collar, with its bow concealed beneath a larger scarf of material tucked under the shirt.

The roots of the bowtie are thus overwritten with royal associations, and indeed, this may only be one of several origins, and may only be a survivor fragment of aristocratic and fashion-industry myth-making and self-legitimation. Its functionality is also overlaid with superstition. As a result, even as the Croatian-soldiers' kerchief, the knotted cloth about the neck signified something beyond itself, beyond its own presence and possible functionality. This surplus of meaning imbues the bowtie with ambiguity: it is both what I will call 'the uniform' (Joseph 1986) of the servant (for example, the *cravate* soldier or a waiter) and it is also part of what I will call 'the costume' of the aristocratic and extraordinary (for example, Louis XIV, a famous lawyer or a well-known orchestra maestro, might well be seen wearing this sign of the extraordinary in images of their day-to-day work). Reduced to any single meaning at the expense of the others, the bowtie appears ridiculous. Yet, if the constellation of contradictory meanings can be kept aloft, so to speak, then the bowtie and its wearer appear to have a flair that is exactly an ambiguous *'je ne sais quoi'*. The bowtie becomes a sign that there is an ineffable 'something more' to the wearer. The ambiguity of this article of clothing's meaning is transferable to its wearer.

Round about the Neck

In some ways, the history of clothing is marked out by the treatment of the neck. The bowtie has been as central to this history as the collar itself or the contemporary necktie. Like hemlines, the bows have been bigger or smaller, obscured the neck with high collars, or revealed it with diminutive bows under turned-down collars. Large, soft, velvety bows appear to be associated with femininity and appear often in images of its exemplars. Thus, to limit our discussion to men in Europe and North America, what bowties can be found in images of culturally-exemplary males? Abraham Lincoln is iconically portrayed as a rugged face sporting a black bowtie and collars turned down. Noble gentlemen and nineteenth-century dandies are said to have sported small bows with winged collars turned up. We find portraits of Oscar Wilde, a famous dandy, sporting such a discreet bowtie (Bristow 1994). A contemporary arbiter of taste, Alan Flusser notes: 'The general rule of thumb states that bowties should never be broader than the widest part of the neck and should never extend beyond the outside of the points of the collar' (Flusser 1985, cited in Spooner 1995:49).

For the purposes of argument, this might serve as a definition of the masculine bow: a performance standard independent of cloth, texture, colour, pattern or even the particulars of the knotting itself and of whether or not the bowtie is clipped on to the collar with mechanical clamps, pre-tied and sewn onto an adjustable strap, or tied and adjusted entirely by hand. Who ties the bow is also not specified, suggesting that the wearer need not actually have tied or even know how to re-tie the bow. Knowledge of the knot itself is presumed, as is knowledge of what a correctly adjusted bowtie might look like – only dimensions and spatial relations are specified.

Most systems for knotting a bowtie drape a strip of cloth around the neck, falling on either side. One end of the cloth is folded back on itself about 15cm and held across the throat. The other end of the cloth is brought over the centre of this folded portion and looped back under and over it once to form a central knot. The free end is folded itself so that the leading edge of the fold can be tucked, folded edge first, behind the existing fold and through the knot, so that the fold ends up protruding on the opposite side of the knot to the first fold, giving a symmetrically constructed bowtie. Thus most approaches construct a type of double-bow: the two ends of the cloth end up sticking out along with a loop each on either side of the knot. Should these ends be aligned with the folds they fall with in order to adjust the bow neatly? Should the bowtie be symmetrical about the centre loop? Should the axis of the bowtie be straight (in line with the shoulders)? Flusser limits himself to the extent to which the folds or 'bows' should be pulled out in a concluding adjustment. The 'look' is everything.

What is the importance of the neck? While the Croatian *cravates* of the 1600s wore their bowtie-kerchiefs as a charm against sword cuts, the neck is a famously vulnerable part of the body for any person or mammal. The tenderness of the skin, its vulnerability to cold, the relatively fragile structure of the spine, and the exposure of the jugular vein are all features which make the neck a key area of attention for the comfort and security of the body. The cultural history of the neck extends this pragmatic fuss over this part of the body. It is not only the 'site' of charms, whether the *cravates'* kerchiefs, religious medals, mementos of self-identity or ornamental rings of beaded strands. The neck is also the object of charms itself: an erogenous zone to be stimulated, stroked and gazed upon. It is a fetish zone and object. Hence the 'charm' of the eroticized neck (e.g. some have commented on 'the lesbian neck' fetish). A curious agreement appears to exist about this. This is more than intersubjective: it appears to extend to what might be called an *intercorporeal* agreement (Game 1996), based on generalizing one's own sensations to others.

This excursus on the neck is important for understanding the conventional definitions of the meaning of the bowtie. Flusser describes the contemporary, 'discreet bowtie' worn with turned down collar tabs (in contrast to the now weddings-only type of formal shirt with a turned-up collar) which does not conceal but rather draws attention to the neck. I will argue that the manner in which the neck is displayed is a crucial detail that inflects the knot with meaning beyond pattern and colour. The relationship between the size of the bow and its wearer's neck appears central to its meaning. Thus, the 'display' and performance of the bowtied male is as much a matter of stance, carriage of the head and posture as it is a question of knots and the size of loops. This 'display' may be accomplished either through the cut and size of the collar, or of the bow, or through the angle of the chin itself. The ambiguous social status of the bowtied-male (servant or patron?) makes the meaning of the bowtie inherently reversible. It can thus be called a liminal signifier, as if on a threshold (*limen*) turned, Janus-like, into both spaces. It is, in Victor Turner's phrase, 'betwixt and between' (1979). Its meaning is susceptible to inversion through rhetoric: the wearer who wishes to appear aristocratic can be lampooned as merely a formally-dressed servant. The wearer can make one of the errors in pragmatic dress codes which Flusser warns of. The meaning can also be inverted depending on the performative competence of the wearer: the bowtie is as much the costume of the professional who wishes to be taken seriously and stand out (see below) as the 'uniform' of the comedian. Or, misunderstandings can be the source of unexpected meanings, as the context in which the wearer sports a bowtie moderates its meaning and the 'image' of the wearer (Davis 1991).

If the liminality of the bowtie is in part linked to the liminal charm-zone of the neck, the bowtie also lies on the corporeal *limen* between the torso and head. Therefore, two axes of liminality might usefully be described (See

Figure 9.1): one, the vertical axis of relations across a spatial threshold such as the neck; the other, the horizontal axis of symbolic meanings about a transition point of complete ambiguity. In the examples discussed above, this 'symbolic axis' of reversible meanings relates to the vertical axis as time relates to space. The spatial axis concerns the relative position of bodies, places and zones – of the head, the neck and the torso. The horizontal, temporalized axis concerns the reversibility of meaning and states from moment to moment as the bowtie is performed and re-coded, its meaning hijacked and re-coded back to the original meaning once again.

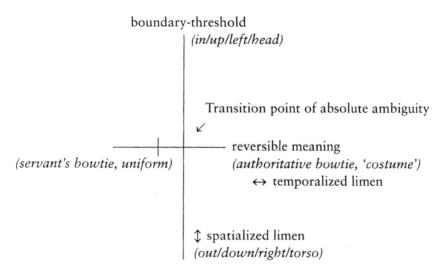

Figure 9.1. Axes of Liminality.

Servants and Masters

As a sumptuary ornament the bowtie has often been used to mark its wearer as someone above the mundane and banal – as a distinguished person. Nobility thus remains a key connotation. The bowtie is 'too special' for most contexts. The contemporary man wearing a bowtie is often accused of snobbery, elitism, of 'putting on airs' and of being 'overdressed'. Being 'overdressed' in a bowtie is hardly to be, for example, too warm or to be simply wearing too many pieces of clothing. The ambiguity of the bowtie is often interpreted within, for example, Anglophone-North American culture, as a signifier of falsity, of Gide-ism, of the dandy whose sincerity is doubted because he cares more for himself than his social relations. Popular opinion suggests that a bowtie shouldn't be worn to a job interview because the wearer may be interpreted as conceited. Is it because its ambiguity is threatening? The 'over'-dressed status relates exactly to the symbolic axis of the bowtie and the reversibility of meaning from one pole (the aristocratic and authoritative) to the other (the servile and uniform). For, in practice, the ambiguity of the bowtie operates in both directions, making the familiar extravagant . . . and also making patrons appear like waiters, clowns or another type of servant and vice versa. In a restaurant or at a formal reception, is the wearer a waiter or a noted patron?

As worn by Charlie McCarthy, the 1950s black-bowtied ventriloquist's dummy or hand-puppet, the bowtie was part of the image of the non-autonomy of a puppet. Ventriloquized, spoken for by a master, and animated by the puppeteer's hand, much of the repartee of this act played on the dummy's direct or indirect proclamations of autonomy and autonomous judgement. The ventriloquist, who operated the puppet as well, played the role of the doubting but dispassionate, reflective interlocutor. Even though the puppet's assumptions of his own autonomy are never directly challenged, the puppet's status is an 'in-joke' shared by the ventriloquist and a knowing-audience. The joke is 'on' the bowtied puppet who is in fact tied hand, foot and mouth to the ventriloquist. Like a clip-on bowtie, the puppet is always clearly just a dummy dressed in the 'costume' of the master.

The bowtie, especially the black bowtie in all its clip-on variations, has proven the preferred *'uniform'* of svelte waiters, obsequious butlers, scrambling bag boys and threatening bouncers: the bowtie is the essential element of a uniform that signifies servitude. It candy-coats the bouncer's threat in the uniform of polite service and chokes off the personal opinions of those in the hospitality industries by clothing them in a uniform and anonymous shell. The 'uniform', below the neck, predominates over any independent thoughts, actions or individual faciality (Deleuze and Guattari 1976) above the neck. The distinction between the 'uniform' and the 'costume' rides on not only the reversible meanings of one axis but the bowtie's associations with the spatial zones of the vertical axis of liminality.

In a performative economy of bodies and signs the bowtie is, in effect, a double-sided index. The instability of its meanings requires a constant effort of maintenance and is always at risk of rhetorical manipulation by *ad hominem* comments. Whereas Flusser discusses the appropriate looping of the bowtie, the key reference is to the wearer's body. His concern is truly *ad hominem*, with the wearer's corporeal embodiment, the coordination of body parts and its performance (Shields 1997). The bowtie-wearer risks being denigrated as attempting to conceal his low economic status or as not having the necessary social status. The bowtie in this case is not just a strategic uniform but an individual *tactic* which has to be 'carried off' by the wearer (DeCerteau 1984). Few of its wearers are fully in control of its meanings. Consider Mickey Mouse – another type of exemplary male (if not by body, by nomenclature and prodigal son-in-the-father's house). In the Walt Disney cartoon 'The Sorcerer's Apprentice' Mickey sports the same bowtied costume as his sorcerer-master, but it proves to be nothing more than a 'uniform' as Mickey loses control of his spells. The apprentice's conjuring commands *him* and determines his action, rather than the other way around. Mickey is shown to be another type of automaton or dummy. The inept sorcerer is soon a victim of his conjuring – and a 'fashion victim' of the bowtie's duplicitous meanings.

The bowtie-as-uniform standardizes the human contact-point of large service corporations who wish to evoke a formal tradition of the nineteenth-century man-servant's relation to his aristocratic employer (gender intended). As opposed to those servants merely engaged to carry out a function, the bowtied man-servant was the personal assistant of the aristocrat and often a trusted proxy in charge of other servants. The contemporary correlate of the bowtied servant is often tied to the semiotic elevation of the status of customer to that of 'master'. This illusion is not a simple prank that beguiles the flattered client. Like the clip-on bowtie, the taxonomic identity of the 'servant' is also 'clipped-on'. The performance of the master and servant relation consists of a complex and delicate performance fraught with opportunities for shattering the illusion. To remain intact, it must 'float', chiffon-like, on a supporting set of gestures of trustworthiness by the servant and delegation by the customer. These are 'gestural' in that they are knowingly understood to be partial performances. For example, a customer at a restaurant may accept the recommendation of the waiter, or a nightclub patron may defer to the authority or instructions given by bouncers. In this situation of 'ironic complicity' (Shields 1989) neither interactant abandons his socioeconomic interest, but rather elaborates a tangential, short-term relationship which is no more than evocative of the lifetime association of master and servant. At the close of, for example, a restaurant meal, the performance comes to a ritualized end with the presentation of the bill – with that great consumer flourish – the credit card which allows the monetary transaction to be ritually hidden.

What then of the bowtie's importance in male formal-wear and in lesbian cross-dressing (Doherty 1995; Fillinyeh 1995; Polhemus 1978)? How does the appearance of 'elegance' of the bowtie operate? For men, the bowtie is the single most important sumptuary accessory to convey an impression of special dress, of the extraordinary, of the formal occasion and the 'elegance' demanded for such events. While the elegance of a man's dress may arguably lie in the cut of suits or even coats, the bowtie is the element which directly proclaims the importance of the occasion, switching a merely nice suit into a 'formal suit'. Yet, even here, the meaning of the bowtie is ambiguous.

Consider, for example, the case of male formal-wear advertising in the twentieth century. The images in such advertisements depict clean shaven, short-haired and often pomaded young, apparently fit, Caucasian males. In general terms they smile, posed in a relaxed and confident manner often with at least one hand in a pocket. They look directly at the camera (and thus at the viewer), yet they are inattentive. They lounge; contrary to the formal implications of their dress they apparently do not attend to their comportment. Swathed in the constricting clothing of discipline, they are momentarily – arrogantly – undisciplined in their poses. The implication of power and prestige derives partly from the ease and comfort they project even while wearing constricting clothes. The bowties can even be undone, un-tied, in these images.

But, the models also smile and look downward in these images: their heads tilted down, necks obscured by square chins. Bent slightly forward, the musculature of their torsos is softened by the folds of generously-cut shirts which are furthermore often pleated. There is a coy shyness to this pose. The effect is to 'sweeten' their appearance: they are 'sweet guys', generally posed together in homoerotic photographs of camaraderie. They are not attentive servants, their composure belies the restrictions of their unusual costume – it is not their habitual uniform. Carefully posed, only the best image of thousands of photos taken in one fashion-shoot is presented. Their stances, the distribution of weight and the coordination between bodies in group photos, indicate their pleasure in the moment: they are at leisure (Rojek 1985; Shields 1997). Elegance achieved in spite of itself, and in this sense 'grace' (understood by Matisse as beauty which has been hidden), is thus a central meaning that can be read from these images. The bowtie or, as more evocatively named, the butterfly-knot, has a long association with grace and lightness.

Louis I. Kahn and the Loop

Centuries after Louis XIV's court-dress innovation, an architect equally obsessed with form, became one of the definitive professionals to wear a bowtie. Since the nineteenth century, painters and tradesmen had worn forms of the bowtie which did not pose any risk of trailing on a canvas or drawing.[1] While some may be familiar with portraits of the French painter Cézanne wearing a loose bow, the famous architectural 'loop' was that of Louis Kahn, the Chicago architect. Bowties flourished in the last decades of the nineteenth century – the high point of the 'Chicago-style' where the skyscraper was invented to fit large businesses into the limited central business district of 'The Loop'. This was Chicago's downtown area delimited on either side by the Illinois River and fronting Lake Michigan. Those large buildings fitted an aggressive business style, to which the bowtie was an ideal counterfoil.

Consider, then, this 'aggressive' bowtie wearer, who strikes an entirely different pose from the aristocrat on the one hand, or the waiter, Charlie McCarthy or the coy formal-wear models on the other. The wearer is often caught in a photojournalist's snapshot: standing with weight balanced, often caught in the midst of a gesture. A middle-aged male, sometimes bearded or grizzled, holds his chin up: the bowtie exposes the neck and chest and presides over a sometimes massive gut. On the other hand one expects revulsion as the prime reaction in a weight-obsessed culture. However, this 'over dressed stomach' below the bowtie can also become the embodiment of authority: a signifier of status and corporealized power. This is also a form of conspicuous expression of class power to over-consume.

Rather than elegant, this is an authoritative loop. The aggressive, bowtied protagonist is a specific assemblage of the body and its ornamentation into a pose completed by the symbolic folds of the bowtie as a marker of prestige. The special significance of this aggressive figure, however, is its link to *bourgeois aggression*. Authority and prestige gloss the nearness of the wearer to the struggle to secure social power and his awareness of this. This is the food-chain struggle to appropriate surplus value and the material wealth which takes the form of not only capital but the *materiel* of reproduction (Lefebvre 1991): the basics of nourishment.

The unusually ambiguous quality of the bowtie has allowed it to act as

---

1. This middle class of bowtie is not simply functional. If it is reduced to its function of 'not trailing' then it again appears a ridiculous concession to a social injunction to wear something at the neck: as a friend jokes, 'bowties make me think of gynaecologists'. The wry hilarity of this comment is that it casts any male in sight wearing a bowtie as 'a gynaecologist', and winks at women's in-group knowledge of the social and bodily discomfort of a gynaecological examination, smuggling another register – what Bakhtin called the carnivalesque 'lower bodily stratum' – into polite conversation (Bakhtin 1973; Cronin 1996). The joke doubles in its destabilizing force amongst those who are part of its knowing-audience by disrupting all semiotic pretence if a bowtied male interjects with 'I don't understand.' From elegant, authoritative figure, the bowtied male fails in such cases to juggle all the meanings and interpretations the bowtie can elicit and drops into a category similar to 'Charlie McCarthy', losing face through semiotic ineptitude and performative incompetence.

an affirmation of rebellious individuality. Despite its aggressiveness and assertion of extra-ordinariness and non-conformism, the wearer appears to maintain his investment in social status and thus in the normative regime of the status quo. In opposition to many proletarian radicals' investment in self-effacing everyday garb of collectivism, the bowtie indicates the self-interest and power of the 'maestro'. Power – cultural as much as economic – is not in this case delegated but 'held' and concentrated – much as a sorcerer might 'hold' a magical spell before it is cast. Architects fall into this threshold or liminal category between the servant and the master: they are both. Musicians are another example. On the one hand they are paid servants, yet on the other hand they are masters of a craft, 'geniuses', whose ability is prized beyond their own loyalty to a master. In this reading, they are, by definition, ambitious, for they are driven to excel and distinguish themselves performatively. They hold cultural power in the form of abilities, not just as 'cultural capital' (cf. Bourdieu 1984). The bowtie marks a middle class of men who have higher cultural and social status, above and beyond their often low economic status. They are 'maestros', the shamans of 'Western' culture whose performative competence in orchestrating the meanings of bowtie are indicative of their competence in other cultural performances.

Louis Farrakhan and the Magical Fold

The bowtie thus marks the 'arrogant performer' – the maestro – who *commands* rather than only pleases. Indeed, commanding or performing the role of a commander is central to the service that this servant offers. At the centre of a public event: a trial, hearing, performance or debate, this performance is the opposite of the role of the paid servant for it demands the attention of the audience, rather than signalling the opposite distribution of attention. As an example, we might take only one of a number of contemporary courtroom lawyers, politicians with reputations for 'backroom' influence such as Arthur Schlesinger Jr. was famed for in Washington DC. Once again, the embodied, physical 'presence' of the wearer and the manner in which he carries off the performance of wearing a bowtie is crucial. That 'presence' is the positioning and stance of the wearer's body in coordination with the bowtie and other sumptuary elements toward the surrounding context and action.

But Louis Kahn is only a way-station on the path to a contemporary example of the ambitious bowtied male: the powerful orator and leader of the Nation of Islam movement, Louis Farrakhan. Farrakhan graduated from a one-time career singing with a calypso band to the podium of race politics without – in a sense – changing his attire. Nonetheless, there was a change, from the bandsman's bowtied *uniform* to the maestro's *costume*. The bowtie is a sumptuary proclamation of status, of being a master, marking the hidden power of the sorcerer. It amplifies the rhetorical power of Farrakhan's speeches and a delivery punctuated by sharp, assertive movements. The bowtie claims respectability and demands the audience's attention to Farrakhan at the same time that he attacks the existing social power structure. Symbolically, the bowtied social critic might be read as seeking membership, but on his own, radical terms. While decrying the status quo, Farrakhan is garbed in the respectability of the establishment and cultural elites. In short a sumptuary tactic complements political and rhetorical tactics.

The bowtie signals a surplus of signification. On the one hand it may be presented for its positive implications and meanings, but it still carries the negative meanings in reserve. But on the other hand, it also suggests that there are even further hidden meanings which are perhaps negative and perhaps positive, which can be conjured out of this sumptuary and semiotic balancing act. There is 'more than meets the eye' and the wearer should therefore be treated with caution.

Crossing-over: Concluding Adjustment

A final case of costuming is the adoption of the bowtie as a signifier of masculinity (out of its many possible signifiers) in lesbian cross-dressing. Or is it masculinity? The attraction of the bowtie is its liminality – its threshold, boundary status – and unstable, double-coding. The bowtie is firmly anchored within the sartorial repertoire of masculinity despite the constancy of bows in feminine dress over the last two centuries. In contrast to the bowtie, the feminine bow has always tended to fall far below the collar-line, covering the breastbone – even lying as low as the sternum. The two are recognizably different even if they sometimes share the same folds. One is overcoded as 'feminine', the bowtie on the other hand is culturally-gendered as 'masculine'. Yet, because the bowtie is ambiguous it is ideally suited to manipulation. In effect, it is not a simple signifier of masculinity at all. It serves as a liminal device which can reverse the meaning of an entire ensemble of clothing and of poses and gestures, not to mention the gender-meaning of the wearer's body. It is a boundary phenomenon, betwixt and between gender identities.

What transforms the 'uniform' into the 'costume'? Attitude and success in carrying it off, is the answer that many give. However, I have argued that it is possible to go beyond a psychological explanation. The answer lies not in the bow or the bowtie, but with the body and the visible coordination of the body and the bow. The line of the chin and the display of the neck transform the garb of the lackey into the power suit. Yet this 'costume' can always be reversed back into its rhetorical double of the puppet's uniform. The bowtie requires a constant performance from its wearer; it requires a constant semiotic effort to arrange the body and the bow to signify and connote in the right direction. If the maestro is arrogant, it is an arrogance that is de facto a site of struggle – a constant adjustment – and yet it must be a concealed struggle. The maestro is thus, like every sorcerer, a master of control and of conjuring.

The bowtie is not 'liminal' just because it is outside everyday garb, but because it is a Janus-faced signifier which, like a threshold (a *limen*) many-times crossed, links the everyday and the extraordinary; the servile and the authoritative; the slave and the master; male and female. It is semiotically unreliable. But, in effect, the bowtie acts as a conduit of semiotic flows: it has a function similar to a lightning rod or conductor, capturing the always approximate arrangement of actants or active elements such as the pose of the body, its posture and comportment, the surrounding context, the other elements worn and the style of bow, into an assemblage glossed as one 'meaning'. These active elements may include what the speaker says and does, stated provocations and the coordination of the body with itself as it resolves the mechanics of mobility and gravity into what we blithely call 'stance'. But the body itself is a key factor which makes its appearance independent of intention or of the postulated status of the wearer as maestro or man-servant.

This 'tale of three Louis' is only the beginning of a critical semiotic audit of the changeable signification of the bowtie. To wear a bowtie is to conjure up a point of balance amongst the unstable meanings, or 'assemblages' which we have surveyed. To point out the unstable, 'assembled' quality of the bowtie's signification is to add a level of complexity which reveals the constructed nature of the bowtie as signifier. It reveals that the concept of a 'meaning' – the bowtie as either a 'uniform', as an elegant or aggressive 'costume' – is a superficial gloss on a fluid arrangement of forces. Balancing the meanings of the bowtie is like adjusting the length of the bow, the final adjustment of the knot.

Bibliography

Ash, Juliet (1995), 'The Tie: Presence and Absence.' In P. Kirkham (ed.), *The Gendered Object*. Manchester: Manchester University Press.
Bachelard, G. (1961), *Poetics of Space*. Boston: Beacon.

Bakhtin, M.M. (1973), *Problems of Dostoevsky's Poetics*, R.W. Rotsel (trans). Ann Arbor Michigan: Ardis Press.

Berger, P. (1990), 'The Suit.' In C. Mukerji and M. Schudson (eds) *Introducing Popular Culture*. Berkeley: University of California Press.

Bourdieu, P. (1984), *Distinction*. London: Routledge.

Bristow J. (1994), 'Dowdies and Dandies – Oscar Wilde and the Refashioning of Society Comedy,' *Modern Drama*, 37(1):53–70.

Cronin, A. (1996), Comments in the Space and Consumption Seminar, Culture and Communication Programme, Lancaster University.

Davis, F. (1991), *Fashion, Culture, and Identity*. Chicago: University of Chicago Press.

DeCerteau, Michel (1984), *The Practice of Everyday Life*. Berkeley: University of California Press.

Deleuze, G., and Guattari, F. (1976), *Thousand Plateaux*. Paris: Minuit.

Doherty B. (1995), 'Fashionable Ladies, Dada Dandies + Clothes and Avant-garde Art,' *Art Journal*, 54(1):46–50.

Fillinyeh S. (1995), 'Dandies, Marginality and Modernism, Georgia O'Keefe, Marcel Duchamp, and the Other Cross-dressers,' *Oxford Art Journal*, 18(2):33–44.

Finkelstein, J. (1991), *The Fashioned Self*. Cambridge: Polity.

Game, A. (1996), Comments in the Space and Consumption Seminar, Culture and Communication Programme, Lancaster University.

Joseph, Nathan (1986), *Uniforms and Nonuniforms; Communication through Clothing*. New York: Greenwood.

Lefebvre, H. (1991), *The Production of Space*, Nicholson-Smith (trans). Oxford: Basil Blackwell.

Mazon, Mauricio (1984), *The Zoot-suit Riots; The Psychology of Symbolic Annihilation*. Austin: University of Texas Press.

McRobbie, A. (1989), *Zoot Suits and Second Hand Dresses – An Anthology of Fashion and Music*. London: Macmillan.

Mort, F. (1980), 'Sexuality – Regulation and Contestation in Gay Left Collective,' *Homosexuality: Power and Politics*. London: Alison and Busby.

Nixon, S. (1992), 'Have You Got the Look: Masculinities and Shopping Spectacle.' In R. Shields (ed.), *Lifestyle Shopping: The Subject of Consumption*. London: Routledge.

Polhemus, Ted (1978), *Fashion and Anti-fashion: An Anthropology of Clothing and Adornment*. London: Hudson.

Rojek, C. (1985), *Capitalism and Leisure Theory*. London: Tavistock.

Shields, R. (1989), *Places on the Margin*. London: Routledge.

—— (1997), 'Feel Good Here?' In J. Caulfield and L.Peake (eds), *Critical Urban Perspectives*. Toronto: University of Toronto Press.

Spooner, John D. (1995), 'Bow Ties: Some Rules of Thumb for the Neck,' *Atlantic Monthly*, (November):46–9.

Turner, V. (1979), *Process, Performance and Pilgrimage*. New Delhi: Concept.

Wilson, Sloan (1976), *What Shall We Wear to This Party?: The Man in the Gray Flannel Suit Twenty Years Before and After*. New York: Arbor.

10

That Barbie-Doll Look: A Psychoanalysis

Jeanne Randolph

I have talked with women who admit to exchanging heads on their dolls when playing as little girls. This has also put the wrong heads on bodies (Kitturah B. Westenhouser 1994:19).

A Brief Introduction to a Psychoanalysis of Toys

Psychoanalysts have been studying aggression in little children since the turn of the nineteenth century, and two theorists of aggressive play, object relations[1] psychoanalysts Melanie Klein (1882–1960) and D.W. Winnicott (1896–1971) have offered provocative conjectures about it. Their work makes a connection between identity formation[2] and playing. Winnicott (1971) discusses play as inextricable from cultural development.

Children develop their understanding of their society's ethos by playing: the toys a society offers to its children valorize the society's ethos. In noting this, psychoanalytic theory is not unique. But psychoanalytic theory also claims that there is something children will bring to their playing. Psychoanalytic theory can interpret the toys society offers the child (such as Barbie™

---

1. Object relations theory developed out of Freudian psychoanalysis – and distinguishes itself from Freudianism by claiming that (1) the newborn's personality forms by interacting with a care-giver who is experienced by the infant not only as a (Freudian) necessity to gratify physical needs; (2) but also as a 'total environment' in which physical *experience* (this includes communication and imagination) is inherently interpersonal experience; (3) not all social experience and not all bodily functions take place in dangerous conditions that behove the human psyche to develop defences, rather (4) many events in the formation of the infant's personality occur in social interactions that are reliably safe.

2. Identity formation is defined here as the picture a person constructs in answer to his or her own question, as well as the question from other people, 'Who are you?'

card games, comic books, colouring books, trading cards) and in doing so will also make a pronouncement about what the child brings to the toy.

The public image of the Barbie™ doll character is disseminated by mass media and ancillary mass-manufactured toys. These representations of Barbie™, whether by verbal advertising copy or aesthetic and formal visual design, are crafted consistent with Mattel Industries' conception of the female persona most attractive to its buying public, girls aged five to fifteen (and the adults most likely to facilitate the doll's purchase). Melanie Klein asserts that children bring their subconscious[3] processes (as well as their consciousness) to their toys, just as adult citizens necessarily imbue their cultural products with subconscious ideas. This essay is about images of the Barbie™ doll and subconscious memories of aggression, indeed of sadism, that these images might evoke. To appreciate as well as analyse Mattel's challenge in verbal and nonverbal product design, it is necessary to entertain the possibility that psychoanalytic theory offers valid observations about ordinary human aggression and defence, gender identity and the bond between infant and caretaker. Klein's work (1930) documents her position on the relevance of sado-masochism to the infant-mother(sic) duo, especially regarding the infant's ordinary maturation into a productive citizen.

Consequently it is possible to explore the role of Barbie™ dolls in the transformation of female infants into women citizens in North American culture. The analysis here, however, is limited to tracing the path that supposedly 'normal' or 'universal' infantile sadistic impulses follow in a culture that idealizes the female as affluent, pretty, hygienic, obedient, cheerful and born to shop.

Klein observed the hunger and satiation of the nursing infant in relation to the mother's power – power to nourish and power to punish. Klein met the paradoxical challenge of offering a verbal representation of the pre-verbal relationship between a baby's bodily function and the mother's physical care.

> The oral frustration which turns the indulgent 'good mother' into 'the bad mother' stimulates [the child's] sadism (Klein 1930:440).
> I have described this early phase of development, the content of which is the attack made on the mother's body with all the weapons that the child's sadism has at its disposal (ibid.:438).

3. 'Subconscious' is used here instead of the idea of an Unconscious. Subconscious could be defined as simple or complex memories and fantasies that can only come to a person's conscious attention through deliberate, concentrated effort, principally introspection, psychotherapy or influence of cultural productions (the arts and entertainment). To some psychoanalysts, the existence of the Unconscious, unlike the hypothesis of a Subconscious, is based on inference, since the workings of an Unconscious are known only indirectly through lapses and contradictions in conscious behaviour.

The little girl has a sadistic desire . . . to rob the mother's body of its contents . . . and to destroy the mother herself. This desire gives rise to anxiety lest the mother in turn rob the little girl . . . and [the little girl's] body should be destroyed or mutilated (ibid.:442).

The proposition of an infantile subconscious teeming with such violence strains credulity perhaps, but the context in which aggression and/or sadism is introduced – Barbie™ 'spin-off' toys, the context of consumerism – offers an intriguing review of aggression[4] as a gendered behaviour and of the infant's acquaintance with sadism.[5]

Children have many incentives to comprehend aggression. According to object relations theory (Hoffer 1950; Winnicott 1949), children do not have the option of being aggression-free themselves or of living on an aggression-free planet. How are children (indeed any of us) to comprehend aggression except by experiencing it and by symbolizing it? All social institutions supply means to comprehend aggression, and toy making is one of those institutions.

One Way to Read Toys

During all phases of maturation people inevitably act aggressively and receive aggression from others while concurrently their society contextualizes and interprets aggression. In this way society offers its citizens some choices for when and how they may become aggressive. And also, of course, citizens are offered a way to interpret aggression of which they themselves are the recipient. It is in this sense that aggression is 'comprehended', not only by its enactment, but also by its depiction. If, according to psychoanalytic theory, infants are born sadistic, what happens to sadism, that special aggression which is meaningful because by definition it involves another living being? Surely sadistic reflexes must be organized and interpreted by and for infant girls as they mature into children and thence into socialized adults. I am wondering how sadism, the infantile version of aggression, has been

4. Psychoanalytically, aggression refers to an innate physiological impulse or (Freudian) instinct to destroy something.

5. Psychoanalytically, in object relations theory, sadism would be the version of aggression most relevant to infancy, a pleasure in retaliating against another human's body as a result of deprivation, frustration and/or pain, all of which are said to be registered by the infant's ill-formed consciousness as an attack. According to object relations theory we have no choice whether or not we are born sadistic. The 'choice' that develops through maturation is which things will be the recipient of our sadistic impulses. Object relations theory does not say that humans are purely sadistic, only that they adapt their newborn and subsequent infantile sadistic pleasure to those activities their society designates as available.

navigated by toy makers. I want to rediscover inalienable sadistic impulses, now fitted to the parameters of North American consumerism. Toys such as soldiers with armour and weapons obviously provide children with a way to enact aggression, including sadism. What can be said about girls' toys in which aggression seems 'conspicuous by its absence'? Through their Barbie™ dolls it seems very likely that girls socialize themselves[6] in regard to sadism no less than boys who play with armed and armoured toy soldiers.

The North American shoppers' ethos – and its potential effects on citizens-in-progress – is not so definitively illustrated, however, by Mattel Inc's Barbie™ dolls themselves, for one very encouraging reason: as soon as children get their hands on three-dimensional, tactile toys, the toys are no longer under the strict control of the toy maker (although of course the toys retain some of the toy maker's influence).

Many a Canadian mother has recounted with relief how their little daughters do not necessarily idolize their Barbie™ doll every time they play with it:

'Mom', said one eight-year-old girl, 'I don't want to *be* Barbie, I just want to *play* with a Barbie.'[7]

Informal conversations will often evoke mothers' reports of how daughters modified their doll:

'Bald Barbie.' 'Dirty Butt Barbie.' 'Barbie with "S-E-X" tattooed onto her chest.' 'Naked Jet-Propelled Barbie.'[8]

There are satellite Barbie™ playthings however that are considerably less amenable to such spontaneous, idiosyncratic and childish interventions. Card games, comic books, colouring books and trading cards offer an opportunity to analyse visual and verbal parameters as they become harnessed to a particular ideology.

The purpose of such analysis is not to unmask Mattel's Barbie™ products as mere propagandistic devices. Rather there is a more complex phenomenon that attracts consideration. It is with great effort that Barbie™ product designers create the impression that consumerism is natural, painless and

6. It could be argued by an object relations theorist that children 'socialize themselves' rather than passively receive a repertoire of social behaviours. Adult society has a great degree of control over the means by which children socialize themselves. The Barbie™ doll is thus one of many 'means' made available to girls.

7. I am indebted to Hollis Landau of Toronto, Canada for this quotation from her eight-year-old daughter.

8. Anecdotal, reported to the author in conversations.

safe. Freud thought up the term 'denial' after Shakespeare had already written 'Methinks he doth protest too much.' Suppose that the more relentlessly a particular fantasy about a toy is touted by its manufacturer, the more fruitful will be our inquiry into what the manufacturer has left unsaid.

This brings us to a series of images in *Barbie: A Super Jumbo Colouring Book.*[9] The Barbie™ character is depicted in one of those special chairs on a deep-sea fishing boat. A girlfriend watches as Barbie's™ fishing pole bows under the weight of something caught on the line. The fish must be very heavy, because Barbie™, hardly less slender than her fishing pole, leans back in the chair as if her massive hairdo could serve as counterweight to her catch. On the next page a fish, yanked by a fishing line attached to its smile, leaves the water and soars over the prow of the boat. A third scene on the following page locates Barbie™ on the dock, posing by the fish, which has been suspended on a huge hook. Barbie™ gazes skyward, away from the fish. The cartoon fish face conveys the expression 'Yikes!'

Images of Barbie™

This is as fierce as the Barbie™ character gets in 686 images included in a 190-page colouring book, a 40-card Barbie™ *Shopping Spree* card game, a 31-page *Barbie Fashion™* comic book, an illustrated 1964 Random House novel *Barbie in Television*, 300 Panini Barbie and Friends™ 1992 Trading Cards, twenty Barbie™ *Fashion Play Cards* and four 100 per cent authentic Barbie™ pogs™. It is no surprise. Aggressiveness is considered by North Americans to be a masculine, not a feminine trait. But it is evidence of a monumental challenge to Mattel industries and the designers who illustrate their star product.

Barbie and Friends™ trading card #80, *Queen for a Day!* offers the opportunity to consider this challenge psychoanalytically. The Barbie™ doll has been photographed in her Cleopatra costume, including her wig of ten or so serpentine, shoulder-length braids. *Au verso* the outfit is described as 'Prototype Fashion (Never introduced on the market)' for the Little Theatre collection.

[Elliot and Ruth Handler] used this theatre to launch an acting career for their doll, Barbie. The theatre was sold in 1964 only, with costumes marketed separately. The costumes were designed around childhood fairy tales and were still available through 1965 . . . Four sets of stunning costumes make up the theatre series. The

9. Cambridge, Ontario, 1991, pp.84–6.

outfits were designed to sell the Little Theatre and the theatre sold the costumes. The combination of outfits and theatre sold the dolls (Westenhouser 1994:95).

The Egyptian Queen is a tainted figure, however, who could not easily be pasteurized. Cleopatra's erotic powers and livid suicide-by-snake could not have been sufficiently bleached or prettified, apparently, for her to slide out of the shadows of sex and violence into the relentlessly upbeat stream of Barbie™ products.

To clarify this psychoanalysis of how Barbie™ is depicted for mass consumption, Barbie™ as sports fisherperson and Barbie™ as Queen of the Nile could be said to illustrate two different rhetorical challenges. The challenge of the former is purging a particular activity (fishing) of its hunting and killing connotations. The challenge of Cleopatra's history is replacing a complex centuries-old literary tradition with a simple narrative of shopping for clothes. These challenges are just two among hundreds. These particular challenges are subsumed under an absolute condition: that the Barbie™ doll image never ever evoke the girl child's memories or fantasies of sadism against the maternal body. The task for trading card #80 designers is similar to the task for whoever designed the common driveway sign, 'Don't even THINK of parking here!' Whether or not a Mattel spokesperson would agree that humans are born sadistic, have infantile sadistic experiences and pre-verbal sado-masochistic memories, Mattel Inc would not want their products to unleash even subconscious fantasies of such goings-on.[10]

The Interpretive Template

Barbie Fashion™ [11] presents an episode in the Barbie™ character's Marvel Comics life. A teacher, Ms Robinson, takes her pre-teen class to The Museum

10. A letter from the author requesting permission from Mattel to use an image of Barbie™ elicited the following response: 'Unfortunately, we will not be able to give you the permission you request. We find that the negative content of the essay is not something that we would want to appear to have authorized or even to appear to be affiliated or associated with in any way. In fact, we adamantly object to what we believe to be an unfair, imbalanced, inaccurate portrayal. Mattel is definitely not interested and would never lend its permission for any material to be used in conjunction with this essay.

'As you know, *Barbie* is an extremely valuable property of Mattel. Please be aware and inform your publisher, Berg Publishing, that we have every intention to vigorously protect all of our rights in this property. To that end our attorneys, while not acting as your legal counsel, strongly recommend that you and your publisher review this matter with your own legal counsel before you go ahead with this essay . . .'

11. Vol. 1, no. 42, June 1994.

of Art to visit '*Barbie in Fashion* . . . a retrospective of the famous fashion model.'

'Welcome to the sixties . . .' says the museum docent (*Barbie Fashion* ™:4).
It was a very exciting time for women because more and more job opportunities were opening up! As you can see Barbie looks great in fashions from any era (*Barbie Fashion*™:5).

History is reduced to 'fashions from any era'. Likewise many other activities, relationships and productions can be reduced and reinterpreted as variations on shopping for clothes. Shopping for clothes becomes 'an interpretive template', a schema that pre-determines the selection and presentation of all details of each Barbie™ product. Analogous to the Little Theatre, the outfits 'sell' the interpretive template, and the combination of the template and the outfits sells the dolls.

Understandably, if Mattel Inc offers an interpretive template that is unambiguously subservient to the values and gender roles of consumer society, Mattel products will be maximally acceptable in the marketplace. Thus, the ancient card game gin rummy is marketed as Barbie™ *Shopping Spree Giant Card Game*, children are urged to '*Collect All 6 Fashion Packs!*' of *New!* Barbie™ *Fashion Play Cards* (a pre-scripted, solitaire variant of 'the exquisite corpse' drawing game) and the back cover of the *Super Jumbo Colouring Book* offers a paper doll Barbie™ in her underwear.

Psychoanalytically, the interpretive template is crucial for two reasons: first, because of its effect on 'free association', secondly because it provides a symbolic format with which the child may comprehend her/his society's assignment of gender in relation to aggression.

Freud coined the term 'free association' to denote a type of thinking that is spontaneously organized according to personal and idiosyncratic memories (in contrast to logic or other modes of formal reasoning). Freud claimed any stimulus could evoke free association, depending, as does the flow of electricity through wire, on the strength of resistance the flow must overcome. The function of an interpretive template is to provide resistance. Consciously and subconsciously the interpretive template solidifies its own, not the child's, happenstance connections between stimulus (product) and memories.

To control the connections between personal memories and brand name products has always been the task of the advertising industry. The purpose of Barbie™ doll packaging, for example, would be to organize the consumer's ideation according to Mattel's interpretive template. Products such as United Colours Of Bennetton Barbie™, accomplish this neatly with the words 's h o p p i n g ! s h o p p i n g ! s h o p p i n g ! s h o p p i n g ! s h o p p i n g !

s h o p p i n g! s h o p p i n g! s h o p p i n g!' and the Bennetton name in trademark typeface on the doll's package and on two tiny paper bags inside. Again, as with the Little Theatre, the package sells the interpretive template and the interpretive template in combination with the tiny shopping bags sells the dolls.

The interpretive template for Barbie™ products resists the flow of free association toward memories of infantile sadism. It is obvious to all who love Barbie™ dolls and to all who mock them[12] that Mattel Inc has chosen to interpret femininity as absolutely devoid of aggression. For example, the packaging, outfits and accessories for Army, Air Force, Navy and Marine Corps Barbie™ present obvious challenges for the interpretive template to detour associations from memories associated with aggression.

According to Mattel's current interpretive template 'Sadistic Barbie™' would be an oxymoron. More to the point here, the interpretive template offers its strongest resistance to images of 'Masochistic Barbie™'. It offers its strongest resistance to the susceptibility of Barbie™ to the child's re-enactment of subconscious, preverbal sadistic memories.

The most fascinating illustrations of this point are found in those images of Barbie™ that, unlike fisherperson, Cleopatra and soldier, ordinarily do not connote violence, but could evoke recollections of frustration, the oral frustration which turns the indulgent 'good mother' into 'the bad mother' (and thus) stimulates (the child's) sadism (upon 'the bad mother').

Page eleven of the Barbie Fashion™ Marvel Comics story provides a subtle example of how the interpretive template offers resistance against the connotation – and therefore any conscious, or visceral memories of – frustration. Two girls are depicted viewing a mannequin on a pedestal in the 1970s section of the exhibition, across from Barbie™ in her Mary McFadden yellow pantsuit and another Barbie™ in white go-go boots wearing 'the popular vest with fringe, fringe and more fringe'. The caption reads 'Here's Barbie's friend, "Malibu Christie," dressed in her U.S. OLYMPIC outfit; all red, white and blue!'

On the pedestal Malibu Christie, the first African-American Mattel doll (sold between 1968 and 1971) is wearing a very short white pleated skirt, bright blue blazer, a scarlet skin-tight bodice with blue neckline, a white fedora, and red high heel pumps. 'Wow', exclaims one of the schoolgirls,

12. February 1996, WWW Site humour-list-request–lists.synapse.net provided seventeen 'Barbies We'd Like to See' which included Melrose Place Barbie: comes complete with her Barbie Dream Apartment, where Skipper and the rest of the gang live rent-free. Other accessories include a bottle of vodka, silk sheets, and an arrest warrant; or My So-Called Barbie: she faces the same troubling issues as regular teens who don't have huge wardrobes, perfect bods, pools, and ponies; Transgender Barbie: formerly known as G.I.Joe.

referring to the huge medallion Malibu Christie wears on a long white ribbon around her neck, 'Look at that gold Medal!' Malibu Christie is sporty, not sweaty. There is no connotation of effort, perseverance or even muscular movement in the style of her outfit or in her pose. This reduction of Olympian athletic achievement to a relaxed, passive 'look', is not new to fashion. It is so familiar that to expect otherwise might seem unrealistic. In this context, however, as Barbie™ herself says, she is being 'a MODEL and a ROLE MODEL'(*Barbie Fashion*™:28). And she proclaims that '. . . the most important things[sic] are to just *be* yourself . . .' (ibid.:28).

The Case of the Missing Masochism

Freud and Rorschach made ambiguity notorious by asking people what they 'saw' in inkblots or other indistinct shapes, situations or phrases. One could say that what Freud and Rorschach proposed is that when we say what we 'see' in an ambiguous image, we are, in a sense, using the inkblot 'to just be ourselves'. Mattel's interpretive template, however, functions to ensure that all images of Barbie™ are devoid of ambiguity. What I am emphasizing is not only the absence of ambiguity but extremism of censorship that actively interferes with any connotation of our most common, ordinary emotions and bodily sensations: physical and social exertion in pursuit of one's needs. The physical and emotional frustration consequent when these needs are not satisfied, is conspicuous by its absence from the interpretive template. Physical and social exertion in pursuit of one's needs is reduced to the acquisition of outfits.

In infancy, according to psychoanalytic theory, desire, its pursuit, its fulfillment *and* its frustration are always subconsciously linked. Especially in children, the memory or image or evocation of one is inextricable from the memory, image or evocation of all the others. And desire, pursuit, fulfillment, frustration are, as Melanie Klein insisted, inevitably linked to *the pleasure of sadistic retribution* when the fulfillment takes too much effort or remains frustrated.

Children are not particularly surprised at evocations of pleasurable vengeance taken upon their mother's body. Children are not necessarily surprised by memories of a maternal body destined, often willingly, to absorb the frustrated infant's scream, first toothless bites and furious little kicking feet. Theoretically, children would not be surprised when offered the opportunity to comprehend their own sadism by playing with a masochistic doll.

Jeanne Randolph

Return of the Repressed: Sadism as Text

It would seem that in the interest of high volume sales Mattel's designers and copy writers are well-advised in their adherence to the so-called interpretive template. The template enforces the idea of 'Good Barbie™' and prevents her turning into 'Bad Barbie™'. The Barbie™ character is depicted living in a totally safe environment. With what can the little girl associate this security except a vast wardrobe and its attendant fashion accessories? Is it possible that Barbie™ doll outfits serve as an impregnable defence? Apparently little girls' sadistic elements go unaddressed.

According to psychoanalytic theory it is entirely possible to sink memories and impulses of any stripe deep into the subconscious. Refusing to acknowledge their existence – by silence and by offering no ambiguous objects or situations with which, in this instance, sadism, can be enacted.[13] It may even seem logical to conclude that products that resist all sadistic connotations, that impede free association, can stop sadistic play before it even becomes an idea or impulse.

According to psychoanalysts, from Freud to object relations theorists, however, if one analyses a phenomenon and its psychosocial context meticulously enough, one will find that the censored element will not disappear. The repressed notion is cleanly 'split off' from its source, only to take form elsewhere, not too far away from the phenomenon at hand. This is what Freud discussed as 'the return of the repressed'.

In this exploration of Barbie™ doll product design and the 'interpretive template' the tragedy of sadism in the human psyche does not go unrepresented after all. On the back of every Barbie and Friends™ Panini trading card is a brief quiz, 'Barbie's Famous Women'. In this unlikely place, the repressed representation of sadism actually returns quite often. It is not of course pinned on Barbie™, or on the little girl who plays with Barbie™. Yet sadism certainly gets represented: as the punishment that women have provoked toward themselves and others throughout history. For many of 'Barbie's Famous Women', sadistic longings are not an ethical dilemma requiring self-consciousness, judgement, emotional maturation or compassion. Sadistic cruelty is what Fate could have in store for any woman at any time:

---

13. Omitting maternity from the so-called interpretive template for example has resulted in a traditionally-garbed Iranian-made doll, Sara, manufactured explicitly to oppose Barbie™ in form (sex object) and 'content'.

BARBIE'S *Famous Women* [14]

'I was killed by Achilles who mourned for me, as I was so beautiful . . . Who am I?'

'I was murdered while pregnant . . . Who am I?'

'I was assassinated . . . Who am I?'

'I was brutally assassinated . . . Who am I?'

'I was assassinated during one of my frequent trips abroad . . . Who am I?'

'I was assassinated by two of my own security guards . . . Who am I?'

'My son had me assassinated . . . Who am I?'

'My performance influenced the man who tried to assassinate the U.S. President . . . Who am I?

'I was sentenced as a witch and burned at the stake . . . Who am I?'

'I was found guilty of treason and beheaded . . . Who am I?'

'I was executed by a firing squad . . . Who am I?'

'I was sent to a concentration camp and executed . . . Who am I?'

'I was guillotined . . . Who am I?'

'I was burned alive by soldiers . . . Who am I?'

'I was tried and condemned to death . . . Who am I?'

'I was one year old when I lost my mother . . . Who am I?'

'I spent the last thirty years of my life in a psychiatric hospital . . . Who am I?'

'Attacks of mental illness led to my suicide . . . Who am I?'

'I died tragically . . . Who am I?'

'I died tragically, strangled when my long scarf got caught in the wheels of my car . . . Who am I?'

'My husband and children were executed . . . Who am I?'

'My husband and I were executed as spies . . . Who am I?'

'We were divorced after just a few months of marriage . . . Who am I?'

'I found city life difficult and died soon after my husband found employment . . . Who am I?'

'I was arrested for voting . . . Who am I?'

'I was excommunicated by the pope . . . Who am I?'

---

14. 'I am . . .' [in sequence]: Penthesilea Queen of the Amazons, Sharon Tate, Alexandra Fedorova, Dian Fossey, Elizabeth of Wittelsbach, Indira Gandhi, Agrippina the Younger, Jodie Foster, Jeanne d'Arc, Anne Boleyn, Mata Hari, Anne Frank, Marie-Antoinette, Carmen Gloria Quintana, Mary Stuart, Anne Bronte, Camille Claudel, Virginia Woolf, Shakespeare's 'Juliet', Isadora Duncan, Nelly Sachs, Ethel Rosenberg, Anne of Cleeves, Mary Gladys Webb, Susan B. Anthony, Elizabeth I, Emma Goldman, Lady Jane Grey, Emily Dickinson.

'I was eventually deported to the Soviet Union by the American Government . . . Who am I?'

'I ruled England for only nine days . . . Who am I?'

'I wrote many poems but only seven were published during my lifetime . . . Who am I?'

Postscript

In a so-called enlightened society, social and psychological scientists can study the consequences and implications for children of the Barbie™ product. In a traditional and/or police state, children are presumably offered dolls whose 'interpretive template' has been equally constrained by religious and other well-defined cosmologies. Although this particular analysis may provoke questions about toys' contribution to the health and ethics of female citizens, my objective has been to test the relevance of psychoanalytic theory to the inextricability of fashion and ideology.

Bibliography

Hoffer, W. (1950), 'Oral Aggression and Ego Development,' *International Journal of Psycho-Analysis*, 31:156–60.

Klein, Melanie (1930), 'Infantile Anxiety-Situations Reflected in a Work of Art and in the Creative Impulse,' *International Journal of Psycho-Analysis*, 18:436–47.

Westenhouser, Kitturah B. (1994), *The Story of Barbie*. Paducah, Kentucky: Collector Books.

Winnicott, D.W. (1949), 'Hate and the Countertransference,' *International Journal of Psycho-Analysis*, 30:69–74.

—— (1971), *Playing and Reality*. London: Tavistock.

Biographical Notes

Anne Brydon is Assistant Professor of Anthropology at the University of Western Ontario, London, Canada. Her research focuses on the social production of perception, discourse, and knowledge as they relate to attitudes toward nationalism, ethnicity, gender, nature and the environment, urban space, and visual art production. This focus has led to investigations of whale hunting, ethnic festivals, gender politics, visual arts, film, travel writing, and fashion production and consumption, and fieldwork in Iceland, northern Europe and Canada. She is just completing a book: *The Eye of the Guest: Icelandic Nationalism and the Whaling Issue*. Her shoes are rather dull, but her hats are marvellous.

Aubrey Cannon is Associate Professor of Archaeology in the Department of Anthropology, McMaster University, Hamilton, Canada. Educated at Simon Fraser (BA, 1979) and Cambridge (PhD, 1987). Research interests include mortuary studies, zooarchaeology, and prehistory of the Northwest Coast and Eastern Woodlands of North America. Recent publications include: 'Two Faces of Power: Communal and Individual Modes of Mortuary Expression' (1995, *ARX World Journal of Prehistoric and Ancient Studies*, 1:3–8); 'Historical Inconsistencies: Huron Longhouse Length, Hearth Number, and Time' (with Colin Varley) (1994, *Ontario Archaeology*, 58:85–101); and 'Archaeology's Public: A Perspective from Two Canadian Museums' (with Debbi Cannon) (1996, *Canadian Journal of Archaeology*, 20:29–38). His involvement in fashion studies developed from PhD research into changes in gravestone design and mortuary display in Victorian England.

Ross Higgins has recently completed a PhD dissertation, 'Sense of Belonging: Pre-liberation Space, Symbolics and Leadership in Gay Montreal,' in anthropology at McGill University. He has written on the coverage of gays and lesbians in the 1950s 'yellow newspapers' of Montreal (with Line Chamberland) and on a sensational gay murder as reflected in French and English language news reports, and has written a forthcoming article on the history of Montreal's gay bars scene and on public sex and the notion of gay community.

Xiaoping Li is a post-doctoral fellow at the University of Toronto-York University Joint Centre for Pacific Studies. She works in the field of cultural studies, and is currently writing about the globalization of culture, contemporary Chinese culture, multiculturalism and the Chinese diaspora in Canada. Xiaoping is one of the fashion lovers in communist China who resisted official management of the body through clothing and hair styles.

Andrea K. Molnar is Assistant Professor of Anthropology, Northern Illinois University, DeKalb, Illinois. She received her PhD from The Australian National University. Her research interests include religion and symbolism, kinship and social organization, development and underdevelopment. Recent publication: 1995, 'Local adjustments and attitudes to development and the environment in West Flores (Eastern Indonesia).' In G. Forth, S. Niessen and J. de Bernardi (eds), *Managing Change in Southeast Asia: Local Identities, Global Connections.* Canadian Council for Southeast Asian Studies.

Sandra Niessen is Associate Professor in the Department of Human Ecology, University of Alberta, largely because the thematic specialization on clothing and textiles in that department complements her interests and research. She is completing the last volume (*The Complete Repertory of Batak Textiles*) of a three-volume corpus on textiles of the Batak people of North Sumatra, Indonesia. In addition to a long-time fixation on Batak textiles, she teaches and researches in the areas of material culture, craft in the global economy, and cultural dimensions of clothing.

Jeanne Randolph is a practising psychiatrist and assistant professor at the University of Toronto. She is the author of *Psychoanalysis and Synchronized Swimming and Other Writing on Art* and *Symbolization and its Discontents*. Currently she is doing research for her next book, *Out of Psychoanalysis*, about intimate friendships between artists and writers in Toronto in the 1980s.

Gordon Roe is currently a PhD candidate at Simon Fraser University in Burnaby, British Columbia, doing ethnographic research on needle exchange outreach programmes and the development of social networks based on attendance at exchanges. He has worked as an artists' model while an undergraduate and graduate student in several provinces and universities in Canada. An ethnography of artists' models was the basis of his masters research at the University of Western Ontario, London, Canada.

Rob Shields is Associate Professor of Sociology and Anthropology, and is acting director of the Institute for Interdisciplinary Studies at Carleton University, Ottawa Canada – where he often wears a bowtie. He is a founding editor of *Space and Culture*. Trained in architecture, his primary interests are related to the social constructions of spatiality and identity. Recent research includes: methodological work on dialogism, *verstehen* and the ethics of qualitative methods; post-colonial and subaltern theories in relation to persona and settler societies; the emergence of 'culture' as a discursive formation; new media and postmodern sociality; changing consumption cultures and their contexts (malls, urban spaces); tourism and cultural syncretism. Publications: *Places on the Margin: Alternative Geographies of Modernity* (1989); *Lifestyle Shopping: The Subject of Consumption* (1991); *Cultures of Internet* (1996).

Ian Skoggard is a graduate of the PhD Program in Anthropology at the City University of New York and presently works as an analyst at the Human Relations Area Files at Yale University. His publications include *The Indigenous Dynamic in Taiwan's Postwar Development: The Religious and Historical Roots of Entrepreneurship* (1996), and 'Inscribing Capitalism: Belief and Ritual in a New Taiwanese Religion' (1996) in Gosta Arvastson and Mats Lindqvist, *The Story of Progress*.

Rebecca Sullivan is completing doctoral studies at the Graduate Program in Communications, McGill University. Her research is on the relationships between gender, religion and culture. At academic conferences, she enjoys guessing who the women religious are in the audience by what they are wearing.

Index

Printed in the United States
220824BV00006B/1/A

9 781859 739693